I am awed by his mythic journey o
towards awakening. Eli relentlessly
challenges his traditional teachings and constantly follows
the sacred path of the spiritual seeker.

A true Godwrestler of the Yehudi tribe, I bow to Eli for
declaring and living his truth: "Any path can lead home.
It is the heart of the seeker not the path that is important."
This book is a fast moving page turner, alive and exciting.
I applaud Eli's honesty, drive and natural story telling
ability.

—Rabbi Sue Morningstar, Ashland, OR

Teachings I'd never known yet somehow recognized as
doors of understanding opened my mind and heart. A
compelling read, Eli's brutal honesty constantly blowing
my mind while traveling through the Revolution of the
Sixties... witnessing the Liberation into true Freedom
bringing me home to my Self! Thank you for taking this
bodacious journey.

—Rev. Sue Adams, Minister of The Lord's Chapel,
Winchester, VA

I couldn't put it down. A raw honest and heart opening
account of a love-warriors journey through chaos and
rebellion into enlightenment. I highly recommend this
book to everyone. It brings us on the journey from the
60s rebellion to 21st century consciousness transformation.
Bravo Eli!

—Dr. Howard Morningstar, Ashland, OR

AN OUTLAW MAKES IT HOME

BY ELI JAXON-BEAR

Dedicated to my life partner and lover, who has dedicated her life to us.

A gift from the Goddess and a goddess in form.

I owe everything to her grace, ferocious clarity and loyalty.

It is by going down into the abyss

that we recover the treasures of life.

Where you stumble,

there lies your treasure.

Joseph Campbell

August 1971

I was holding an M1 Carbine, probably Korean War vintage, which I bought for eighty dollars from a cowboy at a swap meet in Littleton. I stood with my back against the cabin door and held the gun against my chest. I could smell the blue gunmetal oil from the barrel below my nose. I spun, kicked the door open, and jumped out. Holding the gun at waist level, I shot three quick rounds at the mailbox on the dusty road about fifty yards below. I was shocked and amazed to see that I had actually hit it.

I was practicing for what I felt coming. I was a federal fugitive facing a possible forty years in prison, and an unmarked van had started parking in our hidden gulch. I was at the end of my rope.

How did I fall into this dead end where no one gets out alive?

How can I kill in the name of life? became the mantra that haunted me day and night.

Seems like a blink and a lifetime since I was shooting 22s at summer camp. I was a twenty-something, upper middle-class, nice Jewish boy from New York, a year removed from a fellowship in a doctoral program, and now I was hiding out in a cabin in the Red Rock Front Range of Colorado.

I had to reflect on my life, retrace the steps and the path that led me here, to try to find a way out.

Published by
New Morning Books, Ashland, OR 97520

Photography by Eli Jaxon-Bear
Book design by Patt Narrowe

Printed in the United States of America
ISBN: 978-0-985-6911-5-8
Library of Congress Control Number: 2018934579

CONTENTS

PART I

CALL TO ADVENTURE

CHAPTER 1

A Beacon in Brooklyn

Memories come and go, fade in and out, have been told and retold, and change with each retelling. Most memories are like the images that appear on photographic paper in a tray of developer: if they are not fixed, they fade back into shadow.

One childhood memory is burned into my mind with acid. No matter how often I've told it, its indelible imprint is pressed into my psyche like a thumb pushed into soft clay. It marks the crossroads of my life, and it has been my test and my teacher. It formed and framed my point of view.

Beyond testing me, shaping me, defining me, it also gave me a glimpse of something unnamable that I chased for the rest of my life, without knowing how to speak it, or even think of it. That moment, when I was three years old, led to facing my death in a Colorado cabin . . . and to my salvation.

*   *   *

In the winter of 1949, just past my second birthday, my family returned to Brooklyn from Miami. We moved into a red brick, six-story apartment house on Foster Avenue, in Flatbush; we had a one-bedroom on the sixth floor. My first chore was taking the garbage to the incinerator down the hall. I tossed the greasy brown paper bag onto the metal door that opened like an oven. The bag of garbage slid off to fall six stories down to the smoky fire of burning trash in the basement below. I really enjoyed this; there was life in it. Something was burning, and there was a fire. A sign of life burned through the solitary gloom of our small apartment,

On one of my garbage missions, I climbed the stairway next to the incinerator. It led to a large, heavy door, and then to the outside. It was a warm, sunny spring day, and someone in a sleeveless undershirt was washing his car six stories below. Across the way—on the roof of the next building—two men, also in sleeveless undershirts, were lounging in lawn chairs, and drinking out of cans; something I had never seen before. I hoisted myself up onto the ledge to look directly below. At that very moment my mother burst onto the roof, rushed towards me, and screamed as she grabbed me off the ledge. Since then, I have an anus-crunching fear of heights.

I brought a coconut head with me from Florida that was made to look like a pirate with a seashell earring and seashell eyes. When Mark, the downstairs neighbor, came up for a first visit, I rushed out to meet him carrying the coconut head, and it terrified him. He ran out of the apartment crying. I thought it was hilarious. I would later live to regret this style of relating.

Mark Warren and I soon became good friends. He was crucial to what was to be a turning point in my young life. Mark's family had a large wooden box with a tiny TV screen inside. Mark and I watched our first Saturday morning cartoons and cowboy shows together. From Hopalong Cassidy and Gene Autry, to the Red Rider, Johnny Mack Brown, and the Lone Ranger; we drank it all in. My neural net absorbed the cathode ray signal, and I was programmed by the programs.

My favorite cartoon, which played repeatedly, was about a war between good elves and bad elves. The good elves worked in a sunshine factory bottling sunshine, which they launched from catapults as missiles that rained on the bad elves, who sprayed darkness and gloom from giant DDT sprayers. When hit by a bottle of sunshine, the struck elf would say: *I want to be happy,* and start to sing about beautiful sunshine; a song I can still sing. When hit with a dose of darkness, that elf would say: *I want to be sad.* One elf, hit by first sunshine and then darkness and gloom, over and over again, started singing a mantra of: *I want to be happy, I want to be sad. I want to be happy, I want to be sad.* This touched me in some way. I laughed very hard, but inside it struck a chord that I couldn't name. Perhaps it echoed the unbearable loneliness and sadness that pervaded the quiet atmosphere at home.

*   *   *

Grandpa Isaac, my mother's father, was a sometime visitor. He would sit alone at a card table set up in the corner of the living room. I would sit on the floor and watch the dust sparkles in the sunbeams while he played solitaire. These were gentle and quiet times, filled with stillness. I once asked Grandpa Isaac who he was playing against, and he said: *The devil. And the devil always wins.* This gave me pause. Was there a devil? Was there a God?

Once my mom bought me a plastic lifeguard with a key in his back; wind him up, and his arms would spin. *Go put the lifeguard in the water,* my mom said to me in her Brooklyn accent. What I heard was: *Go put the life God in the wada.* As I ran down the hallway to the bathroom, I twisted the key in excitement. The lifeguard's arms fell off because the spring I had been twisting with the key was oversprung. I cried and screamed, but it did no good. I had killed God before I had even gotten him to the water. No one understood; they thought I was crying over a toy.

As well as starting me on a search for God, Grandpa Isaac gave me several lessons in life. First, he taught me how to suck eggs.

He told me that while escaping Russia, to get across the border and get to America, they had to steal eggs from farms along the way in order to eat. If ever I should be eating on the run, with no fire or time to cook, he showed me how to prick a small hole in one end and then suck; it was my first survival skill. He also told me never to bow down to another man, or even to God. But his most important teaching wasn't verbal. I used to sneak in and watch when Grandpa sat at the dinette table, next to the gas stove with the white enamel trim, and injected himself. He was a pharmacist with diabetes so it was never questioned. The sight of the needle going into his skin gave me my second anus-crunching phobia. In all of my drug experiences years later, I never shot up anything. For this I am forever grateful to Grandpa Isaac.

*　　*　　*

My mom grew up an only child above his drugstore and had never been around little boys. She wanted a little white girl of her own she could be friends with, shop with, and dress up in lace and curls. Instead she got me: a scrawny, surly, dark-haired Jew.

In order to help her pass for white, my mom was named Blanche. Her immigrant father didn't want to be perceived as a greenhorn in America, so he changed his last name from something unpronounceable, to Feldberg—because a doctor he knew and respected who worked in the tenements on the Lower East Side was named Feldberg, and it sounded American.

Jews in those days were trying desperately to pass for white. So while my name in Hebrew is Elijah (as pronounced by the Christians), Eliahu in Hebrew, Elie in Yiddish, and Ilya in Russian, my mom named me Elliot Jay. Elijah is the one the Jews are waiting for. At every Seder, a place is set for Elijah in case he should wander in to announce the coming of the kingdom of heaven. I was Elijah wrapped in white bread.

One evening, as the lights of the city were lighting up the darkening sky, my mom sat on her step stool next to the kitchen sink, and mournfully looked out the window. She was wearing her rayon navy-blue dress with small white polka dots and padded shoulders; she modeled herself after her idol, Loretta Young. My mom didn't look like a poor Jewish girl from the shtetl. All her life I heard people tell her how beautiful she was; I agreed. I could see gold flecks in her hazel eyes, and I liked the way she combed her light brown hair into soft waves. I could feel her pain that evening. *Where's daddy?* I asked. *He's working,* she said, and we looked at the city lights on the horizon together. In that moment, we bonded emotionally. She hugged me to her, and in some unspoken way I became her non-verbal confidante about daddy.

Our best times together were when she would read to me. We would lie down on the only bed, and I would cuddle into her warm body and smell the freshness of her hair. One story she told scared me. It was the story of Pandora's box. I don't remember much more than the implication that if I didn't put my toys away, back inside the toy chest in the closet, I was loosing some horrible force of chaos into the world.

My favorite story was *The Pokey Puppy*; I learned to read by following along as mommy read it to me. It was the story of a curious puppy that didn't listen to his mother, and escaped under a hole in the fence. The upshot, as I recall, is that the puppy comes home late, and goes to bed without dessert. It seemed like a good deal to me.

Even though my crib was in their bedroom, and my mother was a modest woman, my mom and dad still managed to conceive a new life right under my nose; she still wanted a baby girl.

My mom's pregnancy slowed her down and allowed me more freedom, which included more time to be in the street. A mother from the building was always supposed to be around watching, but often enough there was no supervision. It was the fall of 1949, and I was approaching my third birthday, and my defining moment.

Instead of staying on the corner of our street as routinely ordered, one day I started to walk down the shady side street into the neighborhood where our six-story brick behemoth had been dropped. Old brownstones flanked one side of the street, clapboard houses with yards and peeling paint on wooden garages the other. Trees created a canopy of cool shade. This was a different world from the barren feeling of Foster Avenue.

Rounding the block on the far side and heading up the next block, I saw my first firehouse. A Dalmatian was lying on the sidewalk outside; I didn't know what to do. A fireman called out that it was okay, and that she wouldn't hurt me. I patted my first dog. It was thrilling—another life with intelligent eyes looking back at me.

By now I was full of myself. This adventure—leaving the known by walking around the block into a different world, meeting firemen, and patting a dog—was almost too good to be true. As I came down the street from the firehouse, I ran by the scary brownstones with their strange cooking smells, to a vacant lot on the corner of Foster Avenue. My apartment building was on the far corner, past the lot; I'd made it back to the familiar world.

The vacant lot had an old tree with a tree house in it, surrounded by rubble, and mounds of dirt and weeds. The boys from my apartment building were there fighting with boys from the brownstones. One of them was hitting my friend Mark. I galloped my way into the fight like a cowboy on a horse. I shouted: *Don't worry Mark. I'll save you!*

I was playing the role of the invincible TV cowboy, the hero, charging to the rescue. The momentum of my run funneled through my arms to my hands, which landed on the chest of Mark's aggressor. He flew backward and hit his head on a rock.

Everything stopped.

Time stood still.

I have no idea how long it lasted but it must have only been a fleeting moment that stretched forever and caught us all in a frozen timeless second. I looked around and saw everyone around me completely still. None of us moved. We are still there, frozen and timeless, a diorama in the story of my life.

In the midst of that eternity of stillness, the only thing moving was a red pool of blood appearing on the rock where the boy's head was laying. I saw it, and it seemed that somehow in my seeing it everyone else saw it as well. Or perhaps we all saw it simultaneously. Only then, once it was seen, did the boy realize that his head was bleeding, and he screamed. His scream shattered the stillness, like a thin sheet of glass can shatter when hit. This shattered crystalline moment sent everyone flying back into motion at full speed, as if the energy of the fight, frozen into stillness, was now unleashed back into the world as a storm. My moment of grand inflation was punctured, and I crashed into deflation and fear. They all started to chase me.

I jumped onto Mark's tricycle and furiously push-kicked my way home. I pulled open the huge old wooden door of our building and ran into the foyer where there was a button to alert my mom to buzz me in through the next locked door. I stood on my tiptoes to reach our button. I pushed it and pushed it and pushed it and pushed it, but there was no response. And then the boys charged through the outer door.

A bigger kid grabbed me by the ears and screamed that I had broken his cousin's head, and started to smash mine into the wall behind me. My body screamed and cried out, but I felt disconnected as I floated out of my body, and didn't feel any pain. I started to see stars, as if I were floating in outer space. I remember having the thought: *This is why they see stars in the cartoons when they are hit on the head.* I found this insight amazing and funny. The next thing I remember, my mother is downstairs and she has chased everyone away. I ran screaming into the building.

The rest of my life was informed by that moment, from the most superficial to the deepest layers of my soul. My mother's authority over me was shattered because she had come too late. Since I could not trust my family for security, I made my own rules and defied my mother in countless ways. It was the start of my being a problem child.

From that moment on, I knew I was a coward. I was not invincible after all. Instead of being a hero, I had turned and run. Now I was terrified of violence, of hurting someone else again, and of being hurt again myself. My identity as a deflated coward destroyed my self-confidence and left me isolated and bereft of social skills. I credit this handicap with keeping me from a successful superficial life. It drove me to despair and beyond.

Although the repercussions of cowardice and destroyed self-esteem were deep, they were not the deepest change this incident brought about. The deepest change was my taste of a reality beyond this world. It was a fully alive moment, a taste of pristine, timeless, conscious silence . . . and I hungered for more.

That moment of timeless stillness never left me. I could not speak of it—and no one ever addressed such a state as I grew older—but it was a gift in that moment of horror. I unconsciously continued to search for it, and since I had experienced it in the context of violent street action, this is where I found it again years later.

CHAPTER 2

The First Crossroads

That traumatic moment in my life was never addressed or spoken of beyond being punished for having left the corner, and being blamed for getting Mark hurt. I never saw Mark again after that as his mother considered me a bad influence. The shock, fear, and pain could not be expressed and so went underground. My acting out against parental authority seemed to just happen on it's own, completely unconsciously; I was just a bad boy. And then, within a blink of an eye, we were out of Brooklyn and the world I had known disappeared. We moved from Brooklyn to Queens where I found myself alone in a hostile world with no tools for survival.

My mother must have been enchanted by Fresh Meadows. Named in the 1600s by the Dutch settlers of Flushing for its fresh water springs and woodland marshes, by the time we heard of it Fresh Meadows was paved over and prepped for the incoming hoards of post-war families. Its name a quaint reminder of another time.

Fresh Meadows was modern: the first development in the United States built explicitly for cars. There was a shiny new school, modern and clean, with a playground and a garden, just a few blocks from our house. But we didn't move directly into

Fresh Meadows, we lived down the street, a block from Utopia Parkway. To the masses escaping the noisy confines of Manhattan and Brooklyn, this area must have seemed like utopia. I caught turtles and frogs in the little patches of wetland that were still left, and fireflies lit up our summer evenings. We didn't yet live in a modern Fresh Meadows ranch house. We lived in a 1930s, Tudor-style, brick row house, in an old Flushing neighborhood. But that wasn't the problem. The problem was the borderline.

Within eyesight of all that was fresh and new and mainly Jewish, we were five houses over the line, and still zoned for PS 107—nine-tenths of a mile, and a universe away. If we had been a full mile away from 107 they would have sent a school bus for me, but to be a full mile away our house would have been over the border, and I could have walked the few blocks to the new school; my first Catch 22, and I was only five years old.

This side of the border—which started on Main Street and ended with my block—was an Irish Catholic, working-class neighborhood, with a sprinkling of Italians. I was the Jew. One day in the third grade I told Mary Irene, who lived across the street, that God spelled backwards was dog. She was not allowed to talk to me again until junior high.

The smart kids in my neighborhood —or the ones with a little money—went to St. Kevin's if they were boys, or to Sacred Heart if they were girls. Kids too poor or too dumb for St. Kevin's went to my school. I was consigned to the bleak, red-brick, four-story lockup they called first grade. When this Dickensian nightmare was constructed there must have been a hill bulldozed to level the ground for the school, and they continued dozing into the hill to make a schoolyard; a concrete pit lined with cold concrete walls. A six-foot wrought-iron fence surrounded the yard. I have actually been in prison yards that were more inviting.

Five years old, with no kindergarten or preschool experience, I walked into a terrifying world. My walk to school started with two long blocks leading to a small cluster of shops. A Bohack's Supermarket started the row, followed by an Irish bar and then a pizzeria. In the early morning sun, the bar reeked of tobacco and booze through its open door. It was dark, quiet, and scary inside. At the pizzeria next door, young wannabe mobsters with their hair in Elvis mode lounged outside, their smokes rolled into their tee-shirt sleeves. Next came the Catholic cemetery: that at least was peaceful. Then came the houses with the smell of cabbage cooking, and the sound of voices shouting, escaping out the windows. This scared me, and I was sometimes chased, but this was just the netherworld. The atmosphere grew darker when I entered the school.

Since I did not have a watch, and I had no idea how long it took to walk to school, I was often tardy. At first my mom got up to wake me and make me breakfast, but I was always nauseas in the morning, dreading the school day to come, and couldn't eat. After a while, my mom gave up. She would wake me and then go back to bed. I didn't really consider time. Whenever I arrived just depended on how fast I walked. I was tardy, tardy, tardy—a word I had never heard before. I wasn't sure how it was different from being late, but it was definitely bad to be tardy.

I had never been yelled at by anyone but my mother until my first-grade teacher, Miss Richter. She was thin and straight as a rod, a grim old maid, with grey hair pulled back into a bun. I remember an assignment to draw a woman. For the dress I used different colored crayons to draw a series of horizontal lines stacked as a skirt. This made Miss Richter angry. *Don't you know how to draw a dress?* she yelled. *Here!* She took a black crayon and drew over my drawing, making a triangle from the waist to the knees that cut off the edges of my lines: I was being trained to stay within the lines.

Miss Richter was my teacher in the second grade as well. One day she announced that James' father had died, and that his mother was on welfare, so we should not make fun of his shabby clothes. I cringed. This news hurt me, and I could never look at James again.

To add to the misery, we were periodically drilled for the coming nuclear attack by Russia. We would hide under our desks and were taught not to look at the atomic explosion, but to keep our heads down.

I remember very clearly the day Miss Richer taught us how to write the alphabet. She was very precise in her instructions. *Now children, put the paper at an angle to the corner of the desk, just like this. Pick up your pencil, and let it rest in the crook between your thumb and your finger. While your third finger holds the pencil against your thumb, use your pointer finger to press down on the pencil. Then hold your wrist like this, so that the point of the pencil comes down to the page at an angle just like this.*

I raised my hand, which annoyed her because it interrupted her flow. *But I am left-handed*, I said.

Stupid boy! Just do what I said with the opposite hand! Now, let's get back to our lesson.

After school, the world of my neighborhood consisted of a one-block area—not the whole block, but just our row of attached houses with an avenue at each end and an alley in the back. It was here, in our back alley, that my neighbors—two older boys, Joey Napolitano and Bobby Chiccorine—welcomed me to the neighborhood by pulling down my short pants so they could see a circumcised Jew. I screamed and cried and tried to fight them off. I was big for my age but still a baby.

Joey had three brothers—Vito, Vincent, and Michael—and a father who was a butcher, and walked around with a cigarette dangling from his lip. Later, it was said that it wasn't only animals that were butchered in the back of his shop. One day Joey's father came out of his garage, which opened onto our alley where we all hung out. He was wearing suspenders with a sleeveless undershirt tucked into his dress pants, and he was holding a large knife and swim goggles. He screamed at Joey: *Didn't I tell you never to leave this in here?* He took his knife to the goggles, slicing them into pieces before throwing them at Joey's head. *Basta fangool!* was my first Italian.

Alfie Fanerio was my first friend in my new neighborhood. He was older, and he taught me how to play chess and ride a bike. He was short and homely, with bad skin but great black, curly hair. I think he was available to be my friend because his peers rejected him. If his grandfather had been an organ grinder, Alfie could have played the monkey. Instead, Alfie's Geppetoesque grandfather sat in their garage all day building ships in bottles.

Once Alfie, Joey, and a few other kids from the block made a stink bomb that we lit and threw at the grouchy lady's front door, three doors down from mine. We all ran for cover. To disguise myself, I switched jackets with Alfie. I wore his black motorcycle jacket, while he wore my Lord Fauntleroy riding jacket—which my mom dressed me in to go with my jodhpurs for God's sake! Her sad idea of dressing up a boy instead of a girl was no more foolish than my idea that putting on Alfie's jacket would disguise me. I knew it wouldn't, but I wanted to wear the black leather jacket with the zippers. Because I couldn't yet cross the street, I ran around the block and hid in a driveway. Of course, I was recognized, and my mother duly informed. On the way home I stepped in dog shit, with the stirrups of the jodhpurs under my shoes; I never had to wear the jodhpurs again, but I did have to give Alfie back his motorcycle jacket.

They must have saved Miss Richter for the first and second graders because she was the nice one. My next two teachers were a nightmare. Apparently the parents at PS 107 wanted the teachers to treat the kids the way the nuns did at St. Kevin's. My third grade teacher was almost as bad as my fourth. They would scream at us, throw chalk, grab us by the ear, and slam our heads into the blackboard. Mrs. Mays looked like Babe Ruth in a bad wig. She was built like him too, except that she had mean-spirited little red eyes. On Halloween she gave apples to the whole class. *Now, children, inside each apple is a penny, except for one, which has a dime. Bite in and see what you get. Who got the dime children?*

I raised my hand. With a sneer she said: *It would be you.* The stabbing pain of that moment stayed with me for years. It was when I started to hate.

What saved me was reading. I devoured books. My first book was *Black Beauty.* I read it twice, and went back to it later for a third time. I cried for the tragic life of this noble creature. My father dug up the musty smelling books of his childhood and I read them all. *Bomba the Jungle Boy* and *The Hardy Boys Build a Giant Cannon* came to life under the covers of my bed. I had a flashlight and would read into the night. Sometimes if the hall light was on, I would lie with my head outside my bedroom door and read by the light of the hall, where my parents would later find me asleep with my book.

By the time of the great change, fifth grade, I was riding my bike to the Fresh Meadows Library and checking out dozens of books. My parents would never have considered trying to get zoning changed because they would never want to draw attention to themselves. They followed rules and kept quiet, but by some miracle the boundary was changed. Suddenly I was in a light-filled room with children like myself, Jewish, middle class, and friendly. My grades soared, and I was well liked by my teachers. I went from the bottom half of a dull-witted class, to the top of a bright one.

One day my mother was called in by my fifth-grade teacher because of a book report I wrote; she wondered if my mother was aware of what I was reading. I wrote about a story of a young Jewish boy who falls in love with a Christian girl during the American Revolution. I was shocked to find this was a problem since it was a book for young adults.

Secretly I had also been reading *A Stone for Danny Fisher* by Harold Robbins and *What Makes Sammy Run* by Budd Schulberg.

My parents were members of the Book of the Month Club, and I avidly read what they didn't have time for. Both these books were about Jewish boys from Brooklyn who start out in poverty, get involved with the mob, marry a gentile, and find the fast life. I loved those books. I finally had a role model of a Jewish boy like me making it out of the neighborhood. But I would never admit to reading these books because they weren't allowed; they were adult fiction. I read them under the covers.

I also read *The Wall* by John Hersey, about the Warsaw Ghetto uprisings. A few years later, *The Last of the Just* by Andre Swartz-Bart completed my Jewish boys in love with gentile blond girls collection. *The Last of the Just* was a real horror story of being caught in the Holocaust. It was at this time that I had fantasy dreams of jumping out of boxcars with a machine gun killing Nazis.

Since I was not a good fighter, to survive on the street I had to fight with my mouth. The put-down was a survival art, and I became a master. I talked my way out of several beatings in the neighborhood—but never with my mother.

Mary Irene, who was not allowed to talk to me because of my God-dog comment—which proved to her parents everything they secretly believed about Jews was true—had her bedroom window directly across from mine. One warm spring evening, she undressed in front of the window. I was thrilled to watch. It was like an early scene in *A Stone for Danny Fisher*, when he falls in love with a Christian girl across the street in Brooklyn as he watches her undress before her window. I could not believe my good luck. It never happened again, but I never stopped checking.

Around this time, I found I could dream and be awake at the same time, aware that I was dreaming. In these dreams I could fly. I soared, not like a speeding bullet but like a kite. I could also dematerialize. The catch with both these powers was that I had to be completely relaxed. So when I flew into Mary Irene's bedroom at night to take her for a flight in her flannel pajamas, if I heard the sounds of her parents coming, I would freeze in fear, unable to disappear or lift off. I had to learn to relax and let everything wash through me as I returned to the calm state that allowed me to be invisible and levitate. Of course I never spoke about this to anyone; it was just part of my interior life. It trained me to face the danger that was to come.

In fifth grade, I found Freud and Marx at the library. I carried *Das Kapital* around with me for a few weeks but couldn't get through the first few pages. I carried it to school anyway, always visible on the outside of my stack; a signal waiting for a response from intelligent life. No one was interested.

Freud was much easier to read—at least the primers that I found were. I liked the idea of an ego, a superego, and an id. I saw how it applied to me. But Freud's proposition of a death wish, and the polarity between the desire for life and the desire for death, made no sense to me at all. While I could not find a death wish in myself, at least Freud gave me something to think about, unlike religion.

We went to a modern temple for Reformed Jews. Beth Shalom, the House of Peace, was on Northern Boulevard, a ten-minute drive from home. For a church it wasn't bad, a modern building with an oddly cantilevered roof, organ music, and singing. Every male in attendance wore a jacket and tie. We were the children and grandchildren of just-off-the-boat Eastern European peasants pretending to be Protestant. No link to anything from the schtetle was preserved—no yarmulkes, prayer shawls, or even Yiddish jokes—instead, a dead Gatsybesque, middle-class, Queens rendition of white people worshipping.

It was so boring I couldn't bear it. It was a lie. The rabbi with his pompous holy-sermon voice sounded to me like a charlatan. I didn't know if there was a God or not, but it seemed to me this had nothing to do with God. It was my great good luck that I didn't get trapped in the net of religion, because by that time I was so strongly identified as a Jew. I wanted to meet mishpucha—a family of warm kindred souls in search of meaning and God. Instead, Temple Beth Shalom was a version of *Leave It to Beaver* without the jokes.

I only found out when he was eighty years old that it was my father's gift to me that I had missed the religion trap. He had been a practicing Orthodox Jew when he went into the military for the Second World War. He brought his tzfillan, titsitz, and prayer shawl into the army and davened every morning . . . until he found out about the death camps. He never spoke of this while we were living together as a family, but in his eighties, he told me that he and God were not on speaking terms. He said that when he found out about the camps, he decided he didn't want a God that would allow his chosen people to be treated that way.

My private search for God was no more successful than the farce at the temple. I once locked myself in the bathroom, the only room where privacy was certain, and asked for a sign. Any sign. Anything at all to let me know there was an intelligent consciousness at the other end. After asking, I listened. I closed my eyes, and I listened. It became very quiet—very dark and quiet. The longer I listened, the more I fell into vast, dark quiet. I heard the silence. Eyes closed or opened didn't seem to matter—I still saw and felt black emptiness. This was not the answer I was hoping for. At that stage, the absence of a sign was no sign at all.

In the Roman year of 1957, the Hebrew year was 5719. I was ten years old and knew that this mirrored configuration of years would not happen again in my lifetime. I believed that I would always remember this year, and so I made a vow. When I examined my life, I saw my own unhappiness and the suffering of everyone around me—family, friends, neighbors. Everyone seemed to be living a lie, faking it. I saw that my parents loved me as their parents had loved them; we had money, and took vacations to

Miami Beach every year, but it made no difference. I felt that I was so emotionally warped and twisted that I would never be happy.

What was the point of passing it on? Perhaps this question was precipitated by my mother's curse. After an episode of screaming at me and spanking me, she said: *Just wait. Just you wait and see how your children will treat you.* This was her painful cry and her way of getting back at me, cursing my future. I saw her point: I did not want to do to my children what was done to me, and given my emotional wreckage, I would surely do just that. I had spent years getting spanked for being bad, until my mother cried and went to bed. Then I had to go to her and apologize to make her feel better. It all seemed so warped. I would never be happy or whole, and I had no idea how to live a normal life—though normal seemed sick to me. Everyone I knew was normal—unhappy and pretending. We could hear our neighbors through the wall when Alan's mother punished him. They screamed at each other, like we screamed at each other, but out on the street none of this was ever mentioned; everyone acted like it never happened. This was normal, and it drove me crazy.

I was ten years old when I made the vow never to have children. I could find no reason to pass along the suffering in my warped psyche. I sent this vow to my future, rightly believing that if I should forget, I would always remember the once-in-a-lifetime mirroring of dates: I would remember 1957 and my vow. It was the first conscious choice of my life, and it has lasted for a lifetime.

At the time, I had no idea of the profound effects this choice would have in my life, how it would affect everything from that moment on. In staying true to that vow over the years,—with many temptations and a few close calls—that ten-year-old boy gave an incredible inheritance to his future. He gave the certainty that I would not have children. This decision meant that I did not have to give my life to supporting a family or having a career.

I added to the vow I was sending to the future another message as well. I had just read a Classic Comic Book about Alexander the Great. It said that a mystic gave Alexander a choice: he could live either a long and wise life, or a short and glorious one. I remember leaning against a maple tree outside at dusk, on the Indian summer day of Rosh Hashanah, in the Jewish new year of 5719. Alfie was leaning against Junior's chopped-down hot rod with a Chinese dragon painted on its trunk. We were just listening to the evening creep into the falling light. I concentrated myself and prayed to the future: *If you get a chance, choose the short, fast life.*

CHAPTER 3

Refusal of the Call

When sixth grade ended, all my classmates went on to the new Fresh Meadows junior high school. Because the zoning hadn't changed at this level, I left the comfort and ease of newfound friends, and took a bus to Junior High School 158 in Bayside: the town past Flushing in the opposite direction from Fresh Meadows. Traveling alone into unknown territory became a theme throughout my life.

My new school had a different population mix: blacks, Italians, and Bayside Jews. My last two years in elementary school had pulled me out of the battlefield long enough so that when I re-entered unknown territory, I was better prepared. I imitated the Italian kids, greasing my hair into funnels on both sides of my head lead to a spit curl down my forehead, wearing taps on my pointy chukka boots, and adopting a smart aleck attitude as a front. I was a wise guy.

Well, I wasn't a real wise guy like my Uncle Jack. Uncle Jack's life was another secret in our family. The entire time that I knew him I could never speak to him about his life. It wasn't until he retired to Miami that he let a few anecdotes slip.

Uncle Jack wasn't really my uncle but my great uncle, my grandfather's youngest brother. Jackie grew up on the streets of the Lower East Side. He made his first money with his boyhood friend Meyer; they were lookouts for Benny Siegel's crap games. Meyer grew up to be Meyer Lansky, the Jewish brains behind the modern mafia. Benny Siegel went on to be called Bugsy, because of his penchant for violence. Together they mobbed up with Lucky Luciano, helping him kill off the Mustache Petes—as the old regime was derisively referred to—and establishing the five families and the modern mafia. Bugsy brought the mob to Vegas (as played by Robert DeNiro in the film *Casino*), and Meyer brought it to Havana. Once, a Manhattan DA was impanelling a grand jury, and Uncle Jack was advised to get out of town for a while. He spent a few months in Brooklyn, where the Manhattan DA did not have jurisdiction.

By the time I knew him, Uncle Jack was an occasional maître d' at my father's Forest Hills restaurant, Scott's. What I didn't know was that he was also working as the right-hand man for Frank Erikson, the Swede: the biggest bookie in the United States. Erikson worked for Frank Costello, the then retired consigliore to Lucky Luciano. My father told me that once when Uncle Jack got into his elevator, someone came in behind him with a gun and took his moneybag. A call was made to Frank Costello, and the next day the money was returned.

So, my uncle was the real wise guy. When he took me to visit his Rego Park studio with a Murphy bed, he let me see his gun. It was lying in the bottom of a drawer he opened to get some old black-and-white photos from the '30s. In one of the photos he was at the Folies Bergère in Paris with a showgirl on his arm. In another, I saw him in a sharp suit and a Borsalino hat, standing in front of his new white car with running boards and a small poodle on the raised front-wheel well. Always impeccably dressed in tailored suits, Italian shoes, and grey pearl cufflinks, he was like Burt Lancaster in *Atlantic City*: a living fossil, carrying in his heart the memories of New York when it had Floy Floy.

Uncle Jack was the only adult who treated me like a real person. He called me *kid* and took me to ball games. He was a Yankees fan, so we got to watch all the great ones of the '50s. During the games, he would buy me a hot dog and tell me to sit tight while he went off to see some friends. When he came back, he always brought a baseball autographed by all the Yankees on the field: Mickey Mantle, Yogi Berra, Whitey Ford, and the crew. Years later, my dozens of autographed baseballs were thrown out, along with my baseball-card and comic-book collection; they were probably worth enough to fund my retirement.

At one of the games in the late '50s or early '60s, a bunch of guys jumped the center field barrier and ran onto the field carrying a banner that read "Support Fidel! End the dictatorship of Batista!" I asked my uncle what it was about, and he said: *Just a bunch of crazy jerks who don't know what they are talking about.* He could have said that they were a threat to Meyer's casino empire in Havana, but it didn't come up. I had no idea that Uncle Jack was working at the games, and that I was his cover.

He also took me to the Russian baths in midtown. I loved the smell of birch, and the various steams and saunas built around a cold-water swimming pool. Again, Uncle Jack would get me settled and then disappear for a while to see some people. Only later, when I watched a movie about the early Jewish mob, and saw a scene in the Russian baths explaining that you couldn't be listened to in the steam rooms, did I realize that yet again I had been the front.

So, in junior high I wasn't a wise guy like my Uncle Jack, but actually more of a smart aleck. I would sit in the back of the room and make jokes and whisper sarcastic comments. I prided myself on not doing my homework, and getting away with it. Only in retrospect do I see that this hardened attitude was a defense born of despair.

One day when I was around eleven, I was with Uncle Jack in the restaurant when two of his friends came in. The three of them stood around me, and my uncle asked me: *Elliot, what do you want to be when you grow up?* I hated these kinds of questions; I found them demeaning. First of all, I didn't want to grow up, and secondly I didn't want to be anything.

A fireman, I sneered. The question made me feel like a trained dog being asked to jump and wag its tail.

Hey, don't be a wise guy, Jackie said.

Okay, okay. I wanna be an Indian chief.

Uncle Jack and his buddies were taken aback for a moment, and didn't know how to respond. After a beat, I said: *Hey, you wanna trained monkey? Find an organ grinder;* they all broke up laughing.

It didn't always go this well in class.

*　　*　　*

Junior high is when I started to make money. By seventh grade, I spent my weekends as an apprentice with two neighbors—both shop teachers—installing attic exhaust fans in the years before mass air conditioning. That was fun! Climbing into attics, helping, becoming someone that could be depended upon—and I liked earning a dollar an hour.

What was more fun was smuggling. Michel Pitou, a neighbor who moved in across the street, became my Fagin. His father worked at the French Embassy in business exports. Michel got hold of a box of thermo-couplers: little metal buttons that became warm and inverted when vigorously rubbed. Put one of these down on a seat, and in a few minutes the metal would cool and snap back into position, popping the disk into the air. Michel sold them to me for a nickel a piece, and I sold them in school for a dime a piece. Soon the whole school was popping its tops.

Next, Michel went to Chinatown and bought mats of firecrackers, which were illegal in New York except during Chinese religious occasions. Fifty packs in a mat cost Michel a nickel a pack. He fronted them to me for a dime, and I took them to school and sold them for a quarter. It wasn't just the money I loved, but also the thrill of sneaking in contraband and not getting caught. Years later, I never crossed a border without smuggling something along with me.

I soon discovered poker, which was how I made my money from seventh grade through college. A game of nickel-dime-quarter with a quarter ante usually made me twenty to forty dollars a week. The summer when I was fifteen, I returned from summer camp with my counselor's paycheck which I'd won over two months of playing poker. I found it was not the cards but the mind that won the game. I didn't realize it consciously, but I could read people, and hide my own emotions; I could tell who was bluffing, and cover my own bluffs.

I remember my experiments with an evasive thought like *Oh no!* when I had a winning hand, or *This is great!* when I had a losing hand, but I found that if I didn't have any thoughts at all, I could see others' emotions more clearly, and they couldn't read mine; I discovered that it was the emotion of the thought that showed on faces.

Of course I didn't win every hand, and not even every game, but I probably won 75 percent of the games until college, where the competition was better. This became part of my training in reading people's energy, and controlling my mind, which became useful decades later.

*   *   *

In junior high, I had my first girlfriend, touched a titty for the first time—although on top of the blouse and bra—and fell in love with girls. I also fell in love with rock and roll, and danced the Mashed Potatoes on a TV dance show as a finalist with my dance partner, Mary Irene—the girl across the street—who got us the tickets. I also began buying my clothes on Jamaica Avenue— Queen's version of Harlem—instead of wearing clothes my mother bought me at Mr. Marvin's, where Marvin flirted with my mom, and sidled into my crotch while measuring my inseam.

Despite being labeled an underachieving problem child, and being sent to my first therapist in the eighth grade, junior high was a peak period for me because I finally had girlfriends. In first and second grades I'd had a crush on Gina Shepard; I loved her ponytail and rabbit front teeth. I can still see her thin cotton print dress with a Peter Pan white collar and puffy short sleeves, but I was too shy to do anything except look at her from my desk. For two years we never spoke, and then she was gone. But in junior high, slow dancing and French kissing became the closest I had yet come to heaven.

In school, I also met my first black friends, who were then called Negros. Benny Peoples was a street kid with raggedy clothes; we teamed up against the Italians. Freddie Paris was an intellectual, a clean-cut, middle-class kid. I remember inviting Freddie to a party at my house, but his mother wouldn't let him come—probably a wise decision on her part given the probable danger of being black in my neighborhood, where I never saw a black person walking down the street. And finally a shout out to Murray the K on WINS radio, who brought the Shirelles and Motown into my life first thing every morning, and Jean Shepard on WOR radio, who kept me company into the night.

After three years of coming out of my shell and making friends, we went on to high school. My classmates all went to Bayside High School, while I went to the newly built school on some of the last wetlands of Fresh Meadows; once again I was a stranger in a new environment. There were 1,800 kids in my class, and almost 6,000 students in the school by the time I graduated in 1964. Most of the students were smart and driven Fresh Meadow Jews, determined to get into the Ivy League.

There were quotas on Jews in those days, and probably on New Yorkers as well, to keep Harvard and Yale from being flooded with thousands of us. I sized up my competition and saw that my chances were zero, and so there was no need to compete. After all, it would mean applying myself and doing homework in subjects I didn't find interesting, and that I couldn't see being useful when I left school. To this day, however, I remember the Gadsden Purchase of 1853 because I was making out with Michelle Block when we were supposed to be studying for our midterms. The Gadsden Purchase was somehow embedded in Michelle's sweet embrace.

If I liked a teacher, and the teacher liked me, I did very well. In seventh grade, I had a crush on Mrs. Susswell, my English teacher and my first African-American teacher. She liked me, so I excelled. In the ninth grade, it was Mrs. Katcher who had eyes like my mother's and encouraged my creative writing; she made me the head of the school yearbook. In the eleventh grade, it was Mrs. Russ, who taught an honors level creative writing class. This was where I met Lisa, who introduced me to another way of life, and set me up for my next major crossroad.

*   *   *

Lisa sat in the back of the class, like me, and started flirting with me. She had long, black hair and wore a black turtleneck over her big-breasted voluptuousness. She winked at me, and I was gone. She was a beat (or *a beatnik* as my mom would say), and had friends that played the guitar and drank Chianti from bottles with baskets woven onto them. Her parents were Trotskyites, and they looked at my bourgeois self with scorn. No point getting into the details of what we got into, except to say that it was sweet, tender, intense, and the most blissful experiences I'd had yet.

In the spring of 1963, Lisa bought us two tickets to see Bob Dylan at Town Hall. Seeing Bob Dylan changed my life. He gave me a point of view that finally made sense of the mad world. He opened my mind, and I have never been the same since. He sang a song about Davie Moore—a boxer who had recently been killed by Sugar Ramos in a championship fight—*who came here from Cuba's door where boxing ain't allowed no more.* The guys with the banner at Yankee Stadium now made more sense than the rest of the world.

Until I saw Bob Dylan, I was an unhappy outcast, bitter and sarcastic, without an alternative vision of possibility. But now, with hundreds of other cheering, singing, like-minded souls, I saw another possibility.

> *Come mothers and fathers throughout the land*
>
> *and don't criticize what you can't understand.*
>
> *Your sons and your daughters are beyond your command.*
>
> *Your old road is rapidly fading,*
>
> *so get off the new one if you can't lend a hand,*
>
> *for the times they are a changin'.*

That night my heart and mind opened to a different view of reality, one that ruled out the possibility of living a comfortable, normal, upper-middle-class existence. I knew that I would never go back as I embraced a new way of life.

That fall, when President Kennedy was assassinated, something broke in the American psyche. Decades do not really start every ten years, but rather when an earth-shifting event changes the psychic landscape forever. Before that moment it was still the Fifties: a black and white, homogenized world, and we really were *still great.* The Kennedy funeral is the last time we came together as a nation of one people, with everyone watching TV and crying together.

After the killing, the Sixties started, the country broke apart and has never come back together again. Civil Rights and Vietnam polarized the population, and the balkanization has only increased since then. The Reagan right-wing counter-revolution corroded and then snapped the fibers of society. It severed the safety net, and monetized the civil net, giving birth to the *greed is good* ethos that we live in today. The rise of red states and FOX news would not have been possible before the rupture. Most of the best left the political field to the paid hacks and the jackals.

The best chance we had to reunite since then was 9/11 when the whole world rallied around us in support. We needed a great leader—a Martin Luther King or a Nelson Mandela—instead we had the craven idiot son, the Usurper, who told us to "go back to shopping," and used the attack as an excuse for a *crusade*, causing a mortal wound to the body of society while destabilizing the world, destroying the last shreds of the Republic and our dignity as a people.

During my senior year in high school, I slipped into my beatnik identity. I was sent home twice: once for my goatee, which was not appropriate for a high school student, and once for wearing jeans, which were not appropriate school attire at that time before the seismic aftershocks reached the mainstream, and everyone was wearing jeans.

Once I was accepted to a college, I thought the last half of my senior year seemed like an even greater waste of time. I cut school a few times to go to Aqueduct Racetrack to bet on the horses, without knowing that this was my uncle's workplace, and that we could have run into each other there. He would have been there placing bets for the Swede to offset the odds, as Angelica Huston did in *The Grifters*.

In the spring of 1964, the New York World's Fair came to Flushing Meadows; I cut school for the opening day. When I got to the Alabama Pavilion, I saw my first picket line. CORE—the Congress of Racial Equality—was picketing the Alabama Pavilion because of the state's racist voting laws. I saw Lila Charney from school on the picket line, and she called to me to join them. I wanted to, but I didn't. I was afraid of the possible consequences. I was afraid of getting arrested and of having a record. This moment of cowardice forced me to examine myself . . . and I didn't like what I saw.

CHAPTER 4

Which Side Are You On?

When the next crossroads appeared in my life, I was primed and ready. I was a different person from the year before when I stood by and watched.

During the summer before college, I started working as a mail boy for United Artists on 49th Street and Seventh Avenue. We all wore jackets and ties to and from work, as if we were in management. When we arrived at the mail room, we would take off our sports coats and don our grey, cotton mail-boy jackets. We personalized and accessorized our uniforms with rolled-up sleeves, tucked-in ties, and pens in our jacket front pockets. We made $47 a week, sorting and delivering mail twice a day, as well as being on call to deliver messages and papers from one office or person to another.

Friday and Saturday nights, I worked as a busboy/dishwasher for 85¢ an hour and 15 percent of the tips at a folk music coffeehouse in Kew Gardens. The coffeehouse was in an abandoned railway station, giving it great atmosphere, with tables set up outside above the empty tracks. Inside were a few more tables and the best music imaginable. Mississippi John Hurt, Lightning Hopkins, Judy Collins, Ramblin' Jack Elliot, Patrick Sky, Phil Ochs, Blind Reverend Gary Davis, and many more played for a small group of devoted listeners. I could not believe my good luck.

I defied my parents and went to the Newport Folk Festival that summer of 1964. Bob Dylan and his then lover Joan Baez, the Swan Silvertones and other great gospel musicians, Earl Monroe and his Mountain Boys, and Pete Seeger and the Jim Kweskin Jug Band filled my ears and heart. I was in bliss. I slept on the floor in the living room of a country farmhouse, where breakfast was included. This was the first time I saw marijuana being smoked. It was on the street, and I was too scared to join in and try it.

*   *   *

The mailroom was where I saw my chance to score. I had befriended Billy, a 19-year-old black kid from the South Bronx. Billy later became my source when I had pounds of marijuana shipped to me at college through the United Artists mailroom. I had no idea what to say to Billy that first time. I had heard different names for marijuana in songs. I didn't know the code, so I asked Billy if he knew Mary Jane.

Mary who?

I mean, do you know where I can get some Mary Jane? I asked conspiratorially.

Billy looked at me for a moment puzzled. And then he lit up.

Oh, you want some weed, he grinned with a look of knowing in his eyes. He said he could get me a nickel bag. I was ecstatic, although I had no idea what that was.

How much will it cost?

A nickel you fool! Five dallahs, he laughed. I laughed with him.

The next day he slipped a little brown pay envelope into my shirt pocket. For the first time, I smelled the pungent bouquet wafting up the front of my shirt. But what to do next? I hadn't a clue. I asked if he would roll it for me.

Sure. Just go across the street and get yourself some Bambú.

I waited for my lunch break, all the while wondering what I'd be buying—this Bambú. Would they know what it was when I asked?

Would they call the police?

When it was time, I nonchalantly walked into the smoke shop on the corner of 47th Street and Broadway. I looked around, as if I knew what I was looking for, and waited for the counter to clear. In a moment when no one else was in the store, I smiled at the old man behind the counter and said, *Give me some Bambú*, with the same inflection and accent Billie used. The man flipped a pack of rolling papers onto the counter.

Little did I know what a small world this city of six million was. It turned out that this smoke shop was a front for a bookie operation, and the man who sold me my first rolling papers knew my Uncle Jack and who I was as well. And so before actually lighting up, my first time smoking was duly noted and passed on to my uncle.

When I returned with the papers, Billie took me into the men's room, where we locked ourselves in a stall and rolled joints. *It's got seeds, okay?*

I had no idea. *Sure, fine.*

So Billie rolled, seeds and all. Only one person saw us in the men's room together: Jaime, the Cuban from the mailroom. He wore tight pants and purple ruffled shirts and a Desi Arnaz pompadour. Jaime grabbed my ass as I walked down the hall. I was shocked, and I jumped. He laughed and winked.

I saw you, he giggled and teased. *I saw you in there with Billie. What about me? I'm not cute enough for you?*

Bunny, the cute blond waitress with a Buster Brown haircut, let me use her apartment above the coffee house to smoke my first joint. I invited Mara Palatsky and could not believe my great good luck when she said yes. To me, Mara was one of the prettiest girls at school. And someone who never looked at me. If our high school had a playing field and a football team, Mara would have been a cheerleader. That she was interested enough in both grass and me was a boon from heaven.

We sat on the couch and smoked. We waited, but nothing happened. So we smoked another. After our third joint, it still seemed like it wasn't working. Then Bunny rushed up to tell us that her friend Roger was coming by for a few minutes and not to let him know. This was just when it came on for both of us. Roger came in and sat in the chair opposite the couch. We both stared at him and grinned. Roger picked up one of my boots that had been lying near his chair and examined it. *Fine boot,* he said and handed it back to me. My arms would not move to take the boot. It was a universe too far away. I just sat there and smiled, and after holding the boot out for an inordinate amount of time, Roger finally put it back down on the floor.

Once Roger left, Mara and I started to laugh. We laughed so hard I rolled off the couch. When I got back up on the couch, our bodies touched. I told her I could feel her skinny ribs, and we both began a fresh round of laughter. I saw through the absurdity of everything, but this time instead of bringing me to despair, it brought me peals of laughter.

For years afterward, I regretted that all I could do with Mara was laugh and feel her ribs. She is probably a Yiddisha grandma somewhere now, but she was my Lauren Bacall.

*   *   *

I won a state scholarship for full tuition to any state school, including Buffalo where John Barth taught. But these schools were all too close to home. I wanted to get as far away from New York as my parents would allow. They made an agreement with me several years before: they would support me until I earned my BA, and then I would be on my own. So when the tiny robin's-egg-blue pill with a Batman sign on it was offered to me, I passed. I knew that if I took LSD, I would never finish college, and I had given my word to my parents.

I was offered early admission to attend the University of Pittsburgh. I was expecting a smaller New York, with the school located in the city, like NYU, where my parents met. The school had Mellon money for a brief moment and was buying high-name faculty to build itself into a major university. They were looking for students like me, with high SATs and mediocre grades, not good enough for the top schools but with potential. (By the time I left the university, Mellon had pulled his money, bankrupted the school, and bought Carnegie Tech, renaming it Carnegie Mellon). Instead of a little New York, I found a backwater steel town with a mediocre college. My Honors English class with Mrs. Russ in high school surpassed any class I had as an English major in the university.

I smoked marijuana in a pipe in the public lobby of the school, without being noticed. They had never smelled it before. I made it my mission to "turn on" the school. By then I was using marijuana as a sacrament. I thought if everyone got high, the madness would end. When someone new was turned on, it was not a casual affair. We would sit on cushions and "meditate" and let the atmosphere contribute to the experience. We smoked for altered states of insight.

Tom Reynolds, Paul DeBois, and I formed Students for Peace, the first left-wing anti-war organization in the university's history. Paul had an off-campus apartment, where the two of us would listen to Miles Davis and smoke grass. Paul was a New Orleans mulatto intellectual who took me to my first jazz club on the Hill, the black neighborhood of Pittsburgh. We saw Cecil Taylor, but as the first set started, someone shot a bullet through the front window – it could have been somebody having a strong negative reaction to the atonal and arrhythmic music Cecil was experimenting with. We ran out the back with everyone else and walked back down the hill.

One day when Paul and I were at his apartment, a phone call came in with news that a bus was going to Alabama to support the civil rights demonstrations happening in Selma and Montgomery.

The previous summer of 1964 was called Freedom Summer, when the Student Non-Violent Coordinating Committee (SNCC) organized voter registration in Mississippi. Three boys—Michael Schwerner, Andrew Goodman, and James Chaney—were arrested in Neshoba County by a Ku Klux Klan sheriff and then disappeared. When the FBI became involved, the boys were eventually found, murdered and buried in a Mississippi swamp. That Andrew Goodman had not only been Jewish but also a student at Queens College, next door to my high school, brought the event directly home to me. To be chased and killed by the Ku Klux Klan in the Mississippi night was the scariest thing I could think of. It happened only a month after I saw my first demonstration at the Alabama Pavilion.

Now, seven months later, just as the phone call came in, Reverend Reeb, a Northern white minister, was beaten to death in Selma when he got off a bus to join Martin Luther King Jr.'s march. The attempts to march from Selma to Montgomery were being blocked by dogs and fire hoses. SNCC was calling for white students to come to Montgomery to risk being beaten with the blacks. The thinking was that if affluent whites experienced the same conditions as blacks, public outcry might lead to federal intervention.

I knew that I was standing at a threshold when Paul got that call, that I would step through a door and leave behind the beaten path of my inherited future. I knew without hesitation that I was on the bus. I was of course very scared. I was putting my life in danger. The photos of the boys dug up in Mississippi were still fresh in my mind, and the footage on the nightly news coming out of Selma was terrifying. I was warned about possibly getting an FBI record that could destroy a future career, but there was still no doubt in my mind that I was on the bus.

We were an integrated bus. This meant that when we stopped to get something to eat at a lunch counter in Memphis, we were turned away. When we stopped for gas and a bathroom break in Birmingham, troopers with German shepherds met us to enforce the use of "the colored toilets."

It was a warm spring night when we rolled through the streets of Montgomery. Ahead of us was a war zone, with police lights flashing, barricades, and state troopers. We had no idea what was going on. I could feel the familiar anus-tightening chill and the tremble of terror in my belly as we approached the police line. The police moved the barricades aside and let our bus through.

We entered a different world. The police's cordoning off of the one road into and out of this black neighborhood made it feel as if the area was both under siege and a liberated zone. The ostensible reason for the police barricade was the previous night, the Ku Klux Klan had come riding down the road on horseback, and up onto front porches, indiscriminately beating and clubbing people. I was naturally cynical and could not yet imagine that this really took place. It was too far from what I believed was possible in America at this time.

Whatever the motivation, the police barricade created an intense and immediate camaraderie. There were no cars. People were standing in the streets in clusters talking. Kids connected the clusters by running through them and up onto the porches, which were full of aunts and grannies visiting, laughing, and worrying. The sense of community was so strong it permeated the atmosphere. United by a common cause, we were surrounded by a dangerous enemy that sought to destroy us. It felt so real and alive compared to everything I had known before. The white-bread existence of my past dissolved in the heart of soul. I felt more at home here than I had ever felt in my life. My petty neurotic concerns were noticeable in their absence.

I was there to be witness and cannon fodder. I was there to put my life on the line and not to fight back. The evening we arrived we went on our first march, to the hospital a few blocks away to use the restrooms that had already been legally integrated by the courts. This was the same hospital that turned away Bessie Smith, who bled to death on her way to the colored hospital in another city. A hostile crowd waited to block our way. We sat on the sidewalk and sang freedom songs while cameramen with 16mm movie cameras slowly walked down the street filming us. The FBI, State police, and every cop with a camera came by with floodlights to get us on film. I'd often seen photos of Mafia dons hiding their faces with newspapers while leaving the courtroom. I couldn't decide if this was the correct tactic for me now. On the one hand, it implied guilt, but on the other, I didn't want my picture in the FBI's files. I tried hiding my face at first, but in the end I smiled and waved.

Jim Foreman, one of the leaders of SNCC and our march leader (the same man you see wearing SNCC overalls and walking with Dr. King in the Selma-to-Montgomery newsreels), negotiated a deal, and we walked in threes to the hospital: a white man on one side, an African-American man on the other, and a black or white woman in the middle. We were spit on and cursed as we walked. We sang our way into the hospital without anyone being hurt— which was a problem because the SNNC's strategy for calling Northern white college students to come to Montgomery was to have us beaten in order to get federal protection for voter-rights activity.

We slept on the floor of the Jackson Street Baptist Church. A truck from SNCC headquarters in Atlanta brought sleeping bags and toothbrushes. That night I witnessed the beginning of the Black Power movement. A radical wing of SNCC was coming to power, and the Deacons for Defense were guarding our church with shotguns, giving rise to the Black Panthers a few years later.

*　　*　　*

The morning after our failed march the mood in the street was heavy with both humidity and dejection. Suddenly, an electric current shot through everyone. I caught it when I saw a wide-eyed eleven-year-old black boy, in a torn tee shirt and raggedy jeans, spreading the news: *The King is coming! The King is coming!*

We packed the larger Fourth Street Baptist Church so tightly that arms were squeezed on either side. The windows were open, and the air was muggy. We sweated as we clapped and sang freedom songs:

> *Ain't gonna let no po'leese turn me round,*
>
> *turn me round, turn me round.*
>
> *I'm gonna keep on walkin'*
>
> *keep on talkin'*
>
> *marchin' to the freedom land.*

For an hour and a half we sang and rocked, and the energy built. Electricity like I had never experienced before, and yet, it felt familiar. I knew it in my bones. Just at our peak, Dr. King entered. His energy matched the room. He not only met it but took it to the next level. Gently, slowly, he built the rock and rhythm, the call and response, and took us all along.

You have seen him on film. His "I Have a Dream" speech will go down with the Gettysburg Address as one of the greatest speeches of our nation. I hardly remember anything he said that day, though I remember it followed along these lines: *By all means keep on moving to freedom. If you can't fly then run, if you can't run then walk, if you can't walk then crawl, but whatever you do you have to keep moving forward.* His basic goodness and penetrating intelligence electrified us, and they still live in my heart fifty years later. And again we sang:

And before I'll be a slave

I'll be buried in my grave

and go home to my Lord and be free.

That night and the next day, I watched a change in leadership happen. The next day Stokely Carmichael led the meeting in the community-packed church. We sang a hymn adapted for the Freedom Movement called "Freedom Table":

We're gonna sit at the freedom table; we're gonna sit at the freedom table one of these days.

Stokely declared, *If Massah don't let us sit at the freedom table, we're gonna knock the legs off of the fucking table!* This was radical. It was Stokely who had just gotten Dr. King to say black instead of Negro, and now he was upping the ante.

Stokely led our next march to the capitol to demand that Governor Wallace and the State of Alabama insure one man one vote. This was a wild march, very different from the earlier one led by Jim Forman. First we ran through the black high school to get the kids to come and join us. We ran through the halls singing:

Which side are you on, boy? Which side are you on? Are you on the side of freedom or an Uncle Tom? Which side are you on?

I remember one girl standing in the doorway of her classroom as kids ran out of the class from behind her. She was crying. She seemed torn between following her heart and listening to her parents—or so it seemed to me.

We were around a thousand as we headed to the capitol in the hot sun. The capitol was in sight, but the police were waiting. They headed us off and cordoned us in. Standing in the gutter, a solid line of men faced us. They wore hard hats. The blue hard hats were state police, the white hard hats were city police, and the red hard hats were the deputized redneck local boys, who wore flannel shirts and slapped billy clubs in their palms. They lined up in an alternating red, white, and blue pattern. Every hard hat had a Confederate flag decal on the front. We sat and sang freedom songs while we passed water up and down the line.

We all stood up when we saw that there was a flanking movement. Stokely and a small group of SNCC volunteers started walking unguarded down the other side of the street to the capitol. I was near the head of the line, and the strategists started at the back. Now they were across the street, and I wasn't sure what was coming. I eyed the deputized redneck in front of me. I could smell the beer on his breath.

Up until that moment I was still solidly in the dream of what it meant to be an American. The unexamined American dream was still the atmosphere I breathed and the lens I saw the world through. Even as a pot-smoking, bongo-playing beat, (as we called ourselves before the birth of hippies and freaks), my life was being lived in the context of the American dream. I was a reformer perhaps, but nothing more.

Suddenly, the whole street dropped into an audible silence. We were shocked into stillness by the horror of what we were now seeing. Riding toward us, down the middle of the street, came the Klan.

We have seen this in movies so many times that it is beyond cliché—yet in real life the scene takes on a monumental quality. The heat waves shimmering off the asphalt as the horses canter in slow motion toward the crowd. The only sound we heard was the clip-clopping of hooves. No one wore sheets, instead most of the men wore cowboy hats; a few wore their state-trooper shirts. The lead rider was a mean-looking old man with a giant cane in his hand. If it were Hollywood, this scene would be too hackneyed to survive, but here he was, riding toward us.

Time opened up and swallowed us in a frozen moment, before they struck.

This moment was familiar. It had been absent for years, but I knew it and loved its return. It revealed a transcendent quality that I could not name and a certainty that things were not as they appeared. Life is a great spaciousness that is ignored in the concentration on what appears in that spaciousness. Yet in those moments when the spaciousness becomes the foreground, a deep joy is brought into the moment of horror.

As the lead rider swung his cane over his head, he seemed to move in slow motion and in perfect symmetry with Stokely as he put his sleeping bag over his head. The THWACK of the cane meeting the sleeping bag resounded down the street and shattered the stillness. A girl screamed, as a glacier-sized chunk of the American dream shattered. I remember so clearly thinking, *This is America. This is happening in America, in 1965.*

Then the horses were on us. People panicked and screamed as they ran, falling over each other and crushing each other in the stampede. Through the chaos I saw a beacon of light. The student organizer from Chattam College was on the steps of the porch of a small white clapboard house. She was singing "We Shall Overcome." She was trying to calm the crowd. She was a hero in the midst of chaos, and I wanted to serve her. I made my way over to her and put my arms over her head to protect her, as we sang together. Suddenly a horse's head appeared over my shoulder, slobbering on the front of my shirt as the posse man swung his State Trooper hard hat at me. I felt the blow to my head from a dissociated space. We were trapped, with the horse up on the porch blocking our escape. A city policeman ran up and pulled the horse off, letting us get away. I immediately felt guilty because I had not been seriously hurt.

My mother saw this on that night's news with Huntley-Brinkley. First they mentioned that students from Pittsburgh colleges were involved, and then she saw me for a few seconds in the news footage flash by from behind a horse. She had my father call the chancellor to demand to know why I wasn't in school.

A message reached me from Pittsburgh that my parents were very upset. I called them the next day to let them know that I was okay. I pleaded that they write and phone Congress to call for federal protection from the violence. My mom said that if I had been in class, where I belonged, there wouldn't be any violence. They were not paying for me to be in Alabama.

The next day we listened to the news on the radio while standing on the porch of the church. President Johnson was sending federal protection for a Selma-to-Montgomery March. He was also introducing the Voting Rights Act in Congress. Johnson, a Texan, was the first politician to say on the floor of Congress that day, *We shall overcome.*

For the moment, we had won, but my vision of America was permanently shattered.

PART II

CROSSING THE THRESHOLD

We had to destroy Bén Tre in order to save it.

—Major Booris in the Mekong Delta of Vietnam,
as reported by Peter Arnett of the Associated Press

CHAPTER 5

Vietnam

Once I chose to get on the bus for freedom, I was led choicelessly and inevitably over the cliff and into the unknown.

Shortly after my return from Montgomery, my freshman roommate Rick Bryan, a great, great grand-something of William Jennings Bryan and an orator in his own right asked if I wanted an all-expense-paid trip to go drinking in Baltimore.

Rick told me his debate partner was sick and couldn't attend the debate tournament at Johns Hopkins University that coming weekend. I learned that Rick had been recruited by the University of Pittsburgh from a high school in Evanston, a Chicago suburb, where he was a champion debater. Pitt gave out four annual William Pitt Scholar debate scholarships to the best in the country.

I had never seen a debate before. Where I grew up, a debate was called arguing, and you got in trouble for it. I was always very good at arguing, so debating seemed like a natural fit. A practice round was set up so that I could have the experience at least once before the tournament.

We drove to Baltimore for the event, and while forty other teams from around the country were in their hotel rooms preparing for the following day when the tournament would begin, Rick and I went to the Gaiety Theater, perhaps the last real burlesque house in the country. The theater featured strippers Candy Cane and Blaze Star, along with baggy pants comics. I was following Rick's lead as we next wandered into a topless bar for drinks.

At the tournament, Rick carried a small bottle of Jack Daniels in his attaché case and took nips between rounds as we walked to our next room. I slowly realized that I was taking the tournament much more seriously than Rick. At one point, he winked at me as he held up a blank card and read from it: *According to Judge Jerome Frank in a court decision*—he was making it up.

I wanted to win, but not that way. I didn't like Rick's approach. I wanted us to work together as a serious team. I became invested and committed and the unspoken leader. Rick followed my lead. Debating became the only serious pursuit I had in college, and for the first time, I became focused and committed.

Two years later, I went back to John Hopkins with a different partner, and we won the tournament. That was the year my political understanding exploded, and I could bring a larger meaning to the shattering experience in Montgomery. In the 1966 to 1967 school year, I debated against the war in Vietnam. Five years before Daniel Ellsberg heroically released the Pentagon Papers, the public record had already revealed the full truth about our nation's war in Vietnam.

Eisenhower said that if there was a popular election in Vietnam in 1954, as agreed to in the Geneva Convention, Ho Chi Minh would have won 80 percent of the vote, so the United States stopped the election. General Westmoreland was on record saying that 80 percent of the forces he was fighting in the Mekong Delta were local people, not North Vietnamese as claimed to the American public to sell the war. The facts of Vietnam were incontrovertible. It was public knowledge that the United States was carrying out an illegal and immoral war of aggression based on a myth of dominos.

Our debate team traveled the country proposing a case that supported the Viet Cong. It was revolutionary, and we were unstoppable. We toured high schools across the United States and Canada. We beat the Canadian national champions as we toured the high schools of Toronto.

We got our pick of tournaments that year, and I chose based on fun, not prestige. We went to the University of Kentucky, and I went to the yearling races at Keeneland, the great horse race track in Lexington, where horsemen in red riding jackets blew horns to call the horses to the track. We drove to Louisville for the Kentucky Derby, where we drank mint juleps and I won a small bundle betting on local jockey Earlie Fires. At the tournament at Vanderbilt University, I went to the Grand Ole Opry and a soul review with Ike and Tina Turner. We went to the tournament at Tulane University because it was the week before the Mardi Gras, and I still remember the thrill of riding a streetcar named Desire on the way to the great restaurants of the era.

I could not believe my good luck. I was traveling around the country, getting mileage for my car and a per diem while carrying out a mission to tell the truth, that the emperor has no clothes. Speaking the truth, especially in high schools, helped to pierce the veil of misinformation clouding the kids' minds. They got it and went wild.

The trophies I won and the newspaper articles written about our victories were a high point for my mother. She made a little scrapbook of the clippings, which I found after her death. But for me, the debates kindled a mission to speak the truth about the lie we had been living.

Victories brought enormous ego inflation because I had no training in debate and was winning tournaments against teams from the best universities across the country. I internally strutted because I was beating the people who had gotten into much better schools than I ever could.

I loved winning. It made me feel great. For a while anyway, at least until I returned from a tournament to celebrate, got drunk, and woke up back in despair. The minor victories and flushes of happiness paled in the face of my immediate future.

The war in Vietnam was driving me mad.

What to do? became the theme of my life. When I graduated, I would be eligible for the draft, yet I supported the Viet Cong against the invading American army. If I did nothing, I was as liable as all the "good Germans" I blamed for doing nothing to stop the Holocaust.

I joined some friends to take a test to become a naval officer, but I couldn't bring myself to take the exam and waited outside for them. They rode out the war as officers on supply ships. But I was crippled by the question, *What should I do?*

I was faced with the draft, my support for the other side, a deep fear of failure and incompetence, and nothing that called to me. I didn't look forward to anything. I wasn't interested in marriage or babies, and I wasn't excited about becoming a lawyer or a college professor, something I could easily do but that simply didn't call to me.

The enormous pressure to choose a way forward and the suffocating sensation that all my choices were wrong and meaningless were the basis of the depression that had sent me to therapy years earlier. And now I was graduating, and nothing had changed.

When I was sixteen, my knee was torn in vengeance in a rugby game at summer camp. It was a game between the waiters (us upper-middle-class Jewish campers) and the kitchen help (street-kid footballers from Newark). Mick, a starting tackle in Jersey, jumped on my leg when it was extended and snapped the anterior cruciate ligament. I had beaten him badly in cards, and this was payback. I always knew it was torn and had never repaired, but somehow I never realized that it qualified me for a medical deferment. This is the nature of ignorance and fate.

As I saw it, it was either the Peace Corps or VISTA, the domestic peace corps. I would get a temporary draft exemption and have an opportunity to do some good. Through VISTA I applied for work on an Indian reservation.

CHAPTER 6

Revolution in the Streets

VISTA sent me to Chicago for training, where we spent our first week living in a YMCA on skid row in the Chicago Loop. Wow! The freshmen dorms and fraternity houses may have been pigsties, but the kids were wealthy pigs who paid for maid service. Skid row was as low as you could go in those days. Alcoholics slid off the curb and into the gutter under the noisy overhead El tracks. It was as if the sun could not find a way into this dark and damp place that smelled of vomit and bad beer. I felt myself grow up. I was cut free of the soft material world my parents provided, and sleeping on a thin bunk bed amid unshaven coughing old men, with a toilet down the hall.

VISTA's training was both theoretical and experiential. Saul Alinsky taught us community organizing and rent-strike organizing. A Blackstone Ranger led my first encounter group—the Blackstone Rangers were a black street gang that was running a large part of South Chicago. As far as I could tell, the encounter group consisted of yelling at each other—and I was quite good at that. If this was what it took, maybe I had found my calling.

After our initial immersion at the Y, those found suitable were moved into local neighborhoods; I was sent to Uptown, an

Appalachian white ghetto. My VISTA supervisor, Peggy Terry, described herself as poor white trash from Alabama. Peggy was running for Vice President with Eldridge Cleaver: the Minister of Defense for the Black Panthers, and the U.S. Presidential candidate with the Peace and Freedom Party.

How fast did that happen? From stepping off the bus as a scared eighteen year old in Montgomery, to three years later working for an Alabama revolutionary redneck woman running for Vice President of the United States with Eldridge Cleaver of the Black Panthers!

Peggy's 26-year-old son, Doug, was the head of a street gang called the Young Patriots. My training consisted of hanging out on the street with Youngblood, June Bug, Hi-Therm, and the boys. Hi-Therm had a brother, Lo-Therm, and the Therm brothers and June Bug were planning a trip to Cuba with the Venceremos Brigades.

The summer of 1968 turned out to be the summer when youth around the world exploded onto the world stage: from Danny the Red and the barricades in Paris, to the Prague Spring, and the Cultural Revolution in Beijing. In the U.S., the explosion happened at the Democratic National Convention in Chicago. The government brought me there, footed the bill while I trained to be a revolutionary, paid my bail when I was arrested and paid my fine when I was convicted. The best part for me of spending a night in jail was that it was with Dick Gregory, the comedian turned social critic, and 10 others in a two man cell.

As barefoot kids played in the rubble of vacant lots, we hung out in the alley, smoked grass, and talked revolution. By now I considered myself a radical, but my first day on the street brought a lesson in attitude. It was a muggy, blistering hot summer day in Chicago when I walked out of my tenement wearing powder-blue Bermuda shorts and sandals. The whistling and catcalls started immediately. I made it about half a block before returning to my sweltering rattrap to change into jeans. My first purchase with my first VISTA paycheck—which covered little more than food—was a pair of work boots. I never appeared in public without my work boots and jeans, a green t-shirt, and a blue denim work shirt.

Haskell Wexler, an up-and-coming cinematographer, was making his directing debut in Chicago that summer. *Medium Cool* was shot in part on our block of Uptown. Doug and the boys got protection money for watching the equipment, which meant hanging out in the alley while the scenes were shot upstairs, and not stealing anything. It all seemed like a play within a play within a play.

One night at Doug's apartment, he was carefully cleaning and spit-shining his worn black cowboy boots, while June Bug played a twelve-string guitar. Doug and his girlfriend—who had Doug tattooed on her calf; the first tattoo I had ever seen on a woman—sang Johnny Cash songs. Doug was a little drunk that night when he took me aside and said: *What would you say if I told you I was a revolutionary communist?* The power of his statement shocked me, sending shivers through my body and mind. I had never heard that spoken before.

Maybe I am too? I bluffed. Doug simply looked at me and smiled. A little later he gave me some big-brother advice about women: *If you are willing to sit and listen to her until two in the morning, you're home free*, he winked.

As for my being a revolutionary communist, I did read Marx in college—not *Das Kapital,* which was still impenetrable—but his humanist and early philosophical writings collected in a book by Erich Fromm. My political science professor had been a CIA operative in Iran. He resigned when the U.S. government overthrew the democratically elected government of Colonel Mosaddiq. This professor taught me that since its formation after the Second World War, the CIA had a then twenty-year-long record of overthrowing democratically elected governments, and supporting military dictatorships and death squads—all part of the national security apparatus to fight communism. I had no idea! I thought the United States was always the good guy; I was so naïve.

This shattering of my view of America brought on a deep despair. This went far beyond Alabama, which was about Southern rednecks and good ole boys, not the nation. I went to Montgomery to get government troops to protect U.S. citizens. In addition to the inhumanity of the South's apartheid, I realized a few years later in class that, as a taxpayer and a citizen, I had a part in the destruction of entire nations and cultures. I played a part in the killing of thousands of innocents, and in denying millions of people around the world the democracy we Americans value and claim to promote.

When I studied the history of Israel, my final illusion was shattered. I always saw myself as a part of a persecuted minority of good-hearted, intelligent people who had a deep sense of moral justice and righteousness that grew out of their own subjugation and attempted annihilation. I grew up certain that we Jews were the good guys. I idealized socialist kibbutz life, while my mother met her girlfriends at Hadassah. But as an undergraduate, when I saw the horror of Israeli policy—its killing and dehumanization of the Palestinians—I became a supporter of the National Front for the Liberation of Palestine, which was far left of Yasser Arafat and the Palestine Liberation Organization, or PLO.

By the time I was on the street with Doug in Chicago, I had read Herbert Marcuse and Franz Fanon, and would have proudly called myself an anti-imperialist and a Marxist. But a revolutionary communist? This was beyond radical; it was an in-your-face statement, and though I never was a communist, I liked it.

When the Democratic National Convention came to town in August I was ready. I had left non-violence behind in Montgomery. By now, both Dr. King and Malcolm X had been assassinated: our leaders were being shot and killed. I supported the Panthers' stand of armed self-defense. If "they" were going to hit me in the head, I wanted to hit them back. I was now more a devotee of Malcolm X than Dr. King—which explains the X in my name today.

Lincoln Park is just a few stops on the El from Wilson Avenue in Uptown. The tribal gathering in Lincoln Park leading up to the Democratic Convention had what I longed for from the Jackson Street Baptist Church: a palpable sense of community that transcended the atomized alienation of day-to-day relationships. The rush of marching down the middle of Michigan Avenue while smoking a joint and chanting: *"The Streets Belong to the People,"* felt like a liberation from all the conditioned restraints of the slavery of middle-class existence. Suddenly my life had meaning: I was acting on a stage beyond the personal, and it felt great.

Giving myself to something larger than myself opened me up in places that I didn't even know were closed and dormant. It was as if a dusty, dark attic inside me was suddenly opened to the full sun from all directions, and what it revealed was a vast horizon beyond measure. But all this was going on just beneath the surface; something I was vaguely aware of but could not directly address. Had I noticed, I would perhaps have said that I was breathing more deeply and more freely because I was less constricted and bound, but I didn't notice.

Each night we would take the streets, and each night the police would take them back, firing tear gas and swinging clubs. The first night of this fighting, I helped Doug and the boys turn over a police car. Another night while we marched down the center of Michigan Avenue, a lone car crept in the opposite direction, engulfed by the surging crowd. The two men in the car glared at us as they pushed against a tide of change. I couldn't tell if they were undercover or Mafioso. People started beating on the car. The car windows were open, and the person in front of me reached through the driver's open window and grabbed the cigarette out of the driver's mouth. The driver jumped out of the car with his gun drawn and started to shoot. I fell to the ground, and then ran for cover. The flash of the first shot, the crack of the explosions that followed, and the smell of gunpowder are still fresh in my mind.

*　　*　　*

When my VISTA training was over at the end of the summer, I was sent to my permanent assignment which was in the poorest black ghetto on Detroit's east side. Nothing in my training prepared me for this, so before shipping out, I was tutored by Leroy, the lieutenant in the Blackstone Rangers who led our encounter group.

One night Leroy invited me up to his apartment. A white girl from my training group was there serving us drinks. The drink of choice that night was a new one for me—cough medicine. Leroy taught me the importance of brand consciousness, as we each drank a few bottles of Romilar. He also explained my survival strategy in Detroit: buy grass from Leroy, and then supply my Detroit neighborhood.

Now, here's what you do, he said. *You go into the corner bar, and you check it out. You dig? You find someone likely, and you say, 'Hey Slick, let me pull your coattail to somethin'. I'm the man. You dig? Now, who is the main man here?' Then you meet the main man, the power, and you say, 'Hey, my man, I am the man! You dig? I got the supply.'*

I nodded. A cough medicine nod. But even in my drug-filled haze, there was not a moment when I believed I could ever pull off what he was describing; I never tried.

The east side of Detroit looked like a city in a war zone. Burned out blocks, abandoned houses, bullet holes in bank windows, and no white people in sight. My partner and I were assigned to the Detroit Commission on Children and Youth, which had a little office off Mack Avenue near Belle Isle. There were two paid staff. One of them was an African nationalist, who was probably a follower of Malcolm, although I can't be sure since he was never there. I only met him once for ten minutes, when his boss from the mayor's office dropped us VISTA volunteers off and he had to be at his desk to greet us. The other employee was Arthur, a 250-pound junkie, who offered me hot jewelry and told me he made money breaking the legs of people who didn't pay their debts. He said if I ran into any trouble, I should just tell people I was a friend of Arthur.

I had not yet unpacked, and my Che Guevara poster was still rolled up on the couch, when two FBI agents paid me a visit to ask about my involvement in the riots in Chicago. Three years earlier, before boarding the bus to Montgomery, this was a fear we all shared—an FBI record. Life was moving so fast, which was fine with me because I didn't expect to live to be thirty—so, full speed ahead.

In Ann Arbor, a short ride from Detroit, I was offered LSD. Before taking the cube of sugar with the acid dropped onto it, I was completely naive about what to expect, how to approach the experience, or what its potential was. I just knew that there would be no going back. My life was a runaway freight, gaining speed and steam, but toward an unknown destination on an unknown track.

I took 100 mics while walking through the ghetto along the Detroit River across from Belle Isle, past barbecue joints and Martin Luther King High School where I was doing draft counseling and tutoring in remedial reading. As I walked along, I first felt a slight nausea, an amorphous fear, and a sensation like falling in an elevator. Oh shit! The elevator became a roller coaster fall, where the earth drops from beneath you and nothing solid remains. I have always hated roller coasters, and there was no way off of this one.

But then a sensation of expansion followed. My body seemed to be floating down the street, as if I was walking on air. Then I realized that I was air, walking on air! It was the funniest thing I had ever experienced; I fell over on the grass near the river, laughing.

That night around midnight, as I was coming down from the acid, I walked alone through the neighborhood. Nobody in their right mind did that, let alone a white boy. The only whites ever seen within miles were police or teachers, and they never got out of their cars. I saw a small group of brothers spot me and head my way. When they got up close enough to see me, they didn't know what to make of me.

When we VISTA volunteers arrived in school each day, there would be a ripple of laughing and calling out, *Here come the hippies!* It was 1968, post Chicago, and by then my hair and beard were Che Guevara length. I wore a red bandanna around my neck or head and a YIPPIE button on my jean jacket. These young brothers didn't know what to make of a white boy on the streets in their part of town, in the middle of the night, looking like I did.

You looking for a woman? the leader asked, while his friends made a circle around me.

No, not looking for a woman, I said.

I was lucid and clear, with no push, no run, and nothing going on.

How much money you got?

I stopped and looked directly into his eyes before slowly saying, *Man, if I had any money, would I be here?*

As we looked into each other's eyes, I could see him acknowledge that what I said made perfect sense. The circle parted. Many years later, I discovered that nothing to push against is an ancient marital arts teaching. I had no idea at the time. I didn't do anything. My mind was quiet, so we could meet eye to eye in clarity.

A few hours after taking LSD the second time, my VISTA partner and I went to see the Detroit premiere of *The Battle of Algiers,* at a special Black Panther showing at Wayne State on the west side of town. After the film, we went to a party of Panthers and movement lawyers. At the party I was tripping and stoned, and when talking with Bill Kunstler and the Panthers, I called myself a revolutionary communist, just over a month after being shocked by the phrase. But once again, I was in over my head. The ante had been raised. Being a revolutionary communist didn't mean shit if I didn't have a gun. Oh, shit!

My third low-dose acid trip was also in Ann Arbor. As it was coming on, two hippie girls, in pigtails and overalls and with paint on their faces, told me that the Hog Farm had just pulled into town and taken over the student union at the University of Michigan. Wavy Gravy was there and saw that I was tripping. He gave me the job of handing out handfuls of candy to everyone who came through the door. I saw how my role as candyman in this street theater gave me a chance to move beyond my shyness and to come out into contact with everyone. I loved it.

A few weeks later, Peggy Terry came to town from Chicago for a church fundraiser for the Peace and Freedom Party. I met Youngblood in the church kitchen, where he used the two hundred dollars raised at the dinner to buy acid from me to take back to the boys on the street in Uptown; three trips, and I had become a dealer.

*   *   *

In January of 1969, after our landlord burned our apartment down to break our rent strike, and we were thrown out of the high school for our anti-war draft counseling and Black Panther associations, I left VISTA. I loved my adventure with VISTA. I loved being on the street and being able not just to survive but to shuck and jive. My self-confidence grew, and I could suss out a situation and deal with it. But I also saw that the experience was no more real than college. I was getting paid to play community organizer and live in the ghetto, but I was not of the ghetto.

To get some working-class cred and shed my bourgeois upbringing, I got a job on the labor gang at U.S. Steel, in Homestead, Pennsylvania. My first day on the job started at midnight. I took the 11 p.m. bus down the hill and across the river to Homestead.

Close to the Appalachian coal mines, the mills spread along the riverbanks for miles. I worked on the labor gang of Open Hearth 4: a quarter-mile of blast furnaces made famous when the workers went on strike to unionize, and Andrew Carnegie's friend Henry Frick was left in charge.

Frick was the head of a private army called Pinkertons. He floated his men down the river on barges and opened fire on the striking workers. A pitched battle went on for several days, with the town siding with the workers against the paid gunmen stranded on their barges during the shoot-out. It was as close to a popular armed uprising as this country came in the late nineteenth century. I learned of the Homestead Strike in high school, and now I was a union man at that very plant.

I arrived early, as instructed, so that I would be on the job at the stroke of midnight. I was taken to the company store where I was outfitted with a hard hat, work gloves, and steel-tipped boots, which were paid for out of my first week's paycheck. A stripe of white masking tape ran down the middle of my hard hat to alert everyone to my status as a newcomer. I still remember my number. It was the only way the foreman ever addressed me: *42578, you're cleaning the flues today. And get a haircut boy, or don't come back!*

I often described my first view of the mill that night to women I wanted to seduce as Dante's inferno, but I realize now that Dante's hell is more ordered. In this hell, trains rolled down the middle of the mill carrying lime and ore. Pig iron carts filled with ore were lifted into gaping blast furnaces. The furnaces flared flames, smells, and smoke for a quarter of a mile, to the end of the open hearth, only to blow out the open end of the mill and mingle with the other open hearths that ran for miles in both directions along the riverbank.

Overhead cranes carried giant vats of molten steel across the back of the ovens, as jack hammers blasted their machine gun rhythms, dynamite blew open nineteenth-century ovens filled with molten steel, and the smoke and dust of the blasts mixed with the general dust, exhaust from the forklifts, and smoke from the stacks of steam engines. It was always smoky, dusty dark amid the flare of molten steel, and the inferno never stopped running, with men working shifts round the clock. I would come off a shift looking like a coal miner, with a rim of white where my goggles had shielded a small portion of my skin from the soot.

And the smell. The smell was of soot and ash, train smoke and brakes, exhaust from forklifts and jackhammers, cordite from the dynamite, and the burning of coal, lime, and ore in the ovens, creating a unique rusty sulphur smell that I will forever recognize with nausea.

To tap an oven, a dynamite charge was placed to blow off the back wall, and a molten river of steel would gush for several stories down into giant vats. There were no walls so that an accidental explosion wouldn't bounce back into the mill. The blasting February wind that blacks called *the hawk* chilled me to the bone. Fires lit in oil drums, now familiar from homeless city-street scenes, were the preferred method to stay warm inside the mill. On my first day shoveling in front of the ovens, the front of my body sweated and burned, while my back froze from the biting cold of the winter river wind.

The sign at the gate said the mill had gone 122 days without a fatality, and 34 days without a serious accident. Someone died there four months ago. They were proud it hadn't happened since, and they were marking the days until the next accident.

On my first lunch break, around four in the morning, I went to retrieve the lunch my girlfriend Jean had packed in a paper bag for me. I took it from the I-beam where I had stored it and discovered a rat had eaten its way through, leaving a hole from one end of the bag to the other. I walked to the canteen for something to drink and a sandwich. It was a quarter-mile walk, a wait, and a quarter mile back, on a twenty-minute lunch break. I learned the value of a metal lunchbox.

To save some money, on night shift they sometimes turned the scrubbers off. If the dirt was so thick when you came out of the mill at eight in the morning that you couldn't see the red flags in the expired parking meters, you knew someone was squeezing the profit machine.

Cleaning the flues meant descending into a pit and having a wheelbarrow lowered in on a winch after you. With a bandana over my nose and mouth, I walked into a tunnel too small to stand up in. I was later told that these flue tunnels were so small because they were built for the twelve-year-old boys who worked in the mills before the union, and that Andrew Carnegie was not a man to waste.

I walked hunched over into the tunnel. The walls on either side were so close that the wheelbarrow had to be pulled in from behind so that it would face the correct direction going out. I discovered that the walls were also very hot, and if you brushed against them, you tcould get burned. Each step was a step onto a foot of fine ash, which made clouds of hot dust when you walked. We didn't have respirators in those days, only a bandana across the face. Whenever we were directly under the blasted-out oven, we were required to shovel a set number of shovelfuls and then bring the wheelbarrow back to have it winched up while another was lowered down. Half an hour at a time in the tunnels was all the union would permit. A ten-minute rest followed, and then another half hour back at it.

One day, to save money, they sent us in early, while it was still scorching hot. I organized a wildcat walk-off, and our crew refused to go into the flue. I was jumped on the street one night soon afterward. Four guys with quart-sized beer bottles broke them on my head. I was fired as soon as I recovered from my injuries.

Before that, though, at 22 years of age, when I had four months on the job, I married Nancy Jean Ednie of Munhall, a small mill town downriver from Homestead. Jean was the fourth child of a retired machinist, John Ednie, from the same mill I was now working in. John started work at the Open Hearth at the age of 16. He was forced to retire at 65 and missed the fifty-year benchmark to retire with a gold watch. He was given a U.S. stainless steel watch instead; he wore it proudly on a chain across his banker's vest. John Ednie suffered two nervous breakdowns during his forty-nine years at the mill, but got through by finding God in the Plymouth Brethren. Nancy Jean told me this congregation was far right of hard-shell Baptists.

Nancy Jean, the fourth of five children, with chalky bones and bad teeth, was homely and shy, with stringy, washed-out blond hair and fair skin. But her eyes were deep and alive, with a flame of intelligence burning bright. We met when she visited friends down the hall from Paul's apartment. She would sleep with me, and we made sweet love together.

We were both John Barth fans: *Giles Goatboy* and *Lost in the Funhouse* still stand out. When Barth came to Pittsburgh's Carnegie Hall to give a reading of his classic *Menelaid*, we went together. He was brilliant, and we were thrilled. But Nancy Jean was too shy to attend the reception that we were invited to afterward.

My mother took our wedding as a personal insult. She was sure I was marrying this shivering wet, poor mousy Baptist to get back at her. She held up the ceremony for forty-five minutes as a no-show. She finally arrived, over-sedated and unsteady; the front she had held up at my bar mitzvah was now cracking and crumbling.

Jean's father asked if it was a hippie wedding, and was reassured by Jean's nearest sister that hippie weddings only happen outside, and we were in Heinz Chapel on the university lawn. I recited a Gregory Corso poem about getting old, fat, and bald. Jean and our friends recited other beat poems as part of the ceremony. Jean's father said we would reap the whirlwind.

It didn't take long for his curse to materialize. While Jean and I were waiting for a bus on a Saturday night, a car pulled up.

Something was shouted out the window, and Jean yelled back in defiance. She then ran for cover, as four locals with beer bottles came at me. Was there some connection with the wildcat walkout a few days before, or was this simply another act of random violence that passes for fun with the mill workers, and marks the streets of Pittsburgh? I will never know, so I assume it was Jean's taunting that brought them out of their car and down on me.

I only know that the first one hit me in the face with a bottle, but it didn't break. I grabbed him with one arm around his neck and started punching, while his friends proceeded to break their bottles over the back of my head. The next bottle hit, with a shattering of glass and a shower of beer and blood. My one thought as I fell into the gutter was *Wow! just like the movies*: it was the same experience of seeing stars that I'd had in Brooklyn when I was a two year old.

I fell into the street from the impact of the bottle, but I still had one guy under me with my arm around his neck. I hit him again. Another bottle was broken over my head. I passed out for a moment, and they ran.

Did I really pass out, or was I faking it to escape? I was faking it, but I always told the story as if I had passed out, to hide my cowardice at not continuing the fight.

Covered with blood and broken glass, I stood up in the street. Cars started honking at me to get out of the way. Jean emerged from the bakery where she was hiding and called a cab to get us to the hospital. The police were not interested in the incident. For them, it was just another Saturday night in Pittsburgh.

I never actively wanted to marry Jean, but I wasn't adverse to it either. We had been living together for around four months when she said that if I really loved her I would marry her and make an honest woman of her. I thought about it: I knew that I would never be happy in this life, so if it would make her happy I was glad to do it. This was the depth of my introspective insight at the time. I was twenty-two and an emotional baby.

Jean applied to graduate school for me, and found that I had been nominated for a Woodrow Wilson Fellowship by my political science professor. With his help they found a place that would give me a full fellowship, including money for our living expenses: I was accepted into a doctoral program at the Graduate School of International Studies in Denver.

CHAPTER 7

One Step Over the Line

Arriving in Denver in September of 1969 was like landing in heaven: the rents were cheap, the sky was clear, and the air actually tasted delicious. To come from the steel mills of Pittsburgh to the still pure Rocky Mountain air felt like being released from a toxic prison back into the sunshine. And such sunshine. Brighter. Crisper. More filled with the scents of the trees and plants. Ponderosa pines, with their psychedelically layered bark of wafer-thin copper sheets, and the hillsides of Aspen, fluttering golden in the breeze, were as far from Homestead as you could be.

I was being paid to be here to get an accelerated PhD directly after my BA. I was getting a doctorate in revolution, with an emphasis in China and Cuba—and it was fun.

My marriage on the other hand had a short aborted life, or maybe it was stillborn. The fall of our arrival in Denver, the Weatherman faction of SDS called for a return to Chicago to challenge the local police to a street fight. Bourgeois kids wanting to be *heavy*. My desire to be heavy led to my job at the steel mill so I could relate.

Jean and I signed up for Days of Rage. She had watched the Chicago riots on TV and was breathless, receiving collect calls from me on the battlefield. Now we had a chance to go into battle together. In retrospect, the complete absurdity of the situation is obvious. Even if it made sense on any level to challenge the police to a fight, Nancy Jean Ednie? A little hundred-pound rag doll with chalky bones?

I got us helmets and billy clubs, and Jean bought her first pair of work boots. A day before we were to leave, Jean came down with a high fever. She asked me to stay and nurse her. I did. She probably saved my life. In that moment, though, when she asked me to stay, I knew our relationship was over.

The marriage had been stormy. Her birth control pills contributed to monthly psychotic breaks, and my dealing lids of grass terrified her. I had no idea how to be in a relationship, and so I withdrew into a book at the slightest upset. Once in the heat of argument, she called me a dirty Jew, and something snapped: it was over. My mother's curse, and her father's prophecy, had come to pass; we reaped the whirlwind after nine months. It was already finished and waiting for the coup de grâce and graceful exit, which came in the form of a fever on the eve of battle.

I had promised never to leave her alone, so I set her up with an old college friend; they stayed together for twenty years, raising a few kids.

As a bachelor again I was cruising, and in April of 1970 I finished my first year as a straight-A student. The work was easy, and I was enjoying myself. It was such a relief from the mills that I could coast and be happy. I had left the stormy streets of Chicago and Detroit behind and was basking in the sunshine.

While walking across the quad in early spring, I came across an unusual gathering. Two former undergraduates were just back from New Haven with Super 8 film that they shot of the street demonstrations around the Bobby Seale trial. I had met Bobby Seale, the Minister for Defense for the Black Panther Party, in Chicago and loved his speech in Lincoln Park. He was being framed in a trial that he eventually won. In response to the film,

I helped form the Central Strike Committee of the University of Denver in support of Bobby Seale.

The Central Strike Committee consisted of six people. Spanky and PJ had brought the film. PJ was a girl, with long blonde hair, rose-colored granny glasses, and a beret with a Che Guevara button on it. Spanky's red bandana held his golden locks, and he wore hip-hugging bell-bottom jeans and a shirt with laces up the front. They looked like they had walked off some sort of *Peace and Love* album cover: a matching set of adorable hippie dolls.

Kenny Jones came from the projects on the east side of Detroit, near Belle Isle, within walking distance of my old VISTA apartment. He had won a basketball scholarship to Denver, but had been thrown off the team after a Black Power demonstration the year before. Moshe was a dropout pot dealer, living in Boulder. Charlotte DeVito, the daughter of a Mafia don from Chicago, wore heavy mascara and looked like a Catholic schoolgirl in rebellion, busting out of her fitted blazer; a look that Madonna would capitalize on decades later.

I was the eldest and the heavy of the group. Now, only eighteen months after my Bermuda-shorts episode, I was a ringleader. I would walk into a lecture hall and catch the teacher's eye, nod in acknowledgement of him or her, and in a voice that filled the room, tell the professor I had an announcement to make. Everyone would stop in stunned silence. I would scan the room looking into their eyes, one by one, and announce a general strike, to start in five days, in support of Bobby Seale. Then I would leave for the next room.

Fate played into our hands when Nixon announced the illegal bombing of Cambodia a few days later. When the school exploded—along with all the colleges across the country—we were ready and in the vanguard.

The chancellor called for a school convocation; he was an avid supporter of Richard Nixon and wanted to keep the campus open at all costs. He took the stage of the auditorium and called for law and order, and peaceful assembly. He spoke long enough for everyone to hear and see the vacuity of his position, and he didn't mention the illegal and immoral war crime of bombing the sovereign nation we were not at war with—much less that it was taking place in that very moment. Maybe he hadn't even gotten to that part, I don't recall, before I felt the adrenal rush of excitement and leapt up onto the stage to interrupt him and call for a walkout. Many thousands got up and left in an uproar.

On the grassy commons outside someone gave me a shovel. I started to dig a hole in the university lawn.

What's it for? somebody asked.

If you are going to build a fire, you need to dig a hole, I replied. That, of course, is not necessarily true, but it is what I said, and in the moment it made sense.

The person who brought the shovel liberated wood and supplies from the art department, and a village slowly came into being. Tepees, forts, and tents went up, turning the campus commons into a counter-culture community.

When the National Guard opened fire and killed students at Kent State who were having a similar protest, the country's campuses exploded yet again. Thousands of ROTC buildings were fire bombed on college campuses across the country. Our demonstration was suddenly mainstream. We called it Woodstock West and entered an agreement with the administration that we wouldn't shut down the school if they didn't shut us down. Soon hundreds of people were living on the campus lawn. A free-food kitchen was set up. Campfires lit the night, and marijuana filled the air.

In response to the Kent State shootings, the largest demonstration in Colorado history marched on the state capitol. As the strike committee, we expected to be allowed to speak. When we were kept off the program by the more moderate elements of the Democratic Party, we took over the podium by force.

My debate training, and watching Bobby Seale in Chicago and Martin Luther King in Montgomery, all came together in my speech, which had a black preacher's cadence, and asked call-and-response questions to build an emotional pitch. I built on the liberal Democrat before me, who finished his limp speech by saying: *Power to the people.*

All these honkeys up here today been sayin' power to the people. Even Nixon in the White House says power to the people. Which people exactly are we here to give power to? Are we talkin' power to the po'leese?

NO!

Are we talkin' power to the corporations?

NO!

Are we talkin' power to the war machine? Are we talkin' power to these honkey congressmen that just spoke?

Each call back of *NO!* built the rhythm and intensity.

So let me give you something to say yes to then.

We have started Woodstock West on the campus of the University of Denver. We have free food, free dope, and free people! Can you say yes to that?

YES! rang from one hundred thousand voices in front of the state capitol.

You are all invited to Woodstock West!

A local rock-and-roll radio station started broadcasting from Woodstock West, and the crazies poured down from the hills to join the party. I love Burning Man and all the attempts to create something unchained and free out in open space, but here it was in the middle of the city, an oasis of campfires, tepees, forts, food, grass, and rock and roll. It was an in-your-face expression of our cultural revolution that ran on as 24/7 living theater. All, from digging a hole in the lawn.

*   *   *

We were tripping on mescaline when we were invited to a meeting in the chancellor's office. The Strike Committee proceeded *to liberate* his office, helping ourselves to whatever he had in his fridge. While we were tripping and camping out in the chancellor's office, an announcement was made at Woodstock West, at the other end of the campus, that the National Guard had been called, and that everyone had to disperse. We were outflanked and missed the announcement.

After a few hours, we realized we had been duped. Still tripping, we wandered off, picking up rocks for our fight with the National Guard. The streets appeared purple, and waved like a roller coaster. The National Guard never came; they weren't needed. Instead, a court order barred us from campus.

The revolt was over. For most, it was just a college lark or an excuse to cut class. For others, it was a statement of outrage at the killing of college students just like them. For some, it was about the war and saying no to the government. But for me, something deeper was cut. I had to examine my life: this was probably my last chance to keep my perch in society.

I remembered being on a night shift with some carpenters at the mill, and we had snuck off to hide behind a boiler for a break. We were covered with soot and our faces were blackened, but I could see the deep creases in the face of one of the carpenters, and the worried concern in his watery blue eyes as he said softly to me, *Get out of here, son. Get out while you can.*

When he said that I knew that I was just playing steel worker, that it was not my destiny, and my heart broke for him because he didn't have the choices I had. My class privilege and guilt ate at me then.

Now the precipice that I faced was this: if I were to give up the fellowship, I would be walking away from an easy comfortable life where everything was paid for.

It won't hurt anyone else, I thought, *if I continue toward my degree. I won't be taking anything from someone else if I show up on campus and continue my doctorate. I'll get to read, teach, influence my students, and do what I like.*

To turn away was to step off into the unknown in a way I had never encountered before; it was no longer a game. My life was on the line. I was growing up. Each choice for freedom led to a steeper precipice, and now I was facing the complete unknown. Too old to start over, and too old to turn back.

I chose then to turn my back on my place in society, and to devote myself fully to the struggle for freedom. My last chance, the last vestige of my privileged life, lay in the graduate fellowship: becoming an academic expert on revolution, and some day perhaps securing tenure somewhere with a wife and kids. A normal life, with *Freedom* remaining an academic subject: that was the trap.

I grabbed my last quarterly stipend and left for the hills.

Once I walked away, I didn't look back: I was choosing the short fast life. I did not expect to live to be thirty, so I could make the most of the years I had left.

PART III

THE ABYSS

Mama, take this badge off of me.

I can't use it anymore.

It's gettin' dark, too dark to see.

I feel I'm knockin' on heaven's door,

Knock, knock, knockin' on heaven's door.

—Bob Dylan

CHAPTER 8

Suicide

I had become a street dealer on the Hill in Boulder, selling grass and acid with my partner Kenny Jones from the Strike Committee. I collected my $800 stipend from my fellowship that fall, and used it to invest in a few pounds of pot. Kenny and I divided it into lids and sold them to the college students who came to the Hill to score; it was an open market for grass and acid in those days.

When the phone call came from my aunt in January 1971, I had been out of contact with my family for over nine months. Having read Carlos Castaneda's books on the teachings of Don Juan, I took the teachings on how to be a warrior to heart: a warrior cut the past and burned his bridges behind him. Faced with no escape, he could then meet whatever came with the attitude that *it is a good day to die*. I thought I'd done this, cut all ties to my past and to society, but there was more to come.

My aunt called the apartment I had moved into with Jean a year and a half earlier. Although I hadn't been in the apartment for at least a month or more—I don't remember exactly—and hadn't paid the rent, I was back now only to discover that my landlord had locked me out. Jean's Vespa was still in the backyard, and I had never moved out. As far as I was concerned, it was still my place. I wrapped a rag around my hand and punched in the glass in the back-door window. Once in, and rolling a joint with Kenny at the kitchen table, the phone rang. It was my aunt—my father's sister Helen—calling to say that my mother was in a coma; it didn't look good. She said there was a ticket waiting for me at the airport.

My Uncle Jack picked me up at JFK. Always dapper in his overcoat and fedora, he looked at me and visibly blanched. I was in my Che-Guevara-in-jeans attire—my first sartorial hit since the ninth grade—but it didn't go over well at home. On the cab ride from the airport to the hospital, Uncle Jack looked at me with ashen horror: *So, Elliot, what do you do now?* he asked.

I'm a revolutionary communist, I smiled.

He digested that for a few moments, and without showing anything more in his face or voice, he replied, *Well, just don't tell your grandpa.*

As we rode together I reflected on the tragedy of my mom's life. Growing up above the drug store in Flatbush she was lonely and embarrassed not to have a real house for a home. Her father was a socialist, and his brother a union organizer for the garment workers; they were content with a simple life. She wanted something more.

She met my father when he was in law school. He was good looking, and from her point of view wealthy. His father, Mike, was a successful businessman. Mike had come to the New York in 1904 through the Ellis Island funnel. Because he was only literate in Russian and Yiddish, at thirteen he was placed in the first grade. Quickly humiliated, he dropped out and began working. Mike's first job was in Hell's Kitchen, loading milk pails onto a horse-drawn milk truck. He rode the subways between jobs, and found that he liked working in deli's because there was always something to eat at night when he slept on the store's floor. By the 1920s, he had married the deli man's daughter and had his own deli on

Columbus Circle. In the 1930s, Fiorello La Guardia appointed him to the New York City Restaurant Commission. Before I knew about his younger brother Jack's livelihood, I once asked my grandpa—who was short, bald, round-faced, looking like what would happen if Edward G. Robinson and Al Capone had a baby—if he knew Lucky Luciano, the leading New York mobster in the thirties. He only said: *Mr. Charles Lucky was a real gentleman.*

Mike's son Bernie was a real catch. In 1946, while mom was pregnant with me, he was working for the Treasury Department while smuggling guns to the Irgun, fighting for a Jewish homeland in Israel. The Jewish gangsters in New York would round up the guns and pass them to my father. He was briefly a hero to my mother then, but that quickly faded away—he could not make her happy, turns out he was made of cardboard. He went into business with his father, and showered her with money; we moved to the house in Queens that she furnished in faux French provincial, but he had no capacity for intimate emotional contact, and this was what she craved most.

She didn't know why she was so lonely, why there was a deep feeling of something missing. In 1960, as my bar mitzvah approached, my mother's mother finally told my mom the truth: she learned that the woman she thought was her mother, grandma Ida, was not her mother but her step-mother.

Ida told my mom that she had no brothers or sisters because her real mother had died in childbirth. Ida—who then married Isaac, her now dead father—could not have children of her own, so she raised infant Blanche as her own child, and Blanche was never told the truth. What a shock! This family secret must have subconsciously burdened my mother, eaten at her, and contributed to her neurotic and unexplainable sadness.

We were making out the guest list for my bar mitzvah when Grandma Ida dropped the bombshell that Blanche had true relatives that should be invited to the party—a whole world of relatives that had been kept secret for thirty-nine years. Her father Isaac had gone to his grave keeping his wife's secret. Then . . . Grandma Ida died just a few weeks before my bar mitzvah.

What a moment: she was devastated by the death of her step-mother and the tragedy of having lived her life without knowing the truth of her family, yet she was supposed to be happy about her son learning the Torah and becoming a man in one of the major milestone's of her family's life. In the midst of the shock and the emotional pain, she put on a perfect face for my bar mitzvah. She was tall, elegant, perfectly dressed and made up. No one who saw her dancing with Bernie, my brothers, or me, could see that she was torn up inside. Everything that she must have been feeling had to be ignored to put on a happy face. And she did, flawlessly. If anyone at the party was subtle enough to detect the sadness in her eyes, it wasn't new; the sadness was always there.

This false life that we all lived was my teacher. I saw the emptiness of everything, and lost all desire to participate. So while it ultimately served me, it crushed my mom.

Now, a decade later, she was in a coma from an overdose of sleeping pills. Her kidneys failed, and she never regained consciousness; she was being kept alive with massive life support.

Before seeing her, I was told that she was unconscious and wouldn't be aware of my presence; that was not my experience. At first I was shocked by the way she looked. Sweat plastered her hair against the side of her head. She had tubes up her nose, and she was chalky pale, with no makeup. Blue veins showed on her temple, and traces of saliva had dried around her parched lips. All of her life she'd taken care of her appearance; she was always made up before leaving the house. Now she was like a beautiful bird that had flown into a glass window and crashed in a bloody mess of feathers. I felt the shame she would have felt knowing she looked like this. Tremendous love welled up in my heart, and I started to cry—not for me, but for her.

I'm so sorry they let you look like this, I told her as I cleaned up her lips and smoothed her hair. Her eyes flickered behind her lids, and I knew she could hear me. I felt our connection. She knew I was there. *I truly love you, and I know that you love me,* I whispered in her ear. *Consciousness lives after death,* I told her. I read to her from *The Tibetan Book of the Dead.* Our hearts and minds touched, and I cried at her bedside.

She was forty-nine years old when she died on January 19, 1971—my 24th birthday. My family would never say it, but the neighbors told me I killed her. I couldn't disagree. In case there was any doubt in anyone's mind why she took her life, she left me a dollar in her will. I had abandoned her. I literally hadn't phoned home.

I had left her behind because I couldn't take her along and give myself fully to the revolution: I had to cut my ties. This was necessary on a logistical level, but also on an emotional one. I had to be willing to give up the neurotic patterns of family by not participating. This was a painful process—cutting the emotional cords that had tied me in knots. The love never died, but the physical connection was severed. And now it had cost my mother's life.

I returned to the temple of my bar mitzvah for my mother's funeral. I sat there and hated the rabbi. We had been in his congregation for twenty years, yet he offered up mindless, mealy mouthings of sorry platitudes, without a single relevant fact from my mother's life. A computer program, any one from our modern era, could have easily surpassed the rabbi by gleaning some anecdotal information about my mother to insert into the formulaic eulogy. By just filling in the blanks with anything at all that was personal to my mom, the computer would beat the rabbi in humanizing and personalizing the eulogy. But a computer, even today, could never get the voice: the unctuous, pontificating, self-inflating voice that covered the complete banality of moral turpitude is something too fine for a computer's ear at this stage.

To ease our pain, my Uncle Max—my Aunt Helen's husband, and the family doctor—gave my brother and me two Seconals each. Uncle Max had helped overdose my mother with the same kindness.

We all gathered at our house for the postmortem ritual of sitting shiva and reciting the Kaddish, the mourner's prayer. That's when I exploded at the rabbi. I couldn't bear his lack of spiritual depth, emotion, humanity: his lack of anything that approached real contact. All holds were off. I called it the gift of my mother's death. The last veils of constraint to be a good son for my mother's sake were gone:

Why did you become a rabbi? I yelled at him as I came down the stairs into the living room. *Easier than being a truck driver? You liked the hours?* I spat the words at him.

The crowd of neighbors and relatives were shocked into silence and disbelief at my rude behavior. That I had killed my mother with my cruelty was now confirmed for them. They thought I was possessed, psychotic, hopped up on drugs, or most likely all three, and they all thought the rabbi a very nice man, just like them.

The rabbi rushed out of the house, and the gathering of friends and family followed after him without looking at me. After the required seven days of mourning, my father threw me out into the winter's snow.

CHAPTER 9

Throwing Out the Baby with the Bathwater

After my father threw me out of our home, I started to make my way back toward Colorado through an ocean of pain. It felt at times like walking under water, dissolving in a sea of loss and suffering.

Yet I found my mother had given me a gift as well. A gift of unimaginable magnitude. I felt so grateful to her.

I realized that her death cut the last strings of restraint. Until then I hadn't realized that, on an unconscious level, my family had still been a part of my psyche. My successes and failures had still been linked to being somebody's son.

I thought the attachment was cut when I left college and stopped taking my parents' money. I felt this more strongly when I joined VISTA, and again when I worked in the mill. But in each step of growing up and individuating, while something deep released, there was still a deeper holding, a deeper binding. A deeper level of unexamined attachment and identification. Each time I individuated further, I thought at the time that the separation from my family role as a son was complete, but each proved to be yet another veil covering something deeper and subtler.

In some way this last break that my mother's death brought was like my experience punching in the glass on the door of my Denver apartment: it wasn't a cut, but a shattering. It was shocking and violent. There was now a plane of reality that was no longer a viable landing place. It had broken into pieces, and dissolved back into a night sea of pain and loss.

Now it really was a good day to die. I felt I had nothing more to live for, and there was no need for me to uphold an image as my mother's son. I was no longer bound to be a good boy. I could go all the way.

In my willingness to make a difference, I believed my mother's death would be meaningful. Instead of it being only the tragic death of an unhappy woman filled with love, longing, and potential, my mother's death would make a difference in the world. It allowed me to give my life fully to the flame of freedom. Living as a spark of freedom, burning full and bright until spent, my life and death would be meaningful, and an homage to her.

To go all the way on behalf of freedom meant I had to be willing to die. My mother's suicide gave me the gift of allowing me to choose a fast life without looking back: it *is* a good day to die. This was not a slogan, an idea, or a belief for me—it really was so. And because it was, I wanted to go out with a splash that would wash waves of freedom throughout the world.

In the next six months, I was arrested three times on six felonies. By August of that year, I was facing a possible forty years in state and federal prisons. Through the grace of the unknown benevolence that was drawing me ever closer, I never spent more than four consecutive nights in jail.

*   *   *

A week before I left New York, I bought a Metro-Mite delivery van that had been outfitted by an LA surfer with windows, curtains, a bed, and painted a robin's-egg blue. It had a bus driver's seat, and a bus-driver handle to swing open the door.

When I stopped in Pittsburgh, I picked up Marshall, a brother needing to get out of town. He told me about the People's Peace Treaty that was about to meet in Ann Arbor: I was retracing my path through my old haunts, making a loop two years—and a seeming lifetime later—from Pittsburgh to Ann Arbor.

In Ann Arbor, as Marshall and I walked into the hall where the meeting was being held, Kenny and Charlotte—from our Denver Strike Committee—walked in from the other side at the very same moment. Had this been a movie, this scene would've been panned as too staged. We had not been in contact about this event—I didn't even know about it when I'd left Colorado for New York. We hugged in the middle of the ballroom, and became the Colorado delegation of the People's Peace Treaty.

The event posters read:

If the Government Won't Stop the War, We Will Stop the Government.

The plan was to present Congress with a Treaty of Peace signed by the American people, and the Vietnamese people, acknowledging that the U.S. government was waging an illegal war against Vietnam. Ron Kovick, a Medal of Honor recipient who had lost his legs in Vietnam, would lead a delegation of the Vietnam Veterans Against the War to present the Peace Treaty to Congress. If Congress did not accept the treaty and stop the war, we would stop the government. We would non-violently blockade the streets of Washington and stop the government by stopping all traffic flow in the city.

Though it proved to be a false alarm, in the middle of our meetings we were warned that we could be raided, so I bought my first gun while Kenny made Molotov cocktails in the van. Kenny, Charlotte, Marshall, and I made our way back to Colorado in my van with a mission to stop the government.

A few weeks later, I was arrested in Denver . . . for eating cookies in a Safeway. I swaggered through the store wearing combat boots, a Bowie knife on my belt, and an in-your-face attitude. I behaved like an arrogant petty thief, but justified it on moral grounds.

Without religion, a fear of hell or of God's punishment, or any other moral order to restrain me, my character flaws went unchecked. I was yet to be humbled, to become aware of my own ignorance, and thereby tap into an openhearted common sense and morality; I was making my own rules, and my own morality.

I had started stealing in junior high school. The bus from school would let us off across the street from Roses' Candy Store. We would stop in for seven-cent cherry Cokes, nine-cent chocolate egg creams, and the occasional candy bar. One day the sweet old couple, the Roses, were gone, and the candy store had new owners.

I realize now that the new owner was an unhappy, fortyish, balding man, living in the back of the store with his wife and children. To us he was short-tempered and mean. Sometimes we could hear him yelling at his family behind the doorway that separated their home from the store. I decided to drive him out of business: my first moral crusade.

To the right of the small candy store's entry was a card table stacked with different sized spiral notebooks for sale. The table was behind the round, red vinyl-covered stools where we would sit and sip our cokes. I would put my schoolbooks down on top of the pile of spiral notebooks before turning to sit down at the counter. When I picked up my books later, I would also pick up a few of the notebooks. I gave them away at school, proving to myself that I wasn't stealing for my own gain. Such apparent selflessness was a way of deflecting my attention from the lack of character I was demonstrating.

Next I started to steal candy. As we sat at the counter drinking our cherry Cokes and talking, I would stuff my pockets with candy bars. I had a sense that this was a matter of principle. When my neighbor Joey Napolitano, in one of his more benevolent moods, once tried to show me how to steal candy bars, I was shocked. I wasn't interested. But now I felt justified: I wasn't stealing to eat a candy bar for free, like Joey. In fact I started throwing the candy in the gutter outside the store, both as a challenge to the candy store owner, and as proof to myself that this was not about being greedy for candy. It never occurred to me then that the rush of the experience of getting away with the crime was what really drove me.

If the new owner saw his candy in the street, it must have broken his heart and his will to continue: after a year and a half, he and his family were gone. The cruelty and arrogance of my "principled stand" had not yet struck home.

When Jean and I moved to Denver, we started stealing from the Safeway; we saw Safeway as the corporate enemy. We supported the grape boycott in support of Cesar Chavez and the Mexican migrant workers, and Safeway was the enemy selling non-union grapes.

Kenny and I had just driven into Denver from Boulder when I was arrested in the Safeway around midnight. Between Kenny's Jimi Hendrix Afro, my appearance, and our swagger, Kenny and I attracted attention. As we shopped I ate three or four cookies out of a box, and then put the opened box back on the shelf. Technically no crime had been committed yet because we hadn't left the store and I could have been planning to purchase the box, but a security cop grabbed us, took us into the Safeway office, and called the police.

I asked to use the toilet. I had a large piece of hash and a hash pipe in my pocket. I considered flushing the hash down the toilet, but thought it would be better to smuggle it into jail. Since I was going in on such a minor charge, I could smuggle it in and share it with the boys in the tank, so I hid the hash in my underwear.

We were frisked and taken downtown. There we were risked again and put in a holding tank. I thought I'd gotten away with it, and took the pipe and hash out to light up. I was very surprised when we were called out for booking and fingerprinting, and didn't have time to hide the pipe and hash before the cop was in view, so I put them in my sock.

Marched around a corner to a bench in front of the fingerprint window, I was told: *Sit down, take off your shoes and socks, and stand over here.* With a policeman watching, I cupped the hash and the pipe while taking off my shoes and socks, and slipped them into the zipper sleeve-pocket of my air force surplus flight jacket, which I left on the bench behind me as I stood to be frisked.

After the fingerprinting, I picked up my jacket and walked back down the hall toward the cell. I was almost around the corner when I had the thought, *I made it.* But the thought came too soon. It was a tell, as they say in poker. A duty sergeant called out from behind the window of the fingerprint counter back down the hall: *Did you check his jacket?*

I was caught. The joke of the cookie bust had turned into something more serious. Now I was facing a charge for smuggling hashish—legally a narcotic—into jail. Felony possession, plus the smuggling, were added to the shoplifting.

Because it was a first offense, I received a one-year suspended sentence, to be served if I got into trouble again—which I promptly did. I was arrested twice more in the next five months.

*   *   *

Instead of going to May Days to stop the government and enforce the Peace Treaty, Kenny and Charlotte chose to join the Venceremos Brigade—a chance to go to Cuba and help in the sugar harvest. Because Cuba was one of my areas of specialization in grad school, I had taken to reading *Granma,* the official newspaper of the Cuban government, and I had been following news about the sugar crop with interest.

When Castro came to power, the sugar cane cutters were the most oppressed class. These jobs were eliminated after the revolution, and former cane cutters were retrained to operate heavy machinery, drive trucks, or trained for other jobs. An entire class of workers disappeared when Cuba no longer had cane cutters, but Cuba was a one-crop economy that had long depended on a crop that now had no cutters.

Volunteers from around the world were going to Cuba to cut sugar cane in our generation's version of the Lincoln Brigades. It sounded like fun, and a great adventure. Now that I was facing jail if arrested again, it seemed like the safe thing for me to do was to get out of town for a while, participate in the revolution in the Caribbean, and let matters cool down in the States.

As much as I would have loved to go to Cuba, however, it felt like a cop-out. I felt that my fight was here in the U.S., in the belly of the beast. I went to May Days instead.

I hitched to Washington, DC carrying a helmet, a gas mask, and a half-pound of Santa Marta Gold—the best pot available at the time. The tribal gathering in DC had the intensity of Montgomery and Chicago, but was now a thousand times bigger; we were growing in numbers and strength, and we never doubted that we would pull this off and stop the government.

For a week, people flowed in from all directions to camp by the reflecting pools—at the feet of Washington and Jefferson. We built fires, set up free food kitchens and medical clinics, and a small city of outlaws came into being. The night before the big action on May Day 1971, we were eighty thousand strong, and we danced to Jefferson Airplane as they sang from their album *Volunteers of America*:

> *All your private property is target for your enemy,*
>
> *And your enemy is ME!*

The next morning, Ron Kovic—in his wheelchair, with his Medal of Honor on his chest—led the Vietnam Vets, including John Kerry, as they presented the Peace Treaty to Congress. When the government refused to acknowledge the treaty, the vets threw their medals onto the floor of Congress—at least one Medal of Honor, Purple Hearts, and other awards for every degree of bravery. The vets then came back and led us into the streets. We were ready to block all the bridges and traffic circles to shut Washington down.

If the Government Won't Stop the War, We Will Stop the Government!

Of course, the Nixon government had months to prepare for our plan, which was public knowledge. On May 1st, Washington, DC was occupied by the 101st Airborne. They were stationed with their jeeps on the grass at the center of each traffic circle, and by every bridge. Police would blow a whistle and point at any blockage, and within moments scooter cops were there making arrests. It was disheartening, and no traffic was stopped. We were losing, and dispirited.

Eighteen thousand of us were eventually arrested. So many that a sports arena was used to hold the overflow—a foreshadowing of Chile a few years later.

I was in a group of six from the Colorado delegation who went to Dupont Circle. We found an oil drum, set it on fire, and rolled it into the street. Within moments there was a whistle, and the police were in hot pursuit. I didn't know the man they arrested from our group—Bill, from New York, had joined us at the last moment. As they were taking him away . . . time stopped.

Everything froze into a silent tableau. It was as if I was viewing a three-dimensional still life, and I could see in all directions at the same moment. I saw clearly what needed to be done. We needed to be inspired, galvanized.

I also realized in that moment that the policeman was my brother. He was playing his role, just as I was playing mine. I felt no animosity toward anyone. I was filled with a sense for the potential of the moment, and knew that something needed to be done. That's when I started my run.

In retrospect, when I see the policeman walking away with his prisoner in tow, I see that it was the same distance from me as my friend Mark had been on the vacant lot in Brooklyn. I realize now that this was a gyre of time, spiraling and repeating itself in some mysterious way. I was playing out my Brooklyn melodrama with a fresh cast of characters, and heavier consequences.

Like Johnny Mack Brown on a horse, I ran-galloped up behind the policeman and grabbed his arms from behind. *Split!* I yelled, and the prisoner fled up a side street.

I turned and ran, as the crowd parted to let me by. I was never a fast runner, however, and my mountain boots and motorcycle helmet didn't help my speed. The policeman's partner came veering in at me, from an angle off the street and onto the sidewalk I was running down. I straight-armed him and knocked him down. I was absolutely amazed. I'd only seen this done in football movies. My dissociated enjoyment of this moment of pain and terror reminded me of the moment when I was a little boy and saw stars as my head was banged into a wall.

Suddenly I was tackled from behind as the policeman I jumped caught up with me. My hands were handcuffed behind my back with amazing speed, like a rodeo rider with a steer. He had neglected to do this the first time, and he had lost a prisoner. He wasn't going to make the same mistake again.

As he picked me up off the sidewalk and led me away, there was an electric crackle in the air. The dispirited protestors had come alive. Maybe five hundred were now clapping in unison and chanting: *Free him! Free him! Free him!*

I turned and saw Cissily, a lanky, long-haired blonde with a horsey Norwegian smile, and sparkling blue eyes. She had been working as a barmaid in Boulder when we met, and had eagerly joined our group. She was wearing one of the motorcycle helmets I had stolen for her, and she was out in front leading the clapping.

I fell in love. Her body, yes, her looks, of course—but it was her fierce seizing of the moment that I found irresistible. In the heat of battle, I had found an ally, and I loved her.

Free him! Free him! Free him!

The arresting officer and I were in the middle of the street, about half way to the traffic circle and the 101st, when the crowd caught fire from Cissily and moved in from three sides. The policeman threw me on the ground, put his knee on my head to keep me in place, and pulled his gun on the crowd.

Don't free me! I shouted. *Game's over!*

I was later taken away from the precinct to the jail in leg irons, with my hands handcuffed to a chain around my waist, and I was charged with two counts of assault on a police officer—a federal offense in DC. Each count carried a possible term of six to nine years in federal prison. There was also my year-long sentence from Denver, which was now in violation: I was looking at a possible nineteen years. I should have been more scared, but it seemed like a movie, somehow unreal as I moved through it and made the best I could of my part.

At the jail they herded all the new prisoners to a shower area where we stripped and sprayed with a hose filled with disinfectant. We raised our arms on command, spread our cheeks, and then closed our eyes. After a cold shower, we were mass dried with large fans, and issued our prison garb.

I was taken in chains to third-tier maximum security. My cellmate was a Black man caught in an armed robbery: he had shot it out and lost. Our cell had a toilet bowl, a metal slab shelf, and a bunk bed. A former inmate had left a color portrait on the wall of a naked Angela Davis. After three days my friends found me and bailed me out; it took a while for them to remember that my ID said Norman Brown.

When I failed to appear for my federal grand jury indictment, my bond was raised to $100,000 and I was listed as a federal fugitive. Four months had passed since my mother's death in January. It seemed like another lifetime.

*   *   *

A federal fugitive already in violation of my suspended sentence, I was arrested yet again in Denver three months later, in August. This was serious. Things were way out of control.

After May Days, our group had dissipated. Four of us hid out for a while in the rugged wilderness of Golden Gate Park, outside of Golden, Colorado. Our cabin was accessible only with four-wheel drive, and in deep snow was not accessible at all. An impossible group of three men and one woman, we did our best to be revolutionary and righteous with one another.

One night I couldn't help but listen to Marshall make love with Cissily. We all slept in the same one-room log cabin. It tore me up. Of course I never said anything about it, and I denied feeling jealous to myself as well. Intellectually I knew that being jealous signaled ownership. I was sure that marriage was a property contract, a relationship of power and chattel, and I wanted nothing to do with it. Yet, here were my feelings nevertheless; my ideas meant nothing to my emotions. All I could do was try to suppress them. I wanted to act as if I didn't notice and didn't care, but I was never very good at hiding my emotions. My passive aggressive moping didn't help anyone, and in the blink of an eye our little collective was over.

CHAPTER 10

Third Strike

Three 'clock roadblock. Curfew.

I've got to throw away,

Yes, I've got to throw away

my little herb stalk . . .

Ain't got no birth certificate on me now.

—Bob Marley, "Rebel Music"

In Boulder, I supported myself as a street dealer. In those innocent days before heroin, crack, and meth destroyed whole swaths of the counter-culture population, you could walk down the street and casually score acid, grass, hash, and mescaline from a dozen different dealers, whether on the hill in Boulder, in the Haight in San Francisco, or on Telegraph Avenue in Berkeley. It was generally a peaceful, non-violent scene.

Selling lids, or ounces of pot, is a hand-to-mouth proposition, and everyone was always looking for the big score. One day a big deal found us. Two friends of Marshall's from Pittsburgh wanted two hundred pounds of pot. We had the guys flying in with the money, and we had a connection who knew the person with the pot: we were the middlemen. Neither side wanted to meet, see, or be seen by the other, and no one was foolish enough to part with either their money or their pot without an exchange. We hit on a plan.

We would meet the boys from Pittsburgh in a Denver motel room, and take a Polaroid of the money spread on the current day's Denver Post as proof that the money was real. We would then leverage this photo to get the two hundred pounds fronted to me for the few hours it would take to drive from Boulder to Denver.

Everything was in place. The pot was there, and the money was there. This could actually work, and we would make enough to get bankrolled and off the street. But when we entered the lobby of the motel to find out which room the boys from Pittsburgh were in, Marshall dropped two grams of cocaine which he had rolled up in his sleeves. In the adrenal rush of making the big deal, we didn't notice them fall.

I first heard of cocaine back in Queens when Dave Van Ronk shouted and moaned his way through "Cocaine Blues," and I knew I wanted to try it. I knew nothing about cocaine then, but after the government had scared me about pot and LSD and I discovered the lie of that, I was willing to try anything once. Watching my grandpa Isaac give himself injections back in Brooklyn had given me a phobia of needles, but if a substance could be smoked, swallowed, or snorted, I was willing to try it.

I tried pure China white heroin—just once. I smoked it, and didn't like it. I tried pure crystal methamphetamine. Chopped it up and snorted it once on each side. It was a fire in my nostrils. I had no idea how much I was doing, and for three days and nights I tripped in my cabin as the cosmic mystery and higher mathematics unfolded themselves. I didn't sleep or eat. After three days, I fell into a gut-wrenching two-day withdrawal, lying in a fetal position. I never tried that again.

I didn't like Tuminol, Nembutal, Seconal, Quaalude or any other downer, or the so-called hypnotics that I tried. Without being told what was in it I was once passed a pipe with angel dust in it and ended up lying immobile for hours. I never did that again.

But cocaine was different. It seemed mild and harmless, and I liked the acceleration it gave to the grass I smoked. I had tried cocaine once, and when a half an ounce was available, I bought it. Marshall and I had just grammed up half of it but not yet sold any of it. We never did. Fate kept us from that.

The kid at the front desk of the motel found the grams Marshall dropped and called the police. We had photographed the money, smoked a joint, and just finished a line of coke when there was a pounding on the door.

I had three grams in the brim of my Irish cap. I rushed for the toilet as someone opened the door and six narcotics cops rushed in with guns drawn. Like many motel rooms, the bathroom door was adjacent to the hall door, so that when the cops came in, I was right there. It was too late to flush.

I put the three grams in my mouth and tried to swallow, but I had cotton mouth, and the glycerin bags stuck to the roof of my palate. One of the detectives recognized me from my previous bust, and pointed and shouted that he knew me.

I couldn't speak. They had their guns out, and our hands were up. I pointed to a glass of water and was allowed to drink. I gulped three glasses while managing to shout about being framed. While I made a commotion, one of the Pittsburgh boys had the presence of mind to hide the money between the mattress and box springs. The police found three empty suitcases, the coke in the lobby, a gram in the room, a Polaroid of $20,000 on that day's paper, and my custom-made Bowie knife with coke residue on it.

I was handcuffed to Marshall in the back of the squad car on our way to the station when the bags in my stomach opened. My teeth started to chatter and my body froze. I bit my hand to keep the noise of my chattering teeth from attracting attention. A passing breeze from an open window sent my body into spasms, but I couldn't let the cops find out what I had done; I didn't want my stomach pumped. I had to bear this without showing anything.

At two in the morning, Marshall and I were in a small interrogation room with the detective who had recognized me from the Safeway cookie bust. Behind his desk was a poster of a large inverted peace sign. The caption read: *Sign of the Hippie Chicken.* I had had a roll of hundreds in my front pocket, and the detective was now examining these bills. *These two look counterfeit,* he said. I asked to look at them. *They're gold certificates,* I condescendingly let him know. *They're actually worth more.*

The detective left the room, and I could hear him talking and laughing outside the door. When he returned, I asked, *How many did you take?*

You hippie motherfucker! You calling me a thief? Hold out your hand, and after I count all the money into your hand, I'm taking you into the back room to kick the shit out of you.

Marshall pleaded, *Oh, leave him alone. He's harmless. He's a nice guy. He didn't mean it.*

I said, *Look, I don't know how many are supposed to be there anyway. I never counted. Just keep it all, okay? I'm sorry.*

The detective counted eighteen hundred dollars in hundreds into my palm, and then unhandcuffed me from Marshall. I took off my glasses and gave them to Marshall to hold as I was led out the door and down the hall. The detective slammed the door of a tiny room, locked us in, and moved toward me to hit me.

I looked into his eyes and showed no fear, no anger—nothing at all. I felt nothing at all. My body was still overdosing on coke. I felt completely empty and at peace. I didn't move. I was fully present and empty as I looked at him.

For some reason, the detective couldn't hit me.

Sit down and shut up! he barked.

Yes, sir, I replied and sat down. He kept me there for several minutes to save face before he took us to booking.

Only in writing this do I realize that this moment with the cop was a replay of my moment in Detroit, when I was surrounded by the Black kids, and remained empty and present. I can't say that I did anything in either case because there was no strategy on my part. These moments were like clues, like crumbs on the trail that drew me closer to my true home.

They held me in the Denver jail for three days of investigation before my arraignment. They were the longest days of my life. I was scared. If the fugitive warrant turned up, I would be extradited back to DC with no possibility of making the $100,000 bail. With no money, and only a public defender, I could do a dozen years on each count in Washington, and then be sent back to Colorado to serve another ten to twenty in a state penitentiary for the coke. It looked like I was in deep trouble and wouldn't see daylight until I was an old man.

I tried rolling and smoking a cigarette with the tobacco and papers the jail supplied. My first cigarette. I smoked it like a joint. It made me feel dizzy and foggy. I never tried a cigarette again.

For the first time in my life, I prayed. I didn't just mouth the words used in temple. There was no scripted prayer to pray. I prayed for help. I didn't know if God existed or not, but if help was available from anywhere in the universe, from conscious beings of a different dimension or a faraway star, or even God, I was in dire need.

After three days, I was bailed out. In those days before computers, the fugitive warrant for Norman Brown didn't turn up. So I was back on the street—still a federal fugitive and out on bail. But I saw that great good luck as a sign. I had complete confidence now that things would somehow work out. I can't say I had faith, because I didn't have faith in anything. Instead, it was a subconscious knowing, a certainty that whatever sprung me from jail would also take care of the rest.

The National Lawyers Guild was having their annual meeting in Boulder when I hit the streets. I managed to connect with Dennis Cunningham who had been my public defender in Chicago. Dennis was a red-headed firebrand, happy to give me advice and a strategy. Taking Dennis' advice, I called my public defender in Washington and worked out a deal to have my bail lowered to its original amount if I turned myself in and appeared in court for trial.

Wearing a short-haired wig, I flew to Washington for my court date. I arrived late because of heavy traffic from the airport. My lawyer and the DA who brought the case to the grand jury were both gone. I called my public defender, and he told me how to get in touch with the judge. Through grace, I met the judge and explained that I just flew in for the day from a lawyers' conference in Boulder and that I had to fly out tomorrow. I asked if it would be possible to hear my case today, and the judge miraculously assigned a DA to meet me, with the instruction to wrap it up. The newly assigned DA to the case did not know that there was television footage of me jumping the officer and the subsequent arrest. He only saw the charges without the file that was taken to the grand jury.

I told the DA the following four sentences:

I was there on that corner.

Several of my friends were also there on that corner.

We all saw what happened.

I will go to trial and beat this case.

Each time he countered with an offer of a deal, I repeated those same four sentences. I repeated them three times, as he lowered the charges, giving me a better deal each time. He then offered me a plea bargain of disorderly conduct. I insisted that I would beat the case. He said, *Look, if you get a fine, I will pay it.*

Internally overjoyed and ready to shout halleluiah, or at least breathe a sigh of relief, I managed to keep a straight face and reluctantly agreed to the deal.

When the original charges of assault on two police officers were dropped, however, the judge said that I couldn't plead disorderly conduct because no charges had been formally filed. This good-hearted judge—a gift from unknown allies—wrote a note saying: *Norman Brown was merely an innocent bystander.* I loved him for this. I was a free man.

Exactly thirty years later, on May 1, 2001, I was invited to give a talk at the World Bank on how best to serve world peace. The World Bank is located on Dupont Circle, where I had been arrested. To get into the World Bank, I needed to pass a background check. Plastic ID cards were then issued and clipped to a red ribbon, which I wore around my neck when I entered the building. Thirty years ago on this day, I was arrested with an ID with the name Norman Brown. A little later, to evade detection, I changed my name to Norman Phillips, and then for almost thirty years, Eli Jaxon-Bear. Thirty years later, they gave my birth name back to me: Elliot Jay Zeldow was printed on my pass, and I wore it around my neck while leading a meditation at the World Bank.

I swear this is true. Of all the possible random events in the universe, how did it happen that the name tag appeared on the anniversary date of May Days? Though by then it was too late, because I was stuck with my hippie name, Eli Jaxon-Bear, honoring Brother Malcolm with an X, and given to me by Kimo, a Mescalero Apache, after we ate magic mushrooms and danced all night on a full moon back on the farm . . . but we haven't arrived there yet.

* * *

I was off the hook in DC, but I still had the case in Colorado to face.

The boys from Pittsburgh had been bailed out the same evening of the bust. They returned to the motel to get their money from under the mattress and left town, never to be heard from again. The charges had been dropped for everyone but me because of my knife with the coke on it and the grams. I felt that the only way to beat this case was to pay off the police.

I started asking around. Our little political collective had been doing karate in Five Points, the Black neighborhood downtown, with the local Black Panthers. A local Panther and I had become friends, and he referred me to his friend who was a bail bondsman. The bail bondsman gave me the name of a lawyer who worked for the policeman's union and was handling a case for one of my arresting officers. For $5,000 the lawyer could take care of this. That was a lot of lids.

Marshall and I ended up in front of the Safeway I had been busted in eight months earlier with a bag full of lids to sell to people leaving the store. We also canvassed the dorms in Denver and Boulder. We sold lids day and night.

What remained of the coke, which I had hidden in a secret hole behind our cabin, was snowed on during one of Colorado's freak August snows. The coke was now mush and could not be sold, so I diluted it with water and filled a nasal sprayer. I used this nasal sprayer when I returned to the police station with my lawyer. We met with the same detective in the same office I had been handcuffed in. I wore my short-haired wig, and apologized and groveled, telling the detective I now saw the error of my ways while using the nasal spray, explaining to the detective that the coke had messed up my nose. I was at war, and this deception was my way of sticking it to the man while I cut a deal.

I agreed to plead guilty as an accessory after the fact to a felony, which is the highest misdemeanor, punishable by two years in state prison. In court the next week, the judge asked me how I pled. I answered: *On advice of my attorney, I plead guilty, your honor.* The judge stared down at me from his bench. He did not like me. I thanked God he had not been in Washington.

I hereby sentence you to two years in the state penitentiary.

He stopped. My heart sank. My gut sank. This was not a frozen moment of time but an enormous squirm.

I was about to cry out *BUT* when he added, *Sentence to be suspended on the advice of the arresting officer.*

In the elevator leaving the courtroom, I pulled off my wig. The detective standing in front of me turned around and said, *We will be looking for you. We are going to catch you again, and it will be your second offense. Then we'll throw away the key.*

They had overlooked the first offense of stealing cookies and bringing hash into the jail, for which I could have served a year. I kept my mouth shut, my mind quiet, and stared straight ahead.

CHAPTER 11

The Smell of Death

A light snow was falling as I drove away from court. I cut over past Larimer Street, with its skid-row cowboy bars and peep shows, and drove down the west side of Denver. I was driving a '59 Ford pickup with a gun rack in the rear window. I had an M1 carbine with a 30-round banana clip in the rack. It was for show, a statement that I was bad, but now my heart wasn't in it. I was in despair. After the inflation I felt earlier walking out of the courtroom a free man, I now felt exhausted and deflated. I drove past my old apartment on Second and Cherokee and looked up to see if anyone had moved in. It was just two years since Jean and I first moved from Pittsburgh to that apartment.

My God. It had all gone by so fast.

The street leading out of town turned into a two-lane county road heading up into the foothills. I drove past Morrison, with its post office, general store, and 25¢-a-gallon self-serve gas, over the red rock ridge and on to the old stage road that switch-backed down into Kerr Gulch. The cloud of dust from the dirt road announced my arrival.

I was renting a cowboy cabin for $25 a month. I had $300 left after paying off the lawyer and the police; it was enough to last for awhile. The cabin had a refrigerator and a stereo. I used five-gallon jerry cans to bring water from the well down the road, and burned kerosene lanterns at night. An antique potbellied stove, with an ornate Kaiser's cap and filigree ears, provided heat, and I cooked on a wood stove.

On cold nights, before going to bed, I would bring the toilet seat in from the outhouse and leave it by the potbellied stove so that the seat would be warm in the morning.

The cabin was built in the protection of a small ridge. I would climb up behind the cabin past the giant Ponderosa Pines to the red rock outcroppings where I would sit and feel the spirit of the Arapaho, who long ago lived and hunted there. Wildflowers of china blue and baby pink bells filled the meadows at the top of the ridge where I practiced with my M1. I learned to spot the titmouse and Indian paintbrush as I shot at cans. I attribute the deafness my wife accuses me of these days to that time.

While growing up, I loved the rifle range at summer camp. I was ranked an expert marksman for my age group by the NRA. I played ball and the mandatory team sports at camp, but I gravitated to shooting, archery, riding horses, and the lake. All that fun became useful later in my life, but now I was in way over my head. A version of my nightmare of going to my death killing Nazis seemed to be materializing before my eyes.

From what I'd seen in the movies, I thought I should be able to strip the guns, clean them, and put them back together again. I tried with the first rifle—a 30-06 Bolt-Action—that I'd bought in Ann Arbor. I managed to get it into pieces, but had no idea how to put it back together again. I never did.

The biggest room in the three-room cabin was the kitchen, which had a table, three chairs, and a cupboard next to the big old cook stove. Two kitchen windows caught the morning light, and looked out onto the hills and Kerr Gulch below. Walking into the cabin, you entered the sitting room with the potbellied stove, an old couch, a rocking chair, and a stuffed armchair. Upstairs was the bedroom: a small loft built into the roof of the A-frame. There was room enough for two mattresses, some shelves, a small chest of drawers, the stereo, and my records.

Sometimes in the morning I'd find water frozen in the kitchen. Once the fire was lit in the cook stove, I would make hot cereal and put on a soup and some grain. Then I would cut firewood. I tried to keep at least a week ahead of the wood I was burning, but since the cabin had plywood walls and no insulation, and it sometimes snowed for days, I burned quite a lot of firewood.

When it wasn't snowing, there were crisp, clear skies, and sun by 10 a.m. I would take a book and hike up to the red rocks to read in the sun. I still loved reading, and read a small library of spiritual books from the bookstore in town. I read everything from the theosophists through all the paths to the Tibetan Buddhists. *Beelzebub's Tales to His Grandson* by G. Gurdjieff, *In Search of the Miraculous* by P. D. Ouspensky, *The Tibetan Book of the Great Liberation, The Tao Te Ching,* and Carlos Castaneda's Don Juan books became my teachers. When Don Juan said that a warrior has no past, I used my high school and college yearbooks for kindling.

I was 24 years old, but I felt like an old man. I was both scared and paranoid. I never knew if anyone I met might be an undercover agent. I sold my pickup to throw the authorities off my trail, bought a green '59 Willys Wagon jeep, and changed my name to Norman Phillips. I retreated to my solitude and my books; I was desperate.

I felt compelled to put my life on the line to stop the genocide of the Vietnam war. I practiced jumping out my cabin door with my M1 at my waist, and shooting at the mailbox down the one-lane dirt road below. I found myself at a dead end that had the smell and taste of impending violence and death.

One day a phone truck appeared in Kerr Gulch. For several days it was parked in a pasture by the side of the road, just around the bend and out of sight of my cabin. But no one in this part of the gulch had a phone.

A week later a plumber came to the cabin door saying he had been called to fix the pipes. I showed him the outhouse. Then an unmarked van took up residence in the gulch. I continued to practice for the coming shoot-out. I could feel the CIA, or the Colorado Bureau of Investigation, or surely the narcotics police were closing in on me.

How do I take a life in the name of life?

I would think of the bombers raining napalm on my brothers and sisters in Vietnam, on both fighters and innocent children, and I would break into sobs. I felt so powerless and hopeless. I didn't know where to turn or what to do.

How do I take a life in the name of life?

Everything that came before had led me to this moment. I could see that each step along the way it was freedom that challenged me: Ready to step off into the unknown? Each step over the edge was scary. I had given myself to stopping racism and war, and ended up here. I felt that the Vietnamese were justified in shooting down the bombers, and if I was truly one with them I should be doing the same. I hated the cowardly Germans who stood by and did nothing during World War II.

How do I take a life in the name of life?

With this question I burrowed into the depths of myself in search of an answer. Without knowing what I was doing, this question became a deepening into the textures of my being to discover what I was really made of.

I knew that I was a coward, yet I also knew that being a coward was no excuse—I saw that clearly when I'd jumped the policeman.

How do I take a life in the name of life?

I truly didn't want to hurt anybody, but this couldn't justify being "a good German."

I was willing to die if it would make a difference, but it seemed dying would make no difference at all. The self-immolation of Buddhist monks in Vietnam, and even of a Catholic priest in the

U.S., had made no difference to the war machine. Their sacrifice just became footage on the evening news.

I was not interested in enlightenment or personal salvation. I was looking for power, for magic, for some way to stop the genocide and mad destruction of mother earth being carried out by the forces of ignorance and greed.

How do I take a life in the name of life?

When I was much younger, I used to dream of flying and being able to disappear. Now what I wanted was the power to stop the madness and violence, but how could I do this? What test had to be passed? What secret needed to be unlocked that would lead to the end of the world's suffering?

I read the Kabbalah and the I Ching, and I learned to use Tarot cards to understand the symbolic levels of consciousness. I didn't know if there really was a God, but I felt in my heart that if there *was* a God, God must not know what was happening down here. He must be busy somewhere else, or taking a nap. In cosmic time, He could turn away for a moment and millennia would pass.

If a God exists, how to get Its attention? I hoped that God would be a superhero interested in intervening in the affairs of the human animals, but I had no faith in it.

CHAPTER 12

Dying for Life

In *The Last of the Just,* André Schwartz-Bart tells the story of the Lamed Vov: the just men that God put on the earth to witness and absorb the suffering here. Lamed Vov's have the full spectrum of lives from famous rabbis, to village idiots, to shoemakers living in obscurity. Hasidic legend says that when a Lamed Vov dies and goes to heaven, his soul is so deeply wounded and burdened by the earth's suffering that it takes the form of a frozen tear drop, which God holds next to His heart for eons as the tear drop slowly melts from the heat of God's love.

It had now been almost one year since my mother's death. My twenty-fifth birthday was approaching. I knew that I wasn't worthy to be a Lamed Vov—I was too arrogant, too rude, too scared—and yet I felt that somehow God must find out what was happening here on earth. I had to send a message. I had to be a witness, a messenger.

As my birthday approached I fasted in preparation. It was my first fast. After initial weakness and dizziness, I became clear, focused, and centered in the great task before me. I spent my days quietly in introspection. My bridges were burned: I had no future, no past, and no attachments of relationship. I was at a dead end, afraid of dying, but ready to die. Since I truly did not believe that

I would live to the ripe old age of thirty, this was as good a time as any to die.

On my birthday, after three days of fasting, I took LSD. I came into the world near midnight, the same time that my mother had died, so around midnight I took the two tiny translucent squares of a gelatin-like substance—windowpane acid: the best of Owsley's famous production—which melted in my mouth. I took 500 micrograms, double the highest dosage I had ever taken, or that anyone I knew had ever taken. People usually took 150 to 250 micrograms, so 500 was off the charts. Today 50 micrograms is considered a dose.

I sat on my bed with my legs crossed and listened to two new records I'd been given for my birthday as I waited for the sacrament to take effect. If someone had planned an initiation for me this would be it. I'd read about the secret rituals of the Eleusinian mysteries in ancient Greece, and of the Sufis in Central Asia, but what I was doing was not an externalized form of ritual— this was free form.

Music had given me so much. From the night I first saw Bob Dylan, to singing freedom songs on the streets of Montgomery, music carried me, inspired me, and nurtured me. Now it was the gateway to my initiation. First, I listened to Jefferson Starship. When I heard them last at May Days, they were Jefferson Airplane, and they were singing about revolution in the streets. Now the Starship were singing "War Movie," a song set in the future that looks back to the near future, only three years down the road:

> In nineteen hundred and seventy-five,
>
> all our people rose from the countryside
>
> locked together hand in hand
>
> all through this unsteady land

to move against you, government man.

Do you understand?

We're gonna roll, roll, roll the rock around.

Lift the rock out of the ground now.

The government troops encircled in the sun gun

found themselves on the run.

From our nation, the rock is raised.

No need to hide from the other side now.

Transformation.

Roll, roll, roll the rock around.

I listened and felt this mythic message was directed at me. This was what I was searching for, an act of magic, a vision of hope. I knew we could not win with guns. This was a shift in consciousness instead. These were my cosmic brothers and sisters channeling a message from the stars. I felt an immediate connection to the heart of this song, while the acid kicked in and started to melt the world.

As the acid rush accelerated, I listened to Jimi Hendrix's *A Cry of Love*. In this last album before his death, he anticipates his death with the song "Belly Button Window":

Well, I'm up here in this womb.

I'm looking all around.

I'm looking out my belly button window,

and I see a whole lot of frowns.

And I'm wondering if they don't want me around.

And then a resurrection of the sweetest kind with "Angel":

Angel came down from heaven yesterday.

She stayed with me just long enough to rescue me.

And my angel she said unto me,

"Today is the day for you to rise.

Take my hand. You're gonna be my man.

You're gonna rise."

This record spoke directly to me. For years afterward, I would have people listen to these records when they took LSD, hoping the music would have the same impact I experienced on my twenty-fifth birthday. I knew that anyone having that experience would be freed. It never worked—except once in that cabin.

The acid came on stronger then, with the force of a rocket, and I fell over backwards. I'd had no meditation practice or living teacher to guide me through such an experience, and I had no grounding to prepare me for what was to come. As I fell backwards, a series of lights, like a strobe, exploded in front of me. I panicked. I had the thought that the cabin was bugged and the CIA was taking pictures of me for propaganda purposes, the way they had when Ché was killed in Bolivia a few months before. I became paranoid, convinced I would not come out of this night alive. But I could use my death to send a message. If there were any conscious beings anywhere in the universe, I wanted to let them know we needed help down here. As I fell backwards, I fell into inner space and entered another reality.

I looked around and it seemed that I was at the bottom of a test tube. I felt myself being poisoned by toxic fumes. If I looked far, far up and out the top of the tube, far, far away again, much farther than the top of the test tube and reaching up into the heavens, there I saw the back of a giant chair leg. It seemed that some boy had created life in a test tube without noticing, and he was now sitting down to dinner. The poison fumes were a by-product of his experiment. I had to let him know we were alive down here. This became a life-and-death mission: to let the boy at the table know there is life in the test tube, and that we're dying from the poisonous by-products of our creation.

I started rocking the tube and internally calling out: *I'm alive. I'm alive down here.* As I rocked the tube, I rose to the top of it. Suddenly a crack opened in space. I thought it might be a tear in the cosmic sheath caused by thermonuclear explosions. This was my chance to deliver the message. To go through this black hole in space seemed to mean death, but there was no time to think about any other choice: I dove upwards and in. Internally shouting, *I'm alive!,* I slipped through a crack in time and space.

I found myself completely alone in a vastness I had no name for. I thought it was outer space. I saw that I was a ball of consciousness, vibrating golden light.

I shouted, *I'm alive!,* and felt it echo through the universe. I had no form, and there was no world beyond endless space. There was only the shout, *I'M ALIVE!,* echoing through emptiness, forward and backward in ripples of time.

I instantly knew that all of history led up to this. I saw that life on earth is a dream, a puppet show to advance consciousness to its own awakening. I knew that in truth no one dies. I realized that I am not my body or my thoughts. I saw that souls reincarnate again and again in order to wake up to their true nature as immortal consciousness.

I sensed a deep conscious intent but found no one else. I could see into different dimensions and realms. I directly realized that everything is alive—formless consciousness appearing in and as levels and dimensions of being. I saw that my idea of God had been a childish one.

I was filled with bliss and yet had no substance. I was fully conscious and present in vast emptiness. The dream of three-dimensional reality had completely disappeared.

Meanwhile, my body was still functioning in its dimension, even though I didn't see a body or the world. Don Juan speaks of a dream double, and of being in two places at the same time. I experienced this without any understanding of what was happening. It took me years to be able to see it in perspective: I was conscious in two places at the same time.

My body-mind felt that this realization would save the world and must be passed on. My body-mind also felt that the CIA now knew that I knew, and now they would attempt to kill me before I could pass on the truth about reality. I stood outside the cabin door shouting: *I'm alive! I'm free! I'm a communist!* This was the part of me that hoped to attract enough attention so that they couldn't kill me.

Friends from the cabin down the road came running, afraid my shouting would bring the police. My plan was to bring the press so that the CIA couldn't kill me. I didn't recognize my neighbors as my friends, and my body fought them off. It was two against one, but I had the power of the mad and delusional. I was fighting for the chance to pass on the secret of liberation.

While my body fought, I was descending slowly back into form. I met death in a different dimension on my way back. Death walked down a staircase into the cabin wearing clothes with no body inside them. Death looked at me and said, *So we meet again. We met before, over New York.* Years later I understood this reference to my mother's death, exactly one year before on my birthday. At the time it made no sense. I felt that I had to fight death to stay alive in a human form in order to pass on what I had realized; while my body was fighting my friends on one plane, I was fighting death on another.

Never having practiced mantra or meditation, I repeated a phrase that distilled my understanding of manifestation: *It is only a matter of matter in motion. It is only a matter of matter in motion. It is only a matter of matter in motion.* This mantra grounded me back into my body just at the moment when my body turned from fighting my friends to face the cabin door. With my legs straight out in front of me, sitting upright on air, I sailed through the cabin and out the kitchen window at the back. My head hit the wooden jam of the window as my body sailed through. I still have a scar from the stitches on my now-balding head.

I knew in that moment that I was going to make it alive. I left the body again and laughed at death, shouting, *I'm still alive motherfucker!*

When I came back into my body, my friends were standing over me in the kitchen, staring wild-eyed at me. I asked them what was wrong, and they told me my head was bleeding from hitting the window. I told them not to worry, I could stop that . . . and it stopped. They told me I was safe, so I relaxed. I left my body again because I was still not through battling with death.

Death was lulling me to sleep. How good it would feel to finally stop the struggle and drop into a deep sleep. I had done enough, I had made it, and now I could just collapse into a soothing, restful sleep. Instead I yelled, *Still alive, motherfucker!*

When I came back into my body this time around I was on a hospital gurney. I had no idea how I got there. A doctor was coming at me with a syringe, and a nurse was reaching for my arm. *Who do you work for?* I shouted. I thought the CIA had me and that my body was about to be killed.

Who do you work for? I shouted again, as they told me to calm down, that everything would be all right. When the nurse grabbed my arm, I threw her through the wheeled partition. I threatened to destroy the solar system while they subdued me with a shot of Thorazine. When the doctor shaved my head for stitches, he said, *We're going to make you look like a monk.*

Thorazine is the fog machine; it kept me sick in bed for three days.

When I recovered, I knew I had to leave everything behind, and find someone somewhere who could teach me; I knew that there was more. I was sure that somewhere there were beings who could show me what I had not yet realized, and teach me how to share what I now knew. I set out to find them. I had seen the early hippies flooding to India, but I thought that if India held the key it would have been discovered by now. I chose to look elsewhere.

Me and Mom

Uncle Jack

High School Graduation

WPDU Picks Top Pair At Debate

The William Pitt Debate Union (WPDU) held intramural debates last week to determine the top teams in the Union and assignments for the October debates. Elliot Zeldow and Ken Holecko won first place ranking.

Zeldow and Holecko will represent the Universiey at the University of Kentucky invitational

For color photos, video clips and more, go to:

outlawmakesithome.org

Dr. King speaking in Montgomery

March 14, 1965, Montgomery

March 14, 1965, Montgomery

Dr. King and James Foreman (in overalls) from SNCC

August 28, 1968
During the Democratic national convention in Chicago, 10,000 anti-war protesters gather on downtown streets and are then confronted by 26,000 police and national guardsmen. The brutal crackdown is covered live on network TV. 800 of the demonstrators were injured.

Battle of Chicago, 1968

Youngblood of the Young Patriots,
Chicago, 1968

Chicago

Chicago

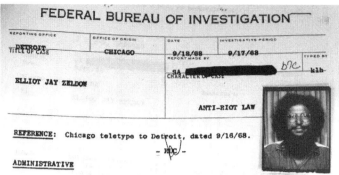

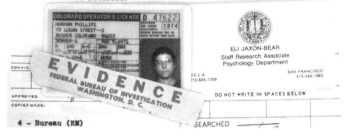

FBI record collage

May Day poster

101st Airborne Occupy Washington DC, May, 1971

101st Airborne Occupy Washington DC,
May, 1971

May Days, 1971

The hills beyond Paruru, Peru, 1972

Tio who worked on the
hacienda and lived in
our courtyard

Neighbor

Our courtyard

When I lost my horse in the hills

Oregon commune

Looking like a rabbi

Homeless in LA, 1974

Bolinas communal house, 1976

Bolinas, 1977

Bolinas, 1977

Soldiers offering me a beer,
Beijing, 1982

Shirfu demonstrating Chin To Toe

Kids offering ice cream

Beijing grandpa

ChoShoJi Zen Temple, Kyushu Japan

Temple hallway

O'Ji'isan, ChoShoJi Zen Temple

Zendo of ChoShoji

Uncle Henry

Thanksgiving in Clarksdale, with Toni and her Dad

Esalen Institute

8:45 AM 7-1-90

The Ashok Group

Page 1

Dear MR ELi - Jaxon

I hope this letter will find you in best of sprit.

I am sending you the following Three address of three famous Sufis. After meeting them you will find many more.

I could not contact in Delhi. I am writing

this letter to you in my flight to Imphal

① Khush Hal Shah
KHUSH HAL SHAH
MORNA VILLAGE
CHILA GAHA.
MUZAFFAR NAGAR
Uttar Prades

रमशी हाल ए शाह
मोरनी गाँव
मुजफ्फर नगर
उत्तर प्रदेश

خوشحال شاہ
موضع گاؤں نی
جیلا گاؤں مظفر نگر
۔ یو۔ پی

Sufi letter, page 1   Sufi letter, page 2

With Papaji, Hardiwar, April, 1990

Papaji

With Papaji and Gangiji

For color photos, video clips and more, go to:
outlawmakesithome.org

PART IV

THE ODYSSEY

. . . gently down the stream.

Merrily, merrily, merrily, merrily.

Life is but a . . .

CHAPTER 13

Into the Unknown

I set off for Peru in search of a secret brotherhood in a hidden monastery in the then uncharted Andes east of Cusco. On my way south, passing through Mexico, I spent a few days at Bara de Navidad—a small fishing village with no tourists and a white sand beach in front of a fresh-water lagoon. It was March 1972, the moon was full, and Rosario, who ran a fish grill on this spit of beach, invited me for a drink.

We drank tequila together, and when we were properly oiled, Rosario sang me a Mexican love song. I didn't speak Spanish, but it wasn't hard to communicate. I understood that now he wanted me to sing something. I sang Bob Dylan's "Tom Thumb Blues":

> *When you're lost in the rain in Juarez*
>
> *and it's Easter time too,*
>
> *and your gravity fails*
>
> *and negativity don't pull you through,*
>
> *don't put on any airs when you're down on Rue Morgue Avenue.*
>
> *They got some hungry women there,*
>
> *and they'll really make a mess out of you.*

We toasted each other and wandered off into the night. Me to my sleeping bag on the beach, with a foreboding sense that wherever I was going, I would have to go through Rue Morgue Avenue.

Another test? Another initiation? I didn't know. Was I making this all up? It could be, but everything made sense—the way it does in dreams. I didn't know who was running the show or dreaming the dream, but I knew my part.

My first day in Lima, I met a Chilean who offered me some pot. We went to his room and smoked. It wasn't very good pot, but it was good to be connected. In return I offered him some LSD. I had brought fifty hits of Windowpane across the border by Scotch-taping them to a roll of unexposed film. I had pulled the film far enough out of its canister to tape on the Windowpane, and then wound the film back into its canister so that it looked like a normal roll of unexposed film.

I gave this Chilean a hit when we got to my hotel room. He popped it in his mouth before I could stop him. *You too, right?* he asked. I just wanted to give him a gift; I wasn't planning to trip in that moment. But at this point I couldn't refuse. It would be bad form. So my first evening in South America, I took LSD. My new friend and I walked through the darkened streets, wandering about in this strange new city of Lima. We rounded a corner and suddenly the street was lit by floodlights, and we heard the horrible noise of diesels revving and men shouting, as tanks and troops filled the streets. A few blocks away, students were marching, chanting, and waving red flags as they headed toward the confrontation. We had come out onto the boulevard behind the tanks, so we were invisible observers of this coming clash.

I felt like I had walked onto the wrong sound stage. I had just left all this behind.

We turned around and headed back the way we came. We walked all night.

In the morning, while coming down from the acid, the shock of seeing the troops in the night hit us. We drank a bottle of Pisco—a Peruvian distilled alcohol—and drunkenly staggered off to score some grass in Plaza San Martin, the Times Square of Lima. We passed out in the morning sunshine, on the grass in front of the statue of Bolivar.

When I came to, a policeman was kicking my foot. In retaliation for the fight last night, they were rounding up hippies. I tried waking my friend because I couldn't speak much Spanish, and I had left my passport at the hotel. My Chilean friend was out cold. I had to grab him under his arms and help the police carry him into the paddy wagon.

My first day in South America and I'd landed in jail. It seems I couldn't outrun my past.

In jail I met someone with a festering gunshot wound from the night before. It was only a graze on his leg, but it had not been treated. The next day, when we were released, I met him again in the plaza where we'd been arrested, and gave him a tube of Neosporin for his wound. In return he gave me the name of his cousin in Cusco, and told me he was someone who could guide me into the mountains. He also gave me general directions for finding his cousin in the metzitzo barrio.

After a long bus ride from Lima, passing through several small cities, climbing out of the plains through a 14,000-foot pass over the front mountain range, I found myself in the verdant and peaceful valley of Cusco, the past capitol of the Inca Empire. I found a room in a hotel a block off the central plaza. The two-story Spanish colonial style hotel had an open central courtyard. My room, in the upper corner, had a small balcony above the street. My front door opened to the veranda that circled the courtyard and led to the toilets and showers at the far end. My room had electricity but no running water. A washbasin in my room stood on a table in front of the balcony.

I spent the next several days exploring Cusco. I would start each day going to the Indian market for breakfast. Under a warehouse-sized corrugated roof with no surrounding walls, Indian women sold produce from the jungle to the north, and temperate river valleys that surrounded Cusco. I had my first taste of cherimoya: a lumpy-looking, misshapen green jungle fruit, which tasted like delicious custard. I also discovered quinoa, avocados, and cilantro.

Outside the market, in the cobblestone gutter, several Quechua women sat with pots of food. For half a sol—worth a little more than a penny—I could get a plate of cooked greens and baby potatoes. I would squat in the street next to the woman I'd ordered from and eat. She'd sit on the high curb with her feet in the cobblestone street. She had three plates and three spoons. When someone finished, she dipped the plate and spoon in a bucket of water and then wiped them on her apron. Next I would go to the juice ladies: eight or nine women with Champion juicers made carrot juice, orange juice, and veggie combos on request. A giant glass, almost needing two hands to hold it, cost three soles. I ate this way daily and never got sick.

When I acquired a Primus kerosene stove, given to me by a passing tourist, I began to purchase and prepare some of my meals. I enjoyed quinoa, potatoes, corn, onions, garlic, beets, and fresh Fava beans, along with avocados, bananas, honey, and yogurt.

In the market I found a brown alpaca poncho, and a worn and patched alpaca scarf. I bought a brown felt cowboy hat, with a small woven hatband of native design. I also bought a net bag to carry my groceries in, and a shoulder bag with large stripes of chocolate-and-cream-colored alpaca, which I used for years as my luggage. It cost a quarter and for thirty years it never lost its alpaca fuzz.

I was deeply drawn to an old Quechua belt. Quechua belts are four-inches wide and six-feet long, woven on a backstrap loom, and wrapped like a cinch multiple times around the waist before tying. The one I liked had the muted colors of age, and its geometric pattern told a story that never repeated itself. Every day I went to the weaving market and bargained with the man selling the belt. The weaving market was the only place where I saw men, metzitzo men, engaged in commerce. After five mornings of negotiation, I finally bought the belt for 250 soles, about eight dollars, which was a fortune for me then. My alpaca shoulder bag and my belt are all that I have left from that time. They live now at the bottom of my chest of drawers.

Once I was properly clothed, I wandered through the barrio looking for the address I was given in Lima. None of the streets had names, and the houses had no numbers. Finding cousin Mario didn't seem likely, and yet, standing in the middle of a dirt road wearing a cowboy hat, army surplus jacket, striped dress pants, and black leather dance shoes with no socks, was Mario, grinning wildly at me. We recognized each other from a block away.

A few years earlier, Dennis Hopper had been in Cusco to shoot a film. Mario had been a gofer. Mario could speak English as well as Spanish and Quechua, and he knew his way around. In exchange for his expertise, the film crew had turned him on to LSD.

The first thing Mario said to me when we met in the middle of the street was, *Tienes acido?* I told him I did. I also told him I was on a spiritual search, looking for a hidden brotherhood of light in the back mountains. Mario was just preparing to leave for his mother's village and invited me to go with him.

At 5:30 the next morning, we met at the truck plaza behind the Indian market. While the few tourists went north to Machu Picchu and south to Lake Titicaca by train, we found a truck going to Paruro: the end of the line due east into the mountains. We climbed into the back of the flatbed along with Quechua women and their restocked supplies, a few live chickens, and some campesinos returning from a trip to the big city. Mario asked me if I had the acid. Knowing what was coming this time, I gave him a half, and I took the other half as we settled in for our journey.

CHAPTER 14

Shangri-La

It was a perfect April day. Wildflowers and chamomile spread from the roadside. We clung to the one-lane dirt track climbing high above the river valley below. The truck ground its gears as it climbed out of the Cusco Valley and we looked out on the terraced hillsides cascading 12,000 feet down.

We stopped for lunch at a tiny village built by the road. As a gringo, I was a rarity. A woman invited me to have sex with her daughter. They thought an American baby would change their luck. I passed on the offer while the girl blushed.

Paruro was a ride back in time, an adobe village with no running water. Most of its people had never even been as far as Cusco in their life. The town did have an electric light, and on festival evenings, to much fanfare, the generator was fired up and a large light bulb turned on in the town plaza.

Standing six feet tall with my full beard and shoulder-length hair, I could have dropped down from another planet among these small native people. I was the first gringo the town had ever seen. And they'd never heard of hippies.

Mario and I shared a courtyard dwelling with an old Indian couple, Tia and Tio. I was slowly learning Spanish and understood only later that this meant aunt and uncle. The couple must have been part of Mario's mother's family. Mario, with his young wife and new baby, moved into the room adjoining Tio and Tia's.

My room was around the corner; my door faced the street and the early morning sun. The room was small, with a dirt floor, no windows, and a thatched roof. At one time it was a grain storage room for the other little dwellings in the courtyard. I enjoyed sitting in the morning sunshine on the soft worn flat-river stone that was my front step and watching the town go by on the street. On school days, the kids dressed in their uniforms would come down my street to see this strange creature and practice their English. *Good morning, meester,* was the sweetest sound. I was in heaven.

Tia wore the same clothes every day: a large full skirt of indeterminate color and great age, with several petticoats to fill it out; a white cotton embroidered blouse; and a shawl of thin red stripes held with a safety pin. Her hat was the hat of her home village: a wide, white sombrero, with the front pinned up.

Tio worked on the hacienda for ten soles a day, which at the time was worth around 25¢. He also wore the same clothes every day: a pair of raggedy pants that came down to his calves; a worn, patched, alpaca poncho; an alpaca hat with earflaps; and rubber flip-flops on his feet.

Each morning, Tia brought us coals from her fire to start ours. In exchange, every few days, I would take her large earthenware jug down to the river and bring water back to her. I learned which river was for drinking, which for washing—the women beat the clothes clean on rocks—and which water was *sucio,* or dirty.

I learned the word *sucio* on a day when I was on my way to wash my clothes in the river. As I passed out of town, the mayor, drinking a warm beer in the morning, called out, *Gringo! Sucio!* and he laughed and laughed. I learned then that *sucio* meant dirty and that there was a clean part of the river upstream. Gordo, the mayor, thought it was hysterical that I didn't know the difference. Stupid gringo that I was.

Mario's mother, who now lived in Cusco, owned a share in a community farm. We spent two days working the potato harvest. At the start of the day, a mud oven was made in one corner of the field, and potatoes and large fava beans were put in to cook. After the oven was fired up, we unearthed the rows of potatoes with a tool that looked pre-Columbian in its antiquity: a stout branch worn smooth with a piece of metal inserted in the end. No doubt this same hand plow was used with a stone before there was metal.

At lunchtime, the oven was opened, and we all sat together to eat hot potatoes and beans. No salt or condiment of any kind was used or needed to make it delicious. It was as if I had died in the cabin in Colorado and was reborn into a land of peace and beauty, where I was seen as harmless, and at worst as a curious oddity. I could finally relax completely. I wasn't wanted by the law, and I wasn't doing anything illegal. No one was looking for me.

The weather was perfect, a cool but sunny alpine spring—or so I thought at the time. I didn't know that it was fall, as it is on the other side of the equator. I was there for what I thought was the summer solstice of Inti Raymi, which I learned later was the winter solstice celebration. Even as we harvested potatoes, I thought it was a spring harvest.

I had stepped back into another time. The air was sparkling clean, and the place was deeply quiet. There were no machines, no hum of Western civilization. No radios, no TV, no electric wires, no traffic noises. Once a day a truck would come into town from Cusco. That was the only motor to be heard if someone was close enough to the road to happen to hear it. In this clarity of stillness, I felt a deep connection with everything alive that is sweet and true.

When we finished our work, the harvest was divided up. Mario, his wife Maria and I were given one sack of potatoes. The sack was made of the same material as my shoulder bag: stripes of undyed cream-and-chocolate-colored alpaca. The potato sack came up to my chest, and must have weighed a couple of hundred pounds. Everyone stood around and watched me, while they winked and smiled at one another. I couldn't budge the sack of potatoes, and this made everyone laugh. The oldest man in the group, standing perhaps five feet tall, with wiry skin and bones, finally backed up to the sack, which was as big as he was. He grabbed a corner with each hand, and with a shout, he hoisted the sack onto his back, while he bent from his waist. It stuck out several feet, both in front of him and behind him, hiding his small body. He looked like a sack on legs as he trotted to the truck to load it on for us.

I was invited to the school to speak English. No one had heard a native English speaker before, including the teacher. I played volleyball with the kids as well. The schoolteacher, Esperanza, invited me to her home for dinner. The school children serenaded us from outside, and after they left, Esperanza played a windup Victrola by candlelight.

Esperanza had relatives in New Jersey, which she imagined a fine place. She thought that if she could only get there she had a career ahead of her as a hair stylist. Esperanza was plump and sweet and inviting, and she thought I might be her ticket out of there. I was a perfect gentleman. My mind was on one thing and I couldn't afford distractions.

After my first week in Paruro, there was a festival. We all drank *chicha*, a lightly fermented corn beer. Like all the beverages in Paruro, from Fanta to bottled beer, it was warm. Mario told me that the women in the village made the chicha by chewing corn and spitting it out to ferment. I found it tasty enough for warm spit, but would have preferred it cold.

Chicha, in Quechua, means water of life. As I sat in the shade at the plaza and drank, I thought of the Japanese word for tea, *cha*; the Indian word for tea, *chai*; and the Hebrew word for life, *chai*. The Chinese word for spiritual energy is *chi* and for tea *cha*. I wonder how this can be explained? How did the Incan culture—clearly separated from the rest of the world since the last great Ice Age—happen to use *chicha* to mean water of life? Either all language has a common root, or it's all done with mirrors. Whatever the logical explanation, somewhere it is a joke, like the fact that the Chinese word for head is *toe*. Somewhere they were laughing, while I drank my warm corn beer and considered the roots of language.

I went to jail in Paruro as well. Paruro was the county seat, the last town with a government presence, and the last stop on the government-maintained road. It was the frontier of the Peruvian state's influence. In addition to the symbolic electric light, the town had a small police garrison and a jail. The jail was an adobe compound where the men lived in hammocks under shed roofs. The front door had a barred window through which women passed food in, and the men passed their weaving out. Several men had backstrap looms that they used to support themselves and their families while in jail.

Soccer games were played in the large open courtyard. Soon after I arrived in town, a guard came by and invited Mario and his gringo friend into the jail to play. Between the guards and the inmates they almost had enough for two teams. They made me a goalie, assuming I must be familiar with using my hands for basketball. Each time we visited the jail, we brought whiskey for the inmates. It was called *aquaverde*, or green water. The local store had two large oil drums with spigots: one painted red, and the other green. Red was kerosene for lamps and Primus stoves. Green was for drinking.

On market day everyone streamed in from the surrounding hills. I bought a horse from a campesino who needed the money for his child's school uniform and supplies; I paid him five dollars. I traded my shaving brush to Gordo—the mayor and boss of the town, whose job seemed to be to sit around drinking warm cervezas—for a cinch, a harness, and two sheepskins. With the harness and sheepskins used as a saddle, I could ride. I soon bought wooden cowboy stirrups and a second larger but skittish horse for seven dollars.

In addition to her share of the community farm, Mario's mother had a very small plot on a terrace a few miles out of town. At sunrise one day, Mario and I rode up to spend the morning harvesting corn and beans. When we were ready to load up our harvest, I approached my horse with my saddle blanket, but she bolted and raced up the hill. I ran after her. Even though I lost her in the maze of foot trails, I continued to run straight up until finally I thought I saw her in the far distance at the head of a waterfall up a steep arroyo. I ran, and my lungs burned to bursting.

I was never an athlete. In college we were required to take one term of physical education, and one of swimming to graduate. PE class started with eight laps around the track; I would get to three and vomit. I dropped out after the first few weeks. I managed to graduate by taking swimming twice with no one noticing.

I don't know how it was possible for my body to run so hard and so long at 13,000 feet, but I finally arrived at the top of the arroyo. I found an old Quechua man on a donkey; it wasn't my horse after all. I tried to ask him about my horse, but I only spoke a little Spanish, and he spoke none at all. Giving up on my horse, I turned around to make my way back, and realized I had no idea where to go; I was completely lost.

I walked down the trail I thought I used to come up, but it eventually took me to a Quechua hut I had not seen on my way up. It was a round hut with a thick thatch roof, and the best views of the lush green valley and snow-capped mountains. A woman came out when she heard me approaching and invited me in for lunch. She, her husband, and young child had already started when I came in. As I sat in the small dark home, smoky from fire, I was surprised to find large guinea pigs running about my feet.

They darted out from the holes under the ledge I was sitting on, and scampered after any kernel of corn that might be dropped. These furry creatures were the primary meat source, eaten only on festival days.

I remember picking up a kernel of corn from the plate of corn kernels and measuring it against my thumb. It went from the tip of my thumb to the knuckle. Each kernel was a thumb-sized morsel to be eaten one at a time. In that moment, I thought of retelling this story in the future, and the likelihood of not believing my own words.

A small amount of soft white farmer's cheese on the plate with the corn was an extra treat, and a sign that this family was doing okay. Through sign language, I tried to ask about my horse. They watched, solemnly, as if watching the performance of a mad pantomiming space man.

I thanked them as best I could and continued down the trail. I wandered down the path, and another home appeared. Once again I was obliged to sit and eat lunch when I tried to ask about my horse. I could not insult anyone by not eating. I promised myself not to ask about the horse again. I felt guilty about the first lunch, let alone two more. There could be a famine this winter with a path of huts of starving families, following the trail of the gringo who ate the threadbare peasants into starvation while searching for his horse.

It was dark by the time I made my way home. Mario and the two horses were waiting. It turned out my horse had darted into a wheat field not far from where the chase began. A farmer caught her and returned her. Everyone knew everything about everyone in this small community.

One afternoon Mario and I were riding back into town when we saw some campesinos in a high meadow taking a break from working their field. We dismounted, and I brought out the jug of aquaverde. We passed the jug while I asked about their crops and their lives, with Mario translating. The oldest of the group asked permission to hug me. I hugged him back, and he started to cry. He said he had heard of John Kennedy, and he thought that he must have been a good man, but he'd never met a gringo before, and couldn't imagine that such a one could care at all about people like him. I cried with him. My heart was bursting with love and compassion for the suffering endured daily. They asked me to sing them a song. I sang "You Are My Sunshine."

Months earlier I had been in the full-blown nightmare of prisons, surveillance, and life-or-death choices. Now, in the blink of any eye, here I was in a different world.

The full moon of April was upon us. I fasted for three days, then I made my way alone up the mountain ridge behind town to spend the night. As dusk fell, I took my sacrament, my holy fire, the divine messenger of the gods.

For the only time in my life, I heard the divine music of the heavenly spheres, an angelic otherworldly harmony that filled me with bliss as the world melted and the acid took effect. I announced my presence to the heavens, quite literally, saying, *Okay. I am here. Now what?* There was no hallucination or visual distortion, only a very clear message: the crazy man in the plaza isn't crazy. *When will he be there?* I asked. The answer was, in the morning.

Where did this message come from? I can't say. My own mind, of course, but what distant cosmic dimension played a role? I couldn't be sure. I only knew that this was the sign I was looking for.

I believed that the universe is conscious and that there is a chain of being. I wanted to believe in a cosmic space brotherhood, dedicated to peace, love, and enlightenment, that was guiding Earth to awaken. Was it true? I didn't know. Was there really a Hidden Valley deep in the Andes, a Shangri-La of spiritual immortals? I didn't know, but I saw nothing better and no other hope, so I intended to find out.

At the first lighting of the sky, just before dawn, I walked down from the ridge and again walked onto the sound stage of another movie. Riding up out of town, making his getaway before light, was a horseman. We met on the trail and looked at each other. He wore a Mexican-style sombrero and two cartridge belts crisscrossed his chest. His pistol was in a holster on his hip, and he had a handlebar moustache. He looked me over and didn't know what to make of me. I saw the thought of kidnapping and ransom flicker across his mind, but I was too unknown. Who knew what forces it would bring down on his head? I nodded and smiled, and we went our separate ways.

That morning the crazy man, *el loco hombre* as he was known in Paruro, was in the plaza. He had flowers in his hat and behind his ears, and he sometimes shouted or recited poems. I had noticed him the afternoon our truck pulled into town, but he had not been around since.

As I approached him now, he asked me, *Are you here on a mission?* Mario translated. I said I was. *Is it a mission of the state?* I said it wasn't. *Is it a mission of the spirit?* I said it was. *Good,* he said. *I live at the end of the world. You must cross the rainbow bridge to reach it.* I told him I would come, and then he was gone. Yes this actually happened. I was not tripping. How this happened, I can't say.

Before I could head out into the unknown, I needed some money for supplies. I returned to Cusco to sell my camera, a 35mm Minolta I'd bought in Chicago to document the fight with the police in the summer of '68. I'd used up my only real roll of film shooting the sights of Paruro and the surrounding countryside.

Cusco was now awash with spiritual seekers. Some were looking for the hidden city of Paititi, supposedly somewhere in the Madre de Dios jungle on the border with Brazil. Others were searching for the space brotherhood, and still others for signs in the Inca ruins. A few were even searching for the Hidden Valley I was looking for.

One of the many esoteric books I'd read in my Colorado cabin was an out-of-print copy of the *Secret of the Andes,* purportedly written by Brother Philip, who describes being taken to a brotherhood living a Shangri-La existence in a hidden valley somewhere in the uncharted Andes between Cusco and Lake Titicaca. He claimed that this valley refuge would attract and be open to messengers of the New Age. These messengers would be called to leave the world behind in pursuit of a deeper goal.

One group of seekers that had been called was staying in my old room at the Colonial Hotel. Randy, a beautiful and beatific Black man with Rasta curls, had been the head of a small band of hash dealers on a houseboat in Sausalito. He and his Swedish girlfriend had migrated to Otavalo, in the jungle of Ecuador, where they helped set up a clandestine LSD lab with someone they called Crazy Richard. They had ridden to Peru on horseback from Ecuador. Riding through the Peruvian jungle to the north of Cusco, where the river from the 18,000-foot mountains makes its way to the Madre de Dios, they found a shaman who gave them ayahausca, also called *Ya Hey.* The shaman also showed them how to prepare it.

Five of us spent the afternoon together taking turns mashing the ayahuasca vine with a mortar and pestle. When it was thoroughly mashed, we put it in a large pot and cooked it down for hours, until there were only five cups of liquid left. Each of us drank a cupful. It was the bitterest thing I have ever tasted; one sip and my whole face puckered up in revulsion. I continued to drink.

As the light of day faded, one of the five, who had been quiet and in the background of the candlelit room, now asked, *Are you Elliot Zeldow? I think I knew you in high school.*

Before I could answer, nausea struck. I was thrown onto my back and held on to the floor for fear of falling off. Waves rocked the universe, tossing the room at strange angles. I heard people vomiting around me. I was flying through blackest space, clinging to the floor, which was the only solid object left in existence.

After maybe an hour or more—impossible to know without a clock or a watch—I felt re-congealed enough to move. I announced that I was going to bed, and headed off to my hotel on the other side of the plaza. It seemed that the effects of the vine were wearing off. I was somewhat disappointed. I had heard of ayahuasca experiences with jaguars and the return of Mayans, but I didn't have any vivid hallucinations.

I got to my room and undressed in the dark. When I turned on the light, I saw someone sleeping in my bed. I assumed there had been a mistake. Since I was in a room with two beds, I thought that perhaps they rented out the other bed. This had never happened to me before, but my explanation seemed reasonable. However, this stranger was sleeping in my bed, not the unused one next to it.

Excuse me. You are in my bed. No response. So I tried again, louder. No response. So I tried in Spanish. There was a sudden movement, and a man sat up. His head was shaved, and he had a goatee and a black cape. Two more figures emerged beside him.

I repeated myself: *Esto es mi cama!*

They spoke among themselves in Spanish, but I didn't understand what they were saying; at best I had a pidgin knowledge of Spanish. I threatened to get the hotel manager, and they laughed.

I went to find the night clerk, however my clothes had disappeared, so I went out naked. I woke up the night clerk, who'd been sleeping behind the desk in the office. The sight of a naked gringo claiming to have strangers in his bed did not predispose the clerk to do anything. He wouldn't move from behind his desk.

I returned to my room. Two beings were now on my bed, and the bald man with a goatee and black cape was on the other. The two were wearing rubber Halloween masks, and were draped in towels that folded into the bed sheets. I couldn't be sure, but they seemed to be women. They were talking quietly among themselves. I overheard the bald one say, *He's too strong now. We can't.* I heard this, but it didn't register.

I suddenly noticed that my shampoo was gone. I left Colorado with one bottle of Hain's Avocado Shampoo and had been assiduously doling it out to make it last as long as possible. It had been sitting on the night table by the bed, and now it was gone. I walked over and picked up the black cape. There, on the bed, was my shampoo. Then I got mad. I said, *Okay, look. I have been nice with you. I've talked to you all night, but this is too much. When you were sleeping in my bed I was polite, but now you are trying to steal my shampoo? This is too much! Now, get out. Now!*

The helper on the other bed finally addressed me and said, *Don't worry. He's leaving.*

Then they disappeared. As they dissolved, I lunged for them and grabbed a towel. I put the towel under the bed as proof of their existence, then I got into bed and went to sleep.

The next morning I woke up to find the towel still under my bed. On the night table, leaning against my Avocado shampoo, was a note signed, *The coven.* Coven? I didn't believe in witches or covens, but my God, this was real! Here was the towel and a note! It really happened.

I rushed across the plaza to tell the others. As I described my experience, I was standing next to the open second-story balcony window. Suddenly, I jumped back and yelled, *Look out!* as a pack of hellhounds flew in through the open window. They brushed against my chest as they flew by. I realized then that I was still hallucinating. I went back to my room, and the towel and the note had disappeared.

My vision went next. I found myself blind, seeing only dimly. I barely had enough vision to find a bench in the plaza and sit in the sun.

CHAPTER 15

Rue Morgue Avenue

For the next three days I remained blind. My friends brought me carrot juice as I sat in the sun. I actually sunned my eyes—which will probably lead to cataracts and more blindness some day.

As my vision returned, an old German man, in 1930s wire-rimmed glasses and a tailored three-piece suit, made my acquaintance on the bench in the plaza. He was intelligent, articulate, and curious about the world. He bought my camera for a hundred and fifty dollars: the price I had paid for it four years before when it was new. I wondered if he was an old Nazi, perhaps a friend of Martin Bormann. I found that I liked him in spite of myself.

Mario returned from Paruro, and with my newfound wealth we bought supplies for our return to meet the crazy man. Mario mentioned that there was a brujo living in a small town outside of Cusco. We took a bus and then walked for an hour to his tiny village. As we walked up the path to the brujo's hut, we passed a group of women winnowing grain. They used almost-flat, slightly curved baskets to catch the grain they tossed into them. They worked with the efficiency of fry chefs flipping eggs in a pan. Chaff from the grain blew off with each turn.

When we entered the brujo's hut, it was smoky, and we found several sick people lying in the corners of the dark room. One was coughing, while the others slept. The brujo greeted us. I offered him a gift of coca leaves and a small bottle of Pisco. He offered me back some of the coca leaves, and we chewed together in silence. After some time, he took a handful of the remaining leaves and threw them in the air between us. He watched carefully and examined how they had fallen.

You've been in jail, he said in Quecha, with Mario translating. *You will be again, but never for very long.*

How could he know? I had told no one, not Mario, or anyone else. I don't believe in psychics or fortune-tellers, but this man *was* reading me, though he'd never met me before and had no clues or tells. The bad news about future jail time didn't sink in beneath my amazement at the brujo's knowledge. I looked deeply into his eyes. They were bloodshot, old, and rheumy. His deeply lined face was kind, but he also looked worn out. What could he know of my experiences in the States?

You've had bad luck with women. One is still angry at you.

Yes, it was true. Jean was furious that I hadn't sent her Vespa after her or paid her for it. I just abandoned it, and the landlord took it against the rent I owed. I did pack a trunk of her stuff, as she requested, but at the time I was making mad love with nurse Judy from downstairs. It was Judy who packed the trunk for me. I later found out from a furious Jean that Judy had packed dirty dishes and empty pie tins from Safeway.

You are on a spiritual quest to a great valley. You must cross a bridge of some kind. Not an ordinary bridge. A rainbow bridge.

Shivers and goosebumps ran up my body. The crazy man had said a rainbow bridge!

You will make it eventually. Come back in three days, and I will make you an amulet that will change your luck with women.

Three days later we returned for my amulet. As we walked up the path in the village, a large tarantula scurried in front of us. Mario crushed it with his heel; my heart sank. I saw the cruel pleasure in Mario's eyes, and I knew he couldn't accompany me on my journey to find the secret brotherhood.

It was clear to me that the crazy man in Paruro did not like Mario. I knew I should be going alone on this spiritual quest, but in truth, I was afraid to ride off without a translator, a trail guide, or help with the horses. When I saw Mario's cruelty, I despaired, but I said nothing. Fear silenced my tongue.

Farther up the path we heard the music of flutes and a drum— and wailing. When we arrived at his hut, we learned that the brujo had just died. I understood his final gift to me to be the warning in the death of the tarantula. I silently felt his presence, and he felt very happy to be gone. My luck with women would have to wait.

When we returned to Paruro, I found one of the horses had a tender foot. It turned out neither horse had ever been shod. In my complete lack of experience I hadn't noticed. With my new money, I took the horses to the local blacksmith and got them shoes. I also realized that the five-dollar horse we called Pokey was really a packhorse. I decided to give the skittish, seven-dollar filly to Mario and buy a true saddle horse. This meant a visit to the hacienda where the Spanish rulers of this area lived.

We packed our lunch and set off on foot up a mountain path out of town. Mario led the way up through the canyons. All morning we walked slowly upwards on ancient footpaths. This was the trail that Tio must take every day when he walked to work as a campesino on the big ranch.

We stopped to enjoy our lunch next to a trickling waterfall. Some honeysuckle was growing nearby, and Mario showed me how to pull the stamens out of the flowers and then to suck the golden drop of honey nectar at its end. I was shocked by the powerful sweet taste. Was it a different kind of honeysuckle—or is my palate now just too jaded—because I can't find that sweetness in the honeysuckle that grows outside my window today.

We reached Raul Peso Vargas' hacienda in the early afternoon. Raul was a little older than me, maybe thirty. His jet-black hair was slicked back under a black cowboy hat. He also wore a black shirt, black pants, and black cowboy boots. I learned that his father was a retired general, and his brother was a high officer in the Peruvian navy. Rulie, as Raul was known, got the ranch. It spanned rolling hills and fields farther than the eye could see. He was a cold man; I could feel his meanness below the surface. When we met him, he was working alongside his campesinos, moving rocks and small boulders, to build a small agricultural dam. Mario and I joined in and helped them carry rocks until the job was done.

On the walk there, Mario had told me that he was Rulie's cousin, which meant that Tio—who also worked on the hacienda—must be distantly related to Rulie as well. Mario the mestizo, living with the Indians and scrabbling to support his wife and baby, was clearly jealous of his Spanish cousin's wealth. Only much later did I consider that Mario's mother could have been seduced or raped by Rulie's father: such a thin line separates everything, yet only in retrospect do some things become clear. Mario Blanco was neither an Indian name nor a Spanish one. Mario Blanco was the bastard child of Rulie's father. This was why his mother now lived in Cusco, and the rooms next to Tio and Tia were empty. Most people in Paruro had never been as far as Cusco, but Mario's mother was set up in her own little house in the barrio. Most likely, Mario was Rulie's half-brother.

We were put up at the bunkhouse, with the luxury of wooden floors, windows, and a pitcher of water with a washbasin set on a side table against the wall. A crucifix with Jesus twisted in agony was the only decoration.

We sat down for our first dinner with Rulie in his dining room—a real dining room, with a large table and high-backed wooden armchairs. Rulie was shocked when he learned I was a vegetarian. *Well,* he said, slightly offended that I was turning down his hospitality and not giving him a chance to show off his upper-class Spanish steak, *you can have radishes*. So I did. I had a plate of raw radishes for dinner, while the boys had their steak.

I wanted to help clear the plates but wasn't allowed; this was the cook's job. Later when I tried to find my way into the kitchen, I discovered there was no door to it from inside the dining room; instead, there was a serving counter between the kitchen and the house. I went outside and was amazed by the Quechua hut—round and complete with thatch roof, dirt floors, and an oven—that attached to the colonial dining room. An opening in the back wall of the hut allowed food to be passed from one world to the other.

The next morning Rulie gave us a treat. The cook made hot rolls, which we took to the beehives. These bees had no enemies and so no stingers, and they didn't seem to mind our removing some of their honeycombs so that we could drizzle honey on our warm rolls. When the bread was all gone, we chewed the honeycombs. In Paruro, breakfast consisted of leftover soup, or thumb-sized kernels of corn, or potatoes, or fava beans, and occasionally some fresh farmers cheese that I'd buy for a few cents from a neighbor down the lane. But never bread or rolls, let alone honey. This was a morning to remember, gastronomical bliss amidst the scent and sight of the herbaceous greenery all around us.

We walked back to the hacienda from the hives on the hillside to find that the Indian boys had saddled up the horses. We were going to ride with Rulie and see a part of the vast land that was his. Seeing these real horses I realized that my horses back in town were poor Indian ponies. Rulie mounted the same white stallion that had once thrown his father and forced him into retirement with a concussion. I was given a giant chestnut horse with a powerful head. I immediately fell in love with the Peruvian high-backed saddles. The Peruvians draped sheepskin over the seat; the most comfortable saddle I've ever experienced, and perfect for riding up and down the hillsides and mountains. As we headed out of the courtyard and up the first rise, my saddle slipped backward and off my horse. I landed on my back. I hadn't checked the cinch. My fall gave everyone a good laugh. I never forgot to check the cinch again.

As we rode on over a pass to a high meadow, a giant condor circled overhead until it soared away behind the peak looming in front of us. I'd never seen anything like it. Rulie cursed because he didn't have his gun.

The next day Mario and I went for a ride together. I chose my own horse this time—a black gelding with an intelligent face. Mario rode the chestnut horse this time. After a few miles of exploring, we came to a space between the ridges that opened out into a vast valley, gently, almost imperceptibly, sloping downhill. Off in the far distance I could barely make out a shepherd with his flock of sheep.

Our horses took off in full race now. They didn't have bits in their mouths. I was scared at first, but I had to trust my horse. My cowboy hat blew off in the wind, to be retrieved later. We jumped a stream. At first I worried that my horse might step into a gopher hole, or trip over a loose rock. Hurtling at this breakneck speed, how could the horse know where it placed its feet? I had to surrender and ride. In the end, it was the best ride of my life, never to be duplicated.

Rulie and I bargained later, and I gave him fifty dollars for the horse, saddle, and tack. We were both very happy with the deal. What's the horse's name? I asked him. The answer was a punch line to my dream of riding off to find the Galactic Brotherhood of Light—Lucifer. I had to laugh at myself and my mad dream, and I did, to the merriment of those laughing at the crazy gringo.

Several days before the full moon, Mario and I rode out into an unmapped region of the Andes. We rode on an ancient Incan road that had occasional stairways cut into the hill making it impassable for vehicles. There were no vehicles of any kind. The only traffic was the occasional Quechua on foot.

At one point, riding in the still air, we heard something coming our way for quite some time before we saw it. It was a rhythmic thumping and a sound I couldn't really place. The sound turned out to be five Quechua men coming down a dirt track off the steep side of a hill. They were bent over carrying huge bundles of grain that stood out for several feet in front and back. The stalks whooshed a rhythm against the ground, as the men trotted with their breath in unison, like one being. A few moments later, a straggler appeared: an old man who could no longer keep up the pace, yet doggedly trailed behind. I found this heartbreaking. It filled me with pain, compassion, and resolve.

The second day out, we were riding high above a river when we came around a bend to a sight I couldn't believe I was seeing. It looked like we had reached the Holland Tunnel to Jersey. This was an area where the government could not build a road that could handle a truck. What I was seeing was one of many Incan irrigation tunnels which moved water from this valley through the mountain. We didn't have time to stop and explore.

The night of the full moon, we camped near a farmhouse on a bluff over the river. I had been fasting to prepare myself for my sacred LSD. I asked Mario if he wanted to join me, but he declined and crawled into his bedroll. The energy had not been good between us while we rode. Nothing was spoken, but there was a felt uneasiness. We were both excited and frightened by what we were doing. Neither of us had done anything like this before: riding off into the unknown without a map or any sign of where we were headed or what was to come. This sense of the abyss made each of us acutely aware of our own, and the other's, incompetence.

I'd been going crazy these last weeks with bed bugs, which hadn't helped my mood. The bugs were another gift from the jungle that Randy and the gang had brought back. Every night they bit, and I was at my wit's end. I tried staying awake with a flashlight, washing my sleeping bag at the river, and bathing many times, but nothing was successful. As the acid came on, it seemed I was on the stage of a comic soap opera of cosmic proportions. I felt I was beaming to different frequencies, and that beings in other dimensions could tune in for a laugh. I stood naked under the full moon and announced that I couldn't go any farther with these bed bugs. I needed help. Suddenly, it was as if a giant freezer door opened in the heavens, and frozen air landed with a thud. I could feel the tiny bugs freezing in the cold and popping off. I shook out my sleeping bag and turned it inside out.

The sudden frost spooked the horses, and they started to neigh. A baby also started to cry, and I became paranoid. I thought my screaming about the bed bugs had woken the local people (and I wasn't sure if I had been screaming, whispering, or not even making a sound). I was afraid they would come out with torches and blood lust, Frankenstein-like, to find me naked and howling at the moon. Mario was wide-eyed in his bedroll.

Mario! They are coming for us!

I caught him off balance and scared him. His first reaction was to take the acid and throw it in my sleeping bag. In that instant, I knew that for Mario, if it came down to his life or mine, I was a goner. The brujo had warned me with that tarantula. When this realization hit me, something inside me shattered. It reminded me of a time when I walked through an unmarked glass door in the East Village in New York. This time there was no physical glass, but I still felt a shard of razor-sharp pain slice into my liver. I fell to my knees and groaned.

No one came to chase us, but the damage was done. I was in pain. With my arm around his neck, Mario helped me to the nearby farmhouse. We woke the family, and they let us stay in the corn manger under the house. Mario laid me down on top of corn stacked in a crib. He made some mint tea and lit a candle. I could feel his guilt and his fear. Still tripping, I saw myself from above and laughed at the sight: me dying in a manger with my post-Che-Jesus look. I hovered over my body for some time, standing watch. Eventually I fell asleep.

The next morning I was too weak to mount my horse and had to be helped on. Mario and I headed back to Paruro. If this were a horror story, I would say that the coven had found my weakness and struck me down. Maybe they were behind that old woman who gave us dirty water to drink when we rode by in the afternoon. That paranoid projection would be an easy way to get off the hook of facing my own fear, but I was not fishing.

In my heart I knew that I had failed in my mission to reach the Hidden Valley and bring enlightenment into the world. I knew that it was my fear, my need for security, that brought Mario along with me on this quest. Maybe I wasn't worthy to enter the sacred Hidden Valley, but that didn't mean I was willing to give up. I had to return. Alone.

I landed in Cusco with almost no money. I had been supporting Mario and his wife and child as well as our expedition. I thought $150 would go a lot further than it did. My fantasy was that if I had a thousand dollars, I could have lived there for a year. My last asset was my return ticket from Lima to Miami on Aerolíneas Argentinas, the cut-rate airline of the time. The ticket was worth $199, but I couldn't cash in a ticket in Cusco. I needed to go to an Aerolíneas Argentinas counter, and the closest was in La Paz, Bolivia.

Walking through the central plaza of Cusco, I spent my last three cents on an orange and some chocolate, which I bought from the boys with the pushcart making their daily rounds.

I found Randy and the gang still in Cusco when I arrived back. They'd been cut down by hepatitis and were laying low. This reinforced my conviction that the jungle was not for me.

I preferred the crisp, clean air, and the cold, clean water of the mountains. I shopped and cooked for them while they were ill, and they shared their food with me. When they were past the worst of it, they lent me twenty dollars to get to La Paz.

I took the train to Puno, and then the steamer across Lake Titicaca. It reminded me of Humphrey Bogart in *The African Queen*. In the 1920s, a steamship was dissembled and carried piece by piece up to Titicaca: the highest and largest navigable lake in the world. After an all-night cruise, I boarded the bus to La Paz, and two college girls on summer vacation from Vassar picked me up. We checked into a room together in an Indian hotel high up the ridge, overlooking La Paz below and the snowcapped mountains above us on the Altiplano.

> *Sweet Melinda.*
>
> *The peasants call her the goddess of gloom.*
>
> *She speaks good English as she invites you into her room,*
>
> *and you're so kind and careful not to go to her too soon,*
>
> *as she takes your voice and leaves you howling at the moon.*

This song, that I'd shared with Rosario on the beach in Mexico a few months and lifetimes ago, was materializing before my eyes. Both girls eyed me and signaled approval to each other. They were beautiful young women, out for adventure, and I was lonely, hungry, and broke. When they learned my name, they assigned a number to each letter, added these up, divided the sum by some mystic formula, and determined that I was *a five*; they liked the outcome, and looked at me with more approval.

Oh, how I wanted to make love with them both! A dream come true—except that I had been warned by my own singing on the beach a few months before. I knew that this was a test.

When I didn't make love with them, they told me I was too soft. They adopted me anyway, like some kind of pet. They took me everywhere.

One night I sang to them, the same song that had been in my head from the beginning of this quest. Another verse:

> Now if you see Saint Annie,
>
> please tell her thanks a lot.
>
> I cannot move,
>
> and my fingers are all in a knot,
>
> And I don't have the strength
>
> to get up and take another shot.
>
> And my best friend the doctor
>
> Won't even tell me what I've got.

They giggled and took me to eat Chinese food. After several years of being a vegetarian, and not caving in to the temptation of Rulie's steak, I suddenly threw my vegetarianism out the window. I had no money, and they were paying; we ate sweet and sour pork and drank cold beers.

One of the girl's uncles was a ruling general of Uruguay. We took a taxi to meet her mysterious friend, JB. We drove into the heart of the exclusive district in La Paz. The house we stopped in front of had razor wire and broken glass set into a 12-foot-high wall that surrounded the property. We were met at the gate by a large guard with a Rottweiler. JB was the head of something called Freedom House. We entered a garden. On the other side, two couples were swimming naked in a swimming pool. One of them came out of the pool when we arrived and confided in me that JB was probably doing what he loves most: driving around in his jeep with his driver, shooting his gun while tripping on acid. He also confided that JB was a CIA operative, and that if he wasn't out shooting, he was engaged in a coke deal.

JB liked the girls I was with and gave them a bag full of cocaine. Until then the best cocaine I'd ever had came from a drugstore robbery. The junkie who robbed a drugstore in Denver kept the Dilauded and sold me a small vial of USP 86%. Whether it was the quality of JB's cocaine, the high altitude, or the last few months of my clean living, whatever it was the cocaine was electric.

Still, I wouldn't have sex. As tempting as it was—and it was—that part of me was shut down. I felt that opening to it now would keep me from reaching the Hidden Valley, landing me on *Desolation Row* instead. The girls didn't understand. They laughed at me and again called me soft, adding humiliation and shame to my aching lost opportunity.

Every day I went to Aerolíneas Argentinas, and every day they told me they had to cable Mexico City. One day, they told me they now had to cable Miami, and were waiting for an answer. *Please come back tomorrow.* So, for a week I partied with the girls.

After a week, they flew back to the States, with something like two ounces of hidden coke each. When they left, I had no money at all. My twenty dollars were gone. I couldn't buy food, let alone pay for the room we'd been sharing. And every day the airline said, *Tomorrow.* I ranted and raved, and learned the deep meaning of *Mañana.*

It became harder to make the daily walk up the hill out of downtown to the Indian district. I would sweat, and have to stop and rest. It never occurred to me to worry about my health. One day while walking home I had to pee. I walked over to some rubble, where a building once stood, and faced a crumbling wall. My heart sank when I saw that my steaming piss was brown and stank. The weakness I'd been feeling was this.

That night it hit. Hepatitis. Another gift from the jungle. I had a high fever and a deep pain in my liver. I was too weak to make it down the hall to the toilet, so I peed into the bedpan that was supplied under each bed. The smell of my urine poisoned my delirium. For two days I lay in bed in a semi-coma. The second night, I left my body and called for help. I later found out that two people in the states—John Hoyt in Florida, and Squeaky in Oregon—were sleeping when they heard my call for help.

John Hoyt was a blue blood and the son of a federal judge. He was a good-looking all-American towhead. He could have been on a poster for the NFL, or Colgate toothpaste, or on an army-recruiting poster. Instead, John was a member of the Industrial Workers of the World: a labor union, also known as the Wobblies. The Wobblies were the Monkey Wrenchers of their time. I met John when he was working as a miner in Leadville, Colorado. He was a throwback to the 1920s bomb-throwing union of miners and lumbermen. Woody Guthrie and Pete Seeger both sang about the killing of the famous Wobblie Joe Hill. As the song goes, the cops killed him, but his ghost remains: *Where working men are out on strike, Joe Hill is at their side.* John gave me a Wobblie Song Book, where I learned to sing, and still sing, Pete Seeger's "Solidarity Forever."

Soon after we met in Colorado, John stole fifty pounds of dynamite from the mine, which he gave to me. It's likely still buried in a hole that our May Days collective dug in the woods near our cabin in Golden—except for a bag of dynamite sticks I gave to my Black Panther friend in Denver. He gave me a .38 handgun in appreciation. The gun was later stolen. It passed out of my hands without ever being fired, just like the dynamite buried deep in the earth that was never used—more an idea than a destructive force. I last saw John at May Days; he was the one who came up with the money to bail me out. He was a true ally.

Squeaky was now living with John's sister in Oregon. Squeaky had traveled with me on this quest as far as Mexico. He gave me the money for my plane tickets, so I let him come along for as long as I could stand it. When I finally sent him home, I never expected to see him again.

Squeaky and John spoke on the phone and discovered they both woke up in the middle of the night from the same dream: me calling for help from Bolivia. So John chipped in, and Squeaky bought a ticket to La Paz.

My fever broke after three days, and I made my way to the American Embassy. They turned white when they saw my yellow skin, and gave me a wide berth and a forty-dollar loan. I paid the Indian hotel what I owed, and moved into a hotel in town. Now my room had heat and a real bathroom. True to the song I had been living, *my best friend, the doctor,* someone the embassy sent to me would have killed me with his meat-and-potatoes diet. I nursed myself back to health with oranges and one peanut a day. Not about to lose the forty dollars they loaned me, the embassy contacted the airline, and I suddenly received my refund. By the time Squeaky arrived in La Paz, I had paid back the government and returned to Cusco to prepare for another trek to the Hidden Valley. Alone. The embassy told Squeaky where to find me.

CHAPTER 16

Crash Landing

If I have yet to join the hosts of the suicides, it is because
(fatigue apart) I find it no meaningfuller to drown myself than
to go on swimming.

—John Barth, "Night-Sea Journey"

I was sitting on a bench in the plaza in Cusco, chewing a stalk of sugar cane that had just come in from the harvest, when Squeaky appeared. I winced. Squeaky was like my evil twin. Not that he was evil, but he personified all that I hated about myself, my dark side. Everything I tried to keep hidden, he broadcast to the world; in a sense, he was more authentic than I was. On some level, I was still trying to pass as white, but Squeaky didn't notice, or care, that he wasn't.

Squeaky—big-faced, bushy-bearded, and longhaired—was another raging East Coast Jew. He was from a Jersey family of Galitzianers. A put-down in Yiddish is to call someone a *galitziana* behind their back. I later found out that Galicia was the poorest Jewish province in Poland, and that was why the more sophisticated Jews of Warsaw and New York mocked the Jews from Galicia.

Squeaky was wearing a cheap polyester shirt with bad shades of runny colors loudly fighting for attention. I saw him first from behind; his shirt had ridden up out of his slumping jeans, exposing the top of the crack of what nobody wants to see. We greeted each other with a hug and sat on the bench together. We looked like the Smith Brothers from the cough drops, or the Furry Freak Brothers from the Bronx. Squeaky told me how he woke up one night hearing my call for help, about his contact with John, and how they flew him down here to bring me home. I told him I was preparing to go back into the mountains alone.

You can't do that, man! You won't come back. You were just dying of hepatitis a week ago. No way!

I listened but dismissed his words. Over the years, I had learned not to believe a word Squeaky said. I met him, a Denver dropout, through Moshe as part of the marijuana trade. Dealing on the hill in Boulder, I learned the hard way about Squeaky. He would show a sample and quote a price, but everything would be different after you committed. I once drove from Boulder to Aspen when he pulled a bait and switch: *Acapulco Gold? Naw, that stuff wasn't any good, and it's gone. This Michoacan is much better and about the same price.*

On the other hand, I did call for help, and this was who showed up. I hoped that somebody somewhere was getting a good laugh out of this. I wasn't.

My reaction to Squeaky was to become a puckered, uptight, withdrawn prude. To be seen with Squeaky was to be lumped in with him and to be seen as just like him. The funhouse mirror appearing in front of me as Squeaky was a horror show that disgusted me. I had to face that what I couldn't stand in Squeaky was a projection of my own self. Because of this, I couldn't deal with him without taking it personally. I had dealt with my self-hatred by hiding it, but with Squeaky it was in full display, and I was guilty by association.

Eventually, I broke down and came to terms with what was in front of me. Denial didn't make it go away. Squeaky had been talking non-stop. Now I decided to listen. He was offering a compromise between my insistence on heading back into the mountains alone and his desire to bring me back to the States. We would do a magic invocation with LSD and invoke the head of the secret monastery to find out if I should go there or leave Peru.

Squeaky was the only person I knew who, like me, had read Gurdjieff's *Beelzebub's Tales to His Grandson*. He had read most of the books I had and many that I hadn't. In his lucid moments, he was the only one I had been able to discuss matters of consciousness with and get an intelligent and sometimes brilliant response. I agreed to his plan.

We walked for about an hour over the first ridge outside of Cusco and into the open-air gallery of the sun temple of the Inca fortress Saksaywaman, which overlooked the valley. I sat on the ground in the middle of the temple, while Squeaky walked the perimeter of our circle and chanted. This continued for about an hour as the acid began to take effect.

Soon we were seated together in the middle of our circle, which seemed to lift off into the vast night sky, like a flying saucer with no top, hurtling through outer space. In the high altitude, the night's deep black was ablaze with heavenly bodies. Everything seemed close, alive, conscious, and clear. I saw the universe as a sea of conscious love, and all the creatures inhabiting this sea as specks of conscious love. As the rapture overwhelmed me, I began to slip out of my body.

Squeaky saw me leaving and panicked: *Holy shit, man! You just disappeared! Come back! They're gonna kill us!*

His terror shattered the crystalline moment—or so I thought at the time. Writing this now I see that he was expressing the same terror that gripped me the month before with Mario. At the time, I only saw his terror, and I reincarnated into the carnage. It felt like we were sitting on broken glass. Danger was growling and howling now on the perimeter of our circle. It felt as though we were fighting for our lives against an interdimensional evil.

I stood up and felt the *Thwack!* of interdimensional slugs penetrating my body. We fought for hours. I tried psychically calling for help. At one point, it seemed my call was causing static on a military radio frequency. When the intensity of the energy on the periphery of our circle became too strong, I staked my claim in the future: my father was remarrying in a month, and I projected myself there as a life-saving strategy.

I suppose this is what people mean by creating their reality. I consciously created my future return to New York. I stepped into it as a way to survive the moment of being under siege by dark psychic forces. I knew I would go to my father's wedding, and it made my choice to return to my father's house a condition of my survival.

There it was: I was not going to continue my search. All these years I blamed Squeaky for this outcome, but perhaps what he really did was keep me from dying, weakened and alone, in the mountains of Peru.

Once I committed to return, grace stepped in. For some mysterious reason, three Peruvians visiting Cusco decided to take a night hike to Saksaywaman. They walked into our magic circle, and the spell was broken. We returned down the mountain with them. I was so grateful that I offered them all of my possessions— my sleeping bag and jacket—which they graciously declined.

My fate was sealed that night to return with Squeaky. I had failed at my mission. The next day, Squeaky told me he had a 160-acre farm in Oregon where he wanted us to set up an institute. *Like Gurdjieff's,* he said. I winced at his arrogance.

Before leaving, I took Squeaky out to the *campo,* or countryside, where I traded back my beloved horse Lucifer, my handmade bowie knife, my North Face down jacket, and my Kelty backpack to Rulie, who promised to send me alpaca blankets and sweaters in exchange to sell in the States. He never sent anything. Failure piled on failure.

*   *   *

Squeaky and I traveled overland from Peru into Ecuador and on to Columbia. We caught a bus on the Peruvian border that took us into Cuenca, a peaceful and picturesque town in Ecuador. The police chief showed up as we got off the bus and asked me to his office. He told me that there was a new directive not to allow hippies into Ecuador. He wondered if I was a hippie.

Look, I said, *hippies have no money. I have a thousand U.S. dollars here in my front pocket.* I moved my hand toward the pocket of my pants. *Do you want to see it?* I asked, a little arrogantly.

No, no señor, he said, before I could reach for my imaginary cash. *Have a wonderful time in Ecuador.*

We took the wrong bus out of Quito: a fantastic colonial town without any of Lima's rush, noise, or dirt. Instead of heading for the Columbian border to the north, we went west, plunging down from the mountains in a zigzagging, cliff-hanging ride all the way to the coast and the town of Esmeraldas, directly on the equator. Esmeraldas was a banana town, where barges floated down the river to be loaded onto ships. The town also had a small Marine garrison.

It was Saturday night. The only hotel in town was also the whorehouse, and the Marines were in town. It was a raucous party that looked like it would go all night long, as our neighbors thumped our paper-thin walls with moans and groans that drove us out into the night to score some grass.

There was only one road. After a few blocks, it led to a shantytown of poor Black laborers. The first person who took our money for some grass disappeared into a doorway and never returned. We just showed the money the second time, and the runner returned with a large bag of pot.

While exchanging the money for the grass, we were spotted, and a small group hanging out and drinking on a corner moved toward us. When they were within a few feet, I took a note of the local money, a centavo note worth a nickel, balled it up, and with a shout threw it at their feet. As they all scrambled after it, we ran for the road. When the pickup we tried to flag down wouldn't stop, I put my hand into the driver's window and grabbed the steering wheel. He stopped, and we jumped in back, just as the guys chasing us caught up.

The next day we found a place down the beach that rented us hammocks for beds. We smoked our grass and went for long walks along the miles of deserted beach.

We split up in Bogota. Squeaky returned to his farm in Oregon. I took the last of my money to the barrio and bought sheets of Columbian hash that I slipped into the rope soles of my Ecuadorian sandals. Then I flew to Miami.

At customs, the agent took a look at me and said, *I bet you meditate.* I grinned and went through, walking on hash.

I hitchhiked to John Hoyt's little commune in the country, outside of Gainesville near the university. I had a few days of rest, and read a book that electrified me: Joseph Campbell's *A Hero with a Thousand Faces.* Campbell had distilled universal patterns from traditions, stories, and myths throughout the world. I saw that I was on a hero's journey that is an intrinsic pattern in the human psyche.

The first step on the journey is the call to adventure. *Check.*

The next step reveals supernatural aid. *LSD. Check.*

Then follows the crossing of the threshold. *Check.*

Initiation and trials begin. *Check.*

A battle ensues where the dark forces of the psyche are met. *Check.*

The hero earns the mystic reward of eternal life: awakening in my cabin to my true identity. *Check.*

Now the hero returns home to found the kingdom. *Uh oh!*

After the hero establishes the kingdom, he abandons it for the solitude of the eventual apotheosis alone on a mountaintop. Apotheosis is the final absorption of the human psyche back into divinity. It is the loss of personal identity into the divine.

I could not imagine what would motivate someone to abandon the kingdom I had never reached or found. I had gone only so far, and then gotten lost. I did not know where I was now on the cosmic wheel, but I knew I had failed.

What course is there for the failed ones? Was I an anti-hero? Like an anti-Christ? Anti-heroes weren't mentioned in the book. I was searching for a clue to what was next. If I could find where I was on the wheel and see how I got tangled up in time, I thought I could see what was coming. But nothing showed itself to clear my confusion.

I was deflated in defeat. I had returned without the prize of the secret from the Hidden Valley that would have taught me how to pass on the realization of liberation. I was back where I started. My personal realization meant nothing if it could not be passed on.

I had to tell the truth. There was no Hidden Valley, and no one to teach me how to pass on what I had realized. It was all a hallucination, which I knew deep in my heart all along but avoided. I knew it, but I was afraid to know it. My search got me out of town and away from my old life. It swept me into a new movie, a much better reality, but ultimately a dead end.

I would have to do the best I could myself to pass it on. My failed, cowardly, deficient flawed self was all I had. I had to buck up and carry on. There were many moments, like this one, when I did not want to buck up, when I wanted to crawl home, to let someone else take care of me. But there was no choice. All I could do was bear the despair of the dark night of the soul, and carry on. To stop swimming in the night sea was not an option.

CHAPTER 17

Lost at Sea with Bobby McGee

I hitched back to New York and my father's impending wedding. Home for a few days, I received a phone call from Cosacha, the man from high school who recognized me in Cusco. He had returned to New York as well and came to visit. Some of his other high school friends had just returned from Rutland, Ohio, with a marijuana crop and needed someone to sell it for them. With my little brother Eddie, I sold the pot, kept a stash for myself, and made a $500 profit. With the additional sale of the hash I'd brought back, I now had a tidy sum: close to a thousand dollars—the amount I'd wished for to stay a year in Peru. It just came too late.

Inspired by Cosacha, I decided to visit the one surviving friend I had left from high school. I had three best friends when I graduated high school. Little Bobby Bendik was a baby-faced outlaw with a handicap: he was very small. In high school, he looked like he was twelve years old. Although he was older then I was, whenever we cut school to bet on the horses at Aqueduct, I had to place our bets because he looked too young to gamble. His size haunted him and eventually killed him. His freshman year at college he took some acid and went skydiving, but he was too light, and shouldn't have been allowed to jump. He was blown into a river and drowned.

Robert Goldstein, my second friend, was another outlaw with a handicap. He was a hemophiliac. He was also determined not to let anything stop him from living life to the fullest; he taunted death. During his first year at college, he died in a motorcycle wreck.

Victor, my third friend, was the good boy. He was bright and sweet, and we had fun together in high school and college, smoking grass and double dating. I decided to pay him a visit in Binghamton, upstate New York, where he was now a graduate student. When I arrived, I found Victor to be the same neurotic mess he had been when we were in high school eight years earlier. It was a time warp: he still fought with his parents, tried to assert his independence, and collapsed into paroxysms of self-doubt and depression. He hadn't cut his family ties and was still a little boy. He gave me the gift of showing me the road I could have traveled, and I was deeply grateful.

While I was in Binghamton, I was drawn to a demonstration there: a zippie smoke-in on the courthouse lawn. Zippie— apparently descended from yippie—was the grandchild of hippie. But there was no smoke when I arrived on the lawn, only the mirrors on the sunglasses of the local police. I was wearing my poncho, white rope sandals from Ecuador, and my cowboy hat. I had joints pre-rolled in my Indian belt. I lit one after the other and passed them around to get the place going. Within a few minutes, an amp was turned on, and we all started to dance.

I was picked up by a woman who took me home with her to spend the night. Mary Ellen Jones was desperate. She was an Irish Catholic girl, a local with a three-year-old son, Cannon. Cannon's daddy, a former black activist named Azel Jones, had split for the West Coast after being busted for embezzling government money from a Black development project. At three years old, Cannon had given himself the name Cannon Bear; he looked like a baby Rastaman. Sex with Mary Ellen was very good. I also felt Cannon calling for help. I agreed to let them travel with me to the West Coast.

First we hitchhiked back to New York for my father's wedding. When my grandmother saw me with this white hippie woman and her Black Rasta baby, she had only one thing to say—which she didn't say to me. With her heavy Yiddish inflection, she asked my father: *Is it his baby?*

After my father's wedding, we hitchhiked from New York to Rutland, Ohio, to stop at the farm that financed our trip. While there I voted for George McGovern; I'd also voted for him on a New York absentee ballot. We overstayed our welcome at the farm, eating our way through peaches and preserves that were supposed to last all winter. For $65 I bought a 1949 Dodge from a neighboring farm, and we were on the road again.

We hit ice in Michigan, and discovered that the car had a 16-inch tire on one side and a 15-inch on the other: this made for near impossible braking. We sold the car in Ann Arbor and hitchhiked. Standing on the highway singing "Me and Bobby McGee," we were picked up for my only ride in a real trucker's rig, which had a cabin where Cannon could sleep up behind the driver.

Eventually, we made it to Albuquerque, where some hippies took us in. They taught us to dip candles to sell for the coming Christmas. We hitchhiked to Santa Fe and sold candles in the plaza while powdery snow fell. In the plaza, we met a Vietnam Vet who taught us to chant Nam-mjoho-renge-kyo for help from the Buddha. We chanted as we walked. A light snow continued to fall. We had around twenty dollars from our candle sales, but no place to spend the night. We were drawn to walk through a vacant lot and came upon an open field with several motel rooms set in it. There was no office, and no one was around. One of the doors was open, however, and when we entered we found a real motel room, with clean sheets, a hot shower, and a television for Cannon Bear. But we couldn't find an office. We left a thank you note when we took off in the morning.

That morning, just a few days before Christmas, inspired by our success with the motel, we chanted our new chant and put our thumbs out to hitchhike a ride to Taos. A big, burly man with a Santa Claus beard picked us up and told us he had been an anthropology professor at UCLA but dropped out to make toys in Taos. He was going to LA for the holidays, and invited us to house-sit and feed his dog. He took us to his home and gave Cannon Bear handmade wooden toys for Christmas.

The Christmas of '72, in the hills outside of Taos, was the coldest winter of my life. One day my hand froze while cutting wood; it actually stuck to the saw blade.

I met a small band of radicals hiding back in the hills, and they offered us a free home. It was an old adobe with broken windows and holes in the wall that was only accessible with a four-wheel drive or by horseback. Consuelo Orobacho, the shepherd who had lived there for decades, had gotten too old and finally moved to Banos, one of the nearby towns. Mary Ellen and I stood in the center of this freezing adobe and looked at each other in the mutual recognition that we could not stay there.

The house we were sitting had a great luxury: a telephone. I managed to track down my old roommate Jim, who drove down from Colorado with my M1. I traded the gun for a hundred hits of LSD. When the good professor returned, we joined Jim in his jeep and set off for the Morningstar Commune. This was outlaw territory: draft-dodgers, deserters, and various miscreants were gathered there under an anarchist flag. People were always coming and going, so housing was not a problem. We stayed a week.

I organized a group ceremony in the commune's kiva. Someone poached a deer for the occasion—my vegetarianism and celibacy had long fallen by the wayside. I gave everyone who wanted to participate some LSD, and we climbed down the ladder into the darkness of the kiva. It was an anarchist session, with each person going their own way. I couldn't lead or pass on anything to that band of outlaws. I felt shipwrecked, marooned on a sand dune of my own shortcomings, with nothing to offer.

*   *   *

We hitchhiked from Taos to Los Gatos, California, where I dropped Mary Ellen and Cannon off with Azel and continued down the coast. The beauty of Big Sur overwhelmed me. Waiting for another ride, I saw some people gathering for a party at a large house on the cliffs. Three women my age were about to enter the gate when one of them turned toward me for a moment, thinking she recognized me. I could easily look familiar in my beard, ponytail, and jeans. I wanted to pretend I was invited, and walk into the party with her, but I didn't move. I couldn't imagine what they did for a living that made them lucky enough to live there.

I was 26 years old and had no profession, no plan, and no idea how to make a living. I had never considered it because I never expected to live this long. This had been a great gift which allowed me to give everything, but now I was still here, washed up on shore with no way to survive. That day on the cliffs of Big Sur, alone and broke, heading toward another unknown, something inside of me yearned to belong, to be a part of that party, drawn in by the invitation of a pair of flirty dark eyes, to learn the mystery of living there. I longed to return from the cold and barren isolation of the mountaintops and re-enter society. I would never express this to anyone else, though, and barely to myself. I had to keep pushing. There was still a chance to save the world, so I dared not acknowledge my longing.

CHAPTER 18

The Siren's Song

From Big Sur, I went up Highway 1 to San Francisco, along 101 to Interstate 5 to Ashland, Oregon. From Ashland, I hitched to Jacksonville, an old ghost town that was being slowly restored and revived. After Jacksonville, it was another half hour of gentle green hills and orchards to Applegate, a town that consisted of a post office, a general store, and a restaurant all in the same building. I made a call there, and someone from Squeaky's farm came down to pick me up.

It was another fourteen miles up Thompson Creek Road from Applegate. The road followed Thompson Creek gently up toward its source. The valley's orchards gave way to mile after mile of luscious green meadows, horses, cattle, and then more rolling hills and pastures studded with giant oaks. At fourteen miles, a rusted '41 DeSoto at the side of the road was the sign to turn right, into the dirt driveway that continued another half-mile and insured complete privacy for the farm.

Pulling into the farm, we passed a large gravity-fed gas tank on wooden scaffolding. It supplied farm machinery and trucks, and was serviced by the Grange. A large redwood barn on the right was filled with baled and stacked hay. There was a tack room for horse gear and a loft that Mushroom turned into a painting studio.

Across from the barn was a small cabin that Brian and Chris had moved into, leaving the main farmhouse for the rest of the community.

Squeaky's farm was not really Squeaky's farm at all. It was owned by Brian and Chris, who had met Squeaky when they were undergrads in Denver. They had family money, and two babies—Kiva and Che—which spurred them to search for the ideal farm. They studied the sunshine tables and found a valley in a banana belt of southern Oregon: eighty acres of sloping pastures and meadows surrounded by eighty acres of woods. Squeaky had convinced Brian and Chris to make their farm a Gurdjieffian institute, without the bother of Gurdjieff or any of his lineage—just an acid dream.

I felt like I had gone to heaven. This was deliverance into the promised land. I spent the most blissful year of my life up to that point living naked in a tree. Using rope and the seaman's knots I'd learned from a neighbor who had been in the navy, I tied a large plywood platform into the crotch of a magnificent oak tree. I used a rope ladder to enter this magical world, where I sat with the birds, overlooking the land and drinking in the depths of Mother Earth. The ripening of my childhood desire to climb into the tree house in Brooklyn had come to pass.

The oak tree was at the edge of the tree line, with woods proceeding up the hill behind, and a sloping meadow in front giving way to more woods and pastures for as far as the eye could see. The farmhouse was out of sight but just a short walk away, past the fresh-water spring box to the dirt road.

Of course, I was not always naked. I wore my boots as I tromped around the farm doing my chores, and I wore my overalls when I drove the '49 Jimmy flatbed to the dairy in Eagle Point. We would bring fresh organic eggs from our farm, and pick up milk from the Jersey cows pastured in rich clover. The big glass jars of milk came with a full head of cream, which we would spoon off to make whipped cream for our deserts. The good-hearted Portuguese dairyman always bought our eggs for his customers, and sent us off with a free truckload of rich manure, scooped out of the barn with a shovel on a tractor and loaded into our truck. We mixed the manure with our bales of straw and kitchen scraps to make compost for the vegetable garden. The garden was a labor of love run by Mushroom, a former professor of research botany at Rockefeller University, and later one of the pioneers of some of the first organic seed companies: Peace Seeds, and Seeds of Change.

When I arrived on the farm, I put all my possessions on the table at a community meeting, and let everyone know that this was all I had to donate: two ounces of pot, Buddha Sticks from Thailand, Acapulco Gold from Mexico, and a few hits of acid. I was all in.

In addition to the farm chores I took on, like caring for the chickens and helping to patrol and clean the irrigation ditch that ran from the weir on Thompson Creek to our farm, my main job was growing pot. I added the seeds from everyone's stash to my own and prayed to Shiva to bless our holy crop. When Cosacha appeared on the farm, he became my partner in the pot field.

I had never gardened before, but I had a copy of Ed Rosenthal's pioneering *Marijuana Cultivator's Guide*. We dug 150 holes in a small meadow surrounded by trees that stood within a larger meadow surrounded by more trees. There was a natural spring and a pool deep enough to jump in until June. We would sometimes sit in the hot sun on a summer's day and literally watch the plants grow; I was shocked to discover that this did not require time-lapse photography. On certain days, and at certain stages of development, you could see a leaf uncurl and grow to life right before your eyes.

Using the *Tassajara Bread Book*, I learned that I loved making bread, and became the bread baker and granola maker for the farm. We put up preserves, made jellies, and cooked feast after feast with the bounty of our garden. And for some mysterious reason, the women steadily found their way up to my perch in the tree, into the marijuana patch, and onto the meadows of clover.

We were headed into a drought that year. By summer, the pools had dried up and the ditch stopped running. This was serious because once the ditch stopped flowing, it took a lot more water to get it to flow again—our first crisis. We drove up to where our irrigation ditch met Thompson Creek and explored. I opened the water gate for our ditch. This was a serious offense because no one was allowed to touch the weir but the weir master, but we suspected we were being ripped off. Thompson Creek was the only privately owned and operated irrigation system left in the west. It was run by old man Elmore and his three sons.

Because we thought they were stealing our water, a truckload of us showed up to confront them at their home. Their farm had a small junkyard of old cars from the 1930s through the 1950s; they must have had forty to fifty cars in their front yard.

Banded together for courage, we piled out of our flatbed and knocked on the door. The brothers baled hay and must have once played serious football, as their bullet heads did not seem to have necks. One of them could have sent us all to the hospital and not been the worse for wear. Perhaps not wanting blood on the furniture, the old man avoided a fight. We promised not to touch the weir again, and they promised us our fair share.

I decided to fast and focus myself on the weather. I sent my energy into the sky, stirring the air and searching for clouds, and on the third day, it started to rain—I couldn't believe it. I rushed down from my tree, dancing naked and shouting for joy in the fat raindrops. When I went to the farmhouse for a bowl of granola and broke my fast, the rain stopped. The shower burst only in our little valley, but I never tried again.

On full moons, we would gather on the ridge for LSD and tribal drumming until dawn. I was inspired by one of these all-nighters to write a screenplay. I saw it all at once, and wrote it down the next morning. My intent was to change the world by changing the dream we all lived in. I wanted people to wake up to the nature of reality, and to see what was real and important. We could not fight the powers of ignorance and greed with guns or money because they had a monopoly on those, but what we had was the limitless power of love and an understanding of the deep nature of reality.

I called my movie *The Master's Game*. It revolved around a multidimensional game of Go that was being played by two galactic masters. Each stone represented a soul. When placed on the board, that stone/soul created karmic circles and Go's dance of enclosure and entrapment. Playing a stone set off a series of events that seemed unrelated, but that from a larger perspective was the intertwining of souls through multiple lifetimes, linked by either the black or the white stones. I included some lyrics from a Jefferson Airplane song in the ten-page synopsis, so I decided to hitchhike to San Francisco to get permission from the Jefferson Airplane to use their music in my movie.

My last ride into San Francisco happened to take me to the Masonic Auditorium for the first Meeting of the Ways. This was a gathering of different spiritual groups that had sprung up like mushrooms on California's foggy coast from the compost of the psychedelic sixties. At the Meeting of the Ways, I met a fellow grad student from my China studies in Denver. That was only four years earlier, but lifetimes had passed. His name was now Swami Das, and he was a Sufi-Sikh blend in a white turban who did massage. All the different groups in their turbans, saris, and Zen suits were a marvel to see. With my poncho and cowboy hat, I was dressed for a role in *The Good, the Bad, and the Ugly*, except with a joint instead of a cigar.

From the auditorium, I was taken to a benefit for Timothy Leary in North Beach. Leary was in Folsom prison for marijuana charges, and for escaping the country when the Weather Underground broke him out and smuggled him to Algeria. Somehow a film crew had made it into the prison and filmed a brilliant interview with Leary, which was shown at the benefit. Joanna Leary, Tim's jet-setting new wife, whom he met on the run in Europe, hosted the evening in North Beach. After the showing, I met Joanna and offered to help with the campaign to get Tim out of jail. I suggested a fundraiser in Ashland. To show I had something to bring to the table, that night I wrote a response to Tim's short new work *NeuroLogic*. I called mine *Building the Rainbow Bridge,* and gave it to Joanna the next day to pass on to Tim.

I also tried to spend the night in Joanna's North Beach home. I told her I could crash on the living room floor. She would have none of it. *But I'm your brother,* I told her. *My brother is in Switzerland,* she let me know. I don't remember where I slept, but I did buy Joanna breakfast the next morning at Mama's on Washington Square. We spent the afternoon at a concert smoke-in in the square.

Within a few days, Joanna took me to meet Paul Kantner and Grace Slick, the leaders of the Jefferson Starship, at their seaside home in San Francisco. This trajectory from watching the Jefferson Airplane perform at May Days in '71, to listening to their album in my cabin in Colorado in '72, to actually being with them in their bedroom in '73 did not seem possible. They stayed in bed while Joanna and I sat on the bedroom floor, and we passed around a joint of my homegrown pot. When I told them about my story, *The Master's Game,* they loved it. I asked if I could use one of their songs. Paul was interested until I told him which one. *Oh, that's Jorma's song* ended the conversation.

The next day, Paul and Grace took us to see a tai chi demonstration by an 80-year-old master living in the city. His name was Guo. It was the first tai chi I'd seen that had deep energy. I later spent three years studying with Guo's protégé from China, Shirfu Chiang.

I wanted Abbie Hoffman to star in my movie, so Joanna took me to meet Abbie at a party at his lawyer's house. I told him my movie idea and my desire that he play the lead. He liked the idea but was about to go underground because of a cocaine bust. This party was his last appearance as Abbie for many years.

Grace thought the perfect person to play the lead in my movie was David Carradine, who was then starring in the TV show *Kung Fu*. Grace called Carradine the Che Guevara of television. I hitchhiked to LA to meet David Carradine and found his number listed in the phone book. I convinced him to meet me. I hitched up to his home in Laurel Canyon, shared my homegrown with him, listened to him play the piano, and then told him about my movie. He liked it a lot, but it turned out that getting my story into a workable screenplay was something else altogether.

Back in Oregon, we rented Ashland's movie theater and had our benefit for Tim Leary. We showed his film, gave out grass, and collected donations for his defense. In the film, Leary announced the arrival of Comet Kohoutek, which would usher in the New Age. We went for it. Like the cargo cult natives of Borneo who built airstrips to attract the great silver birds that landed during World War II, we dropped acid and projected a new reality for the second American Revolution riding the tail of Comet Kohoutek.

We hoped to win with acid and dreams what we could never conquer with force. I called it global thought-form building. It had about as much power as Peter Pan's *If you believe in fairies, clap your hands*. As much as we clapped, Kohoutek never came.

*   *   *

When our marijuana crop came in, we gave it away. I stood alone and fought for that. I said it was a sacred herb and shouldn't be sold. I had to run Squeaky down, as he headed for the field to grab his share. We gave our seeds away to communes up and down the Applegate and shared our experience of growing.

We formed a non-profit to buy the farm from Brian and Chris for $60,000, the price they paid for it. Four months after the crop was gone, we came up $9,000 short on a $20,000 balloon payment. In truth we could have managed to keep the farm if we really wanted to, but I was finished. I psychically blew it up. The temptation was strong to settle into an earthly paradise, put down roots, and live in a community where I had my own way and was accepted as a leader. I could have lived there comfortably and pleasurably until my mossy old roots rotted out with age.

I said that I would be happier in a muddy hole with true brothers and sisters who were fully committed. The Garden of Eden that this place was attracted everyone who wanted to return to the land without a thought of service or liberation. While it was tempting to take a load off, settle my weary bones down, and go to sleep, it would be a betrayal.

It was a perfect dream except for the elephant in the room: the farm was not serving its true purpose, or at least the purpose that I thought we were there for. I was there in service of world liberation and freedom, not just settling into a comfortable country life. So in the face of the temptation to go to sleep, yet again, I had to internally shout my battle cry: *Still alive, motherfucker!*

I was afraid of stepping off again into the unknown. Each time I was older, with less to show for it. A few years earlier, leaving graduate school was huge, but now I seemed to be stepping off into space again without a grip or a ledge, and I was no longer a kid.

I left the farm with the clothes on my back. I vowed that next time I would have the money. It seemed that those with the money never had the consciousness to serve and liberate, so I set off to make my fortune. Brian and Chris had sold the farm for $100,000, so I decided $100,000 in the bank would be a sufficient goal. When I returned to Ashland twenty years later, I did indeed have $100,000 in the bank. It was enough for a down payment on a house in town, though not a 160-acre farm.

CHAPTER 19

Meeting the Swami

July 1974

When I first heard of Swami Muktananda, I was homeless. All of my possessions fit into my alpaca shoulder bag. I had been house-sitting in a row of old houses on Santa Monica beach, where I'd washed up after leaving the farm. With Highway 1 and the cliffs of Santa Monica behind them, the front yards of these homes opened onto the ocean. The sidewalk between the front yards and the beach connected the community while insulating it from the outside world. Saved from development by the coastal commission, these 1930s beach homes and bungalows were built by early Hollywood for weekend escapes.

I would peddle through the alleys of Santa Monica on a borrowed bicycle looking for fruit trees that I could pick and trade for food at the health food store. I was writing my screenplay, *The Masters Game*, which opened the doors of the small film community of gaffers, grips, and wannabes who lived in these choice but cheap cottages by the sea. I would house-sit up and down the block while working on my screenplay.

When the house sitting dried up, I moved in with Carrie, a lovely, sweet thing, who had a lead in the movie *Cheerleaders II*.

She lived in a household of three women. Two were aspiring starlets; the third was the boss and the economic engine, who kept it together. I had slept with the two starlets but avoided the head lady, and my welcome was wearing thin. No job. No money. No resources. I had nothing with which to support the household except expired food.

I would get a ride to the Safeway in Beverly Hills and go through the dumpsters, picking through the discarded dairy, often still fresh on the sell-by date, along with bruised fruits and vegetables. I would give away some of the yogurt while walking along the row of beach houses and bring the rest home as my offering from the hunt.

I tried selling my blood, but because of my hepatitis in Bolivia, they didn't want it. It was time for a job. I tried Manpower and the State Employment Office, but by the time I spare-changed my bus fare, all the jobs at Manpower had gone to the people with cars. For some reason, it never occurred to me to hustle the money in advance.

I interviewed for a job from the State Employment Office as a chef in an Indian restaurant in Westwood. I went to the library first and wrote down recipes for curried chicken and a few vegetable dishes. I had helped out at the hippie Indian restaurant in Denver and imagined this job would be like that. I hitchhiked to the job interview, where I learned that the head chef was returning to London and three assistant chefs still remained.

You must be able to do four different curries for chicken, beef, vegetables, and fish, and you must supervise the tandoori and of course a different roti for each curry. What can you do?

I showed the manager my recipe cards. He looked at me and asked me to make a chicken curry. I read from the card by the side of the stove as I cooked. They were very nice as we ate chicken curry for lunch, and I then hitched back to the beach.

Besides writing, swimming, and hanging out, I played Frisbee on the beach with Yogi, a Brooklyn boy who bore a remarkable resemblance to Yogi Berra, the homely great Yankee catcher of my childhood. When a new swami came to town, his people went out to gather a group for his meetings. They'd heard there was a yogi on the beach, and so they came to invite us. They drove us to the meeting.

I'd been fasting again for three days. I had no acid and was searching for a sign.

We arrived at a mansion in Beverly Hills and sat in rows. A small Indian man in a wool watch cap and sunglasses entered the room, trailed by bodyguards wearing mirrored sunglasses. My first thought was that this was a CIA scam, a new experiment in mind control to introduce their version of a swami and confuse the spiritual scene.

I had already checked out many of the local gurus, head trips, and wannabes, and I was beyond skeptical about the whole guru scene. I'd read Rajneesh before he renamed himself Osho and felt that anyone on acid could have the same insights he shared in his books. Interesting, but not profound. Rajneesh seemed to be sucking off the potential of the spiritual revolution by channeling it into self-centered drugs, sex, and rock and roll. I did like Bubba Free John's book *The Knee of Listening*, but he also went on to give himself holier names as he inflated to bursting with egocentric madness.

That day in Beverly Hills we chanted for a while, and as I remember it, nothing in particular happened. Then the guru, Swami Muktananda, gave out *prasad*. Prasad is holy food, blessed by the guru and much sought after by devotees. That day in Beverly Hills, he gave us chocolate Fudgsicles for prasad. Although I'd been fasting, chocolate was something I never passed up. Normally, I would never break my fast with chocolate, and low-grade chocolate at that. I preferred breaking a fast with soothing oatmeal or miso broth. But on this day I not only ate my Fudgsicle, I also managed to cage a second. I was even more certain that this scene was a CIA plot or even a cosmic Beverly Hills joke, breaking my fast with junk food.

There had been talk that this guru's spiritual energy, called *shaktipat,* radiates out and affects the lives of those who've been close to him. I didn't pay it any mind. The visit seemed to me to be a dud. Yet within a week of seeing Swami Muktananda, everything totally changed. First, my brothers mailed me a check for $3,000. They had generously offered to share the $10,000 my mother left them in her will, which had just come out of probate. After paying my debts, I had $1,200.

Next, a surfer I played Frisbee with let me know that he was going to Maui and asked me if I would feed his cat and take over his apartment while he was gone. He had Wallace Beery's old top-floor apartment on the oceanfront overlooking the beach in Venice. The apartment was fully furnished with houseplants and the cat. Before leaving, my surfer friend also introduced me to his grass connection.

I needed a car to get a job, so I bought one—a silver '57 Chevy for $200 from the original owner, who was too old to drive anymore. Her son was selling it for her. The car still had the cardboard instructions for using the automatic transmission on the visor.

I next bought a pound of grass. Sitting at my kitchen window overlooking the pavilion on the beach, I saw a bicycle being offered for sale. I traded some pot for a silver Schwinn Paramount racing bike.

All these events cascaded within a week of each other. I went from being homeless, with no money or prospects, to living in the oceanfront apartment of a thirties movie star, owning a classic silver car and silver racing bike, and having a job. The job could only be the guru's grace, the mysterious working of the universe. I went from dumpster diving to making a couple of hundred dollars a day, plus enjoying an expense account covering travel expenses and a per diem. No visualization or manifestation practice involved on my part. It was the shaktipat of the guru—and I wasn't even a devotee, didn't particularly like the man, and wasn't interested in seeing him again.

Without a degree in psychology, I now had a job as a staff research associate in the UCLA's Psychology Department. The job posting was never supposed to leave the Psychology Department, but it was summer and some temp made a mistake. I was sitting in the State Employment Office when the job was phoned in. It came in to a caseworker at an adjoining desk, and I overheard him repeating the details, while my caseworker hunted for something in a file. I jumped up. *That's my job!* I shouted and went directly to the other desk. The job never got posted.

They were looking for someone who could interview Chicano junkies without getting killed in the barrio and write graduate level reports. I started in East Los Angeles, known as East Los to the junkies I met. I was paid fifty dollars an interview plus mileage and expenses. The junkie was also paid twenty dollars and an extra ten dollars for a bust-free urine sample. I made my way through East LA, interviewing and learning the lay of the land.

At the end of summer, after two months of successful interviews, a new opportunity appeared. I was selected to set up a Northern California office. They wanted me to find a living place and an office to use as a base while interviewing junkies covering the area that spanned from the Oregon border to the Central Valley.

As I made my way north to my new home, I worked my way through the prisons. My first prison was Soledad. My first interview was with a Gang banger being housed in the isolation ward because there was a contract out on him. He wanted me to give him LSD. He said LSD was the only way he could survive. I didn't have any. But I did have my pound of Acapulco gold.

I considered. If I were in prison, I would want whoever was visiting me to bring me this sacred herb. So when I returned for my third day in Soledad, I had two joints rolled for my two interviews in the morning. I waited the extra day so that I could once again go through the procedure of getting into the prison and see where and how they frisked me.

My next stop was Tracy, a hellhole of noise and violence, where Gang-banger Chicano kids from the Central Valley were proving their machismo. I brought a joint and a Carlos Castaneda book to a boy who seemed to be ready for something else in his life.

There's been much controversy over Carlos Castaneda and whether or not he made up his encounter with Don Juan and all the teachings. I have never been interested in this discussion. It doesn't matter. As the dim-witted foil, Castaneda was a perfect channel for a pure teaching, which I have never to this day found wanting.

In San Quentin after giving out joints to various prisoners over several days, I smuggled a joint into death row. Although at the time there was no death penalty in California, death row existed as a prison within a prison, with multiple locking metal doors and a special locking-elevator with guard stations and searches, which was now called the Adjustment Center.

I brought a joint into the hole at Folsom as well, but I was only allowed to speak to the prisoners on phones through a glass wall, while the prisoner was handcuffed to his waist. One convict I met was my age, 27 years old. He was a Central Valley boy, a white greaser who looked like Elvis Presley and was first busted at 19 for holding up a 7-Eleven. He got out three years later at Christmas time, broke, with a wife and a four-year-old daughter, and was busted again for robbing another 7-Eleven. They took down his license plate number as he drove away. Not very bright—like Nicolas Cage in *Raising Arizona*, but without the happy ending. His second offense landed him in Folsom Prison, where he got into a fight with a guard. He would be in the hole for years before he would ever see the outside yard. There was nothing that I could do. There but for fortune. I felt so grateful to whatever it was that saved me from this fate.

For those at Vacaville, Susanville, and a dozen other lockdowns, besides bringing them joints, I did small favors—a box of See's chocolates, an occasional copy of Castaneda's Don Juan—calling a wife for a man in solitary.

But I was unfulfilled. I was writing poetry then. One was about a lonely goose soaring over softly swaying wheat fields, crying for a home. Another, called "Honey Do," ended with the line *but the dew never comes*. It was one of my many dark nights of the soul. Another drive through the night alone.

I quickly saw that the interviews I was conducting had a strong unexamined institutional bias in both the questions being asked and the way they were phrased. These interviews were part of a follow-up study on the long-term efficacy of jail for junkies, California's practice at the time. The questions never addressed the true issues, only a distorted view of effects. So I started to fill in the interviews with additional questions and helped the inmates with their answers. After a few months, I was fired for taking liberties with the reports.

For my home and office, I had taken a room in a commune in Berkeley called the One World Family. When I was fired, I began work as a waiter in the commune's vegetarian restaurant on Telegraph Avenue. It was down the block from People's Park, with its mural of the people's fight with the police that led to the founding of the park. The One World Family commune was a psychedelic Space Brotherhood of Christ Communism, led by the Cosmic Messiah Alan Michael. Enjoying tofu, tantric sex, and imagining flying saucers in the clouds were the brotherhood's primary occupations.

I had to face the horror of the results of our collective psychedelic tripping, from Lazer Farm, to SafeSpace Foundation, to the One World Family. All were good-hearted, well-intentioned attempts to change the course of civilization by waking people up from mass hypnosis, and all metastasized into madness. All the thought-form building and materialization was creating Frankenstein monsters that almost lived.

Soon many would make millions of dollars in self-help books, teaching people *to visualize and create their realty*. Our psychedelic experiment in changing the world for peace was quickly marketed for personal profit. If the millions of eager visualizers of "prosperity consciousness" had been willing to die for Mother Earth instead of trying to buy a better dream for themselves, perhaps we could have had a chance.

CHAPTER 20

My First Teacher

While living with the One World Family, I met Laurie, a 15-year-old redhead who lived with her 20-year-old boyfriend on the floor below. She was open, intelligent, and curious. I shared Castaneda's Don Juan with her. She read it and said she *grocked it*. She also said her mother would like to meet me.

I had been preparing to return to the Oregon hills and wanted a partner to go back to the land with this time. A steady trickle of women had found their way to my room on the top floor of the commune—all prospects. Laurie's mother, Joan, also came to smoke some grass and promptly seduced me.

While I continued to prepare for my move back to the land, I moved in with Joan and her four other children in her home in the Berkeley flats. Joan was 35, with five kids from five fathers, and four ex-husbands, which all began when she was 18 and an aspiring chorus-line dancer. Randy, her firstborn, was now 18 and living on the roof of Shalimar, the Indian Restaurant where he worked in the kitchen. Laurie was living at the commune and had two younger sisters, Nancy, 11, and Connie, 9. Patrick was five. For the next eight months, I lived with Joan and the kids, supporting the family with my unemployment checks from UCLA and later from the profit on a small summer pot garden in Oregon. I was 27, and now I had five kids—the eldest, nine years younger than me.

Joan was a devotee of all male gurus, which extended to all other men as well, under the right circumstances. She said that I set her free by living with her in a fully open relationship with no restraints. I don't believe I had anything to do with it, as she plowed her way through the Berkeley Hills.

While working as a waiter in the One World Family restaurant after being fired by UCLA, I met Rycho Yamada, a Zen Priest who had come to the United States to give Shiatsu to Suzuki Roshi when he was dying of cancer. After the Roshi died, Rycho made his way to Berkeley, where I waited on his table. We quickly became friends. His father was the oldest living Zen master and was ready to turn the Zen temple over to his eldest son, but Rycho was not interested and let his younger brother take the job.

Rycho was teaching Shiatsu classes, and Joan and I both signed up. Soon the three of us were teaching together. I turned Rycho on to marijuana, and together we developed what we called Zen Shiatsu, using the expanded state to go more sensitively and deeply into the meridian lines, feeling the energy and releasing the knots. I still occassionally see practitioners of this form almost fifty years later.

I traded my Chevy for an old pickup, and a regular customer at the restaurant offered to build a house on its bed. He was a capable contractor who quickly built a little, shingled hippie house, with a Plexiglas dome jutting out of the roof that served as an observation tower. Like the Joads in *The Grapes of Wrath*, Joan, her kids, Rycho, and I all piled in and headed for the Oregon hills.

We rented a twenty-five-dollar-a-month cabin in Jacksonville while we scouted for our new home. We were quickly led to Slagle Creek, where we rented sixty acres on the creek. The property was the former home of a commune and still had a sauna and a tree house. The tree house was a huge upgrade from my simple platform. It was a Chip and Dale house with blue shutters, a shingled roof, and a little window box for flowers. We set up a tepee and enjoyed a sweet summer on the land that is now a winery.

With the kids starting school and no running water getting old for Joan, we moved back to the house in Berkeley in the fall. Rycho and I slept on mattresses on either side of the dining-room floor, Joan on a queen foam pad in the living room, and the kids shared the bedrooms.

I saw a flyer on a telephone pole about a tai chi teacher teaching a rare northern style of tai chi. The photo of the teacher caught me. His presence and his chi were undeniable. I'd found my first teacher. Shirfu Chiang was fifty years old when I started taking his class. He looked thirty and moved like a teenager. I later found out that he was the protégé of old man Guo, the eighty-year-old master I saw in San Francisco two years before.

Shirfu started us off with a set of thirty warm-up exercises—deep stretches, from the splits to touching our chins to our toes. After the first week, Shirfu asked me how it was going. I told him I liked the warm-ups and that I did them several times during the week.

Several times? No! Every day. One day's practice, one day gong fu. One day no practice, three days no gong fu.

For the first time in my life I was learning the joy of discipline. Gong fu was made of two characters, the first depicting time, and the second, man. Together they meant moving toward perfection through practice. Shirfu taught me Gong fu.

A true disciple shows his worth by demonstrating the fruits of practice. As students, our test was to be able to touch our chins to our toes. With one leg stretched out in front, we bent over and touched our chin to our toe while keeping a straight back. After six months, I could do the splits and was working on kissing my toe while in the splits. After a year and a half of twice-a-day practice, I could touch my toe with my chin. I wanted to show Shirfu that I was serious.

Unlike other teachers of tai chi who were around at that time, we spent our first three months only doing the warm-ups, as our bodies slowly loosened, our limbs stretched, and our balance stabilized. After three months of the warm-ups came three months of a series of ever more difficult walking kicks. The last one involved double jumps and slapping the foot with each move. It was six months before Shirfu gave us our first tai chi move. His tai chi set was like no other I'd seen, requiring deep stretching and balance and muscle strength. We spent one year learning and practicing the set, the second year doing the set in mirror image, and the third year in super slow motion.

Around the same time that I met Shirfu, Swami Muktananda opened an ashram a bicycle ride away from our house. Joan, who had a nose for gurus and could sniff them out a mile away, didn't know that I'd already met the swami when she took me to meet him at the ashram.

There were only a few dozen of us in the room. Each person went up to meet him and ask him a question or just receive the guru's grace. My attitude toward him had changed by that point. I didn't ask for anything and didn't want anything from him. I went up to thank him for being my bodhisattva brother.

After this short meeting, we were to adjourn to the main hall for chanting the Guru Gita, a Sanskrit hymn. I was leaving to get my bike when the swami came over, put his arm around my shoulders, and invited me to stay. Joan's eyes popped out of her head at this gesture from the guru. I thanked him but let him know I was on my way to my tai chi class. I rode off on my silver racing bike.

But something drew me to the swami, and soon I found myself bicycling to the 5:30 a.m. sitting each day. Darshan with Baba, as I learned to call him, followed the morning meditation. I'd never experienced the power of his energy in my body before. It was called *shakti,* and it was electric and powerful on a level I'd only experienced with psychedelics.

Each morning was a holy shower of golden, grace-filled shakti. After a few weeks of sitting in the mornings, someone recommended that I touch the swami's feet as he left the hall. I arrived early enough one morning for a front-row aisle position and put my hand over Baba's foot as he walked by. He was walking quite slowly, so I did not interfere with his walk. I was amazed to feel the energy rise from my palm up into my arm, up into my head, and down through the rest of my body, like a tingling heat wave, as the inner darkness was lit with light.

I was very cynical and challenged all the teachers I'd met. I first saw Muktananda as a fraud. But my experience was undeniable. His was a power as strong as LSD in human form.

Swami Muktananda's teachings were simple. *Worship me as the God that is in you,* he often said. This was Siddha Yoga. *Siddhis* is the Sanskrit word for spiritual powers. Flying, disappearing, and psychic heat are among the siddhis. A fully realized Siddha transmits his or her spiritual power to their devotees. I understood all of this theoretically. I went through all the motions of worshipping the guru. I worshipped at the guru's feet, learned to chant the Arati in devotional fervor, and yet, in my heart, my devotion wasn't totally true. I could not worship the swami. He held enormous power and magic, but I did not feel love.

One weekend, Swami Muktananda had an intensive for the transmission of shaktipat. He grabbed my head and held it against his leg. I soon felt like I was tripping. After a few hours, an enormous rush of fiery electric steam shot up my spine and gave me a terrible headache. I almost never have headaches. This one was making me sick; I was on the edge of vomiting. The pain was so intense that I couldn't go back for the second day of the intensive; instead, I lay in bed in a sweat.

I felt I was dying. The heat burned me up like a tropical fever, which I experienced years later when I got malaria in India. I needed a glass of water. But Rycho was gone, and Joan was too busy making love with Flashlight to hear me calling for help. The fever broke the next day, and my relationship with Joan was over as well. I packed my few possessions back into my alpaca bag and moved out. This turned out to be part of the guru's gift.

PART V

THE KINGDOM APPEARS

Castles made of sand

fall back into the sea

eventually.

—Jimi Hendrix

CHAPTER 21

The Goddess

Ice Melts My Fire

Berkeley,1975

I love you, I cry

through the spiraling

wheel web of time.

I love you, I sigh

as the petals

burn up my mind.

"Empty is full,"

she whispers back

through a crack

in time and space.

She's my fiery silver queen

carrying diamond sutras in her palm,

which she pawns

on a juncture

of a dimensional interface,

sending the dharmic wheel

spinning

through inner space.

And the manifestor, set director,

High Inspector,

from the kingdom of souls,

sends an equalizer

in fertilizer,

nourishing the sprouts

of the budding seeds

that are singing

diamond sutra harmonies,

in the faithful bliss of unknowing,

yet thanking God all the same.

And the pawns

in the game

are cashed, checkered,

and spun

through myriad mazes

that we've all begun to see.

Yet the diamond queen is familiar,

from other missions of mercy,

on a galactic harvest

and salvage crew.

As the universal mind

plays

polarity duality

with a checkered demon

and a crystal Christ

on a multidimensional

Go board of light.

And the diamond sutras

are singing our name

as they dancing emerge into sight

and another strung-out soul

is beaded on Buddha's necklace

harmonizing a crystal spiral of light.

So sing sweetly

my love,

my earthen vessel

of light.

Your cosmic being

is intergalactically harmonized

and fertilized

by the stars tonight.

As the glass-bead game

is sung

in a magic circle

on the edge of the dawn

on the rim of the crystal

sparkling with life.

— Eli Jaxon-Bear

I felt her coming—from a long distance off. Months before we met, I wrote her the poem "Ice Melts My Fire."

It was November of 1975, and Joan's red-headed daughter, Laurie, was about to have her sweet sixteen. A few weeks before Laurie's party and before I moved out, we went Sufi dancing at Ashkenaz in Berkeley, where Joan picked up Flashlight. Flashlight was from the Yay God! Commune in upstate New York. Tall and thin, with a Jewish Afro, an Anglican nose, and a doctorate from

Yale, the former history professor at Smith had dropped out. He came home with Joan, and a few days later was making love with her in the living room, while I was suffering with my headache and calling for water.

Within days of moving out, I met Toni. Flashlight brought her to Laurie's sweet sixteen. I followed her around the party, reciting my poetry, including my latest poem to her, though neither of us recognized it as such at the time. Toni didn't know what to make of this bearded young man in Oshkosh B'Gosh overalls, looking like Jerry Garcia playing farmhand and reciting psychedelic poems about Shiva. She liked my poem about my fiery silver queen but didn't understand it. I explained that *ice* was slang for *diamond* and a reference to the queen, but it didn't help. This was my mating dance.

Even if she hadn't been beautiful and deep and shining brightly, I would have gone after her simply because she came with Flashlight. I didn't know at the time that she would be my salvation and redemption. At first, I just saw a pretty body. Her hair had turned silver prematurely; it was stunning. Later I would see that people constantly asked her about her hair. Was it natural? How did she do it? While her hair marked her, on the surface at least, my silver queen's hair was not as important as her eyes— deep pools of light, veiled by sadness.

Toni was a dancer. A few years before she had worked as a waitress at one of the early San Francisco fern bars where knockout hippie waitresses dressed in leotards and sarongs. She had been studying African dance for the past year and was now learning massage. At this stage, pretty was not enough for me anymore; there had to be a spiritual connection as well. When she appeared at Muktananda's morning meditation the next day I fell in love. I assumed she was a regular but learned later it was her only time. An old lover of hers from Maui had come to town and he made her take him.

I was house sitting at a grand old North Berkeley home and invited Toni to dinner there. I made pasta and a fresh tomato sauce with English peas. I found a red velvet smoking jacket in my host's closet and wore it. Toni never came. I took off the smoking jacket and invited Joan and the kids to come and eat the pasta.

Toni called later and said she was sick. We made a date to to meet in her apartment in Noe Valley the next day, where I would give her a shiatsu massage. When I arrived, the apartment door was cracked open. I walked in, and she appeared to be asleep in her bed. Later she told me she was hoping I would see she was ill and go away. But I thought the gods were smiling on me and gave her a massage instead. In those days, a massage was always a prelude to a kiss.

My second date with Toni was in Bolinas at her ex-husband's house. Her eight-year-old daughter lived in the house, and it was mom and dad who rotated in and out of the house for half a week each.

My instructions were to phone from downtown Bolinas when I drove in from Berkeley to get directions up to the big mesa. Downtown Bolinas consisted of two streets. I had never been there before but as soon as I arrived I knew I was home. This was an outlaw hippie town on the coast of Marin County, cut off from civilization by a winding mountain road. To this day the Bolinas Border Patrol takes down all signs pointing to Bolinas. I was soon a member of the patrol.

On one side of the street was Smiley's Schooner Saloon, founded in 1862, when Bolinas was a port for shipping redwood to build San Francisco. Across the street from Smiley's was Scowley's, a greasy spoon for hippies, fronted by a wooden sidewalk just like the Wild West. On a bulletin board next to the pay phone were two cards. One advertised a room for rent and the other a car for sale. I called both numbers and then drove up to see Toni.

We smoked and flirted, and I told her my war stories. We were near the stereo, where she was about to put on Bobby "Blue" Bland, when we saw a long electric spark arc between us. Neither of us had seen anything like that before, and we haven't since. We took it as a sign, a prelude to making love. Before we made love, we lit a candle and dedicated our love-making to the enlightenment of all beings. I invoked Padmasambhava, a Tantric mystic and magician who was instrumental to the establishment of Tibetan Buddhism. I saw Tara, the goddess of compassion, in front of me looking back at me with eyes of love. As we made love the depth of the pleasure and bliss was extraordinary.

After we made love, we walked in the twilight and found the house with the room for rent. I took it. I also went on to sell my pickup and buy the car for sale, a '67 Fiat for $350.

Murray, who owned the house, lived in the basement and used the garage for metal sculpting. Chad lived in the cottage and made raku pottery in the driveway. The main floor of the house had two bedrooms and a shared bath between them. I was on one side, and Beth, a chocolate-colored beauty and Arica Yoga instructor, was on the other side.

I was suspicious of the bounty pouring into my life.

My move to Bolinas was the end of the journey that had started in Colorado and spanned thousands of miles and lifetimes of changes, adrenal rushes, pushing through, close calls, and running on empty. I was burned out and grinding the gears. This move was my final collapse.

Toni fell in love with me first. I was enjoying great sex with a beautiful woman I believed I could also enlighten. On my 29th birthday, I had to choose between Toni and Beth. My frustrated desire in Bolivia had ripened.

There really wasn't a choice to be made. The purity of Toni and her sharp intelligence were undeniable. It wasn't just her outward beauty that drew me, because Beth was a beautiful queen as well, but the depth of Toni's soul. Three months later, Toni changed her name to Toni Bear and moved into Beth's room when Beth moved back to the city. To afford the move, she sold her wedding silver. I later saw the wedding announcement that brought in that silver. Toni came from an old family in Clarksdale, Mississippi. Her father was a former FBI agent. Her husband was a doctor from Memphis society, and Toni had been a high school homecoming queen. She'd had it all but left it all, inspired by the movie *Woodstock*.

My first Thanksgiving in Clarksdale reminded me of Woody Allen and Diane Keaton in *Annie Hall* when he visits her family in the heartland. Like Woody, I imagined that Toni's family saw me as a Hassidic Jew sitting at their dinner table. After several Bloody Marys and before grace was said, I looked around the table at Toni's family. These were real white people. One of Toni's uncles had been the head of the White Citizens' Council in town, the businessmen's branch of the Klan. When her father was stationed in New York, he petitioned J. Edgar Hoover for a transfer because he didn't want Toni to have the stigma of New York on her birth certificate. She was born a few months later in El Paso.

I had imagined introducing myself to Toni's father:

Hi. How ya'll doin'? You probably heard of me. I'm the New York commie Jew outside agitator who came down here and stirred up your Nigras a few years back. Now I'm sleeping with your daughter.

Instead, we all had more Bloody Marys and watched Ole Miss play football on the TV.

*   *   *

At parties Toni loved to entertain and make her friends laugh. She was willing to be the butt of her own jokes and often would make up things that never happened, that reflected badly on her, just to keep the story moving in a funny way. This made me angry. I didn't want her to present herself in that light. I wanted people to see the radiant goddess I saw. I didn't want her to be seen as a dizzy Southern belle. Someone once called her the bauble on my arm. This was the only issue we fought about in our first year together.

In fact, our first year together was the most blissful year of my life. Later Toni told me that she realized at that time that to be with me she had to be into what I was into, so she studied with Shirfu Chiang too. We started teaching his Taoist yoga warm-ups five mornings a week at the community center in Bolinas.

Shirfu was also an acupuncturist, an herbalist, a painter, and a calligrapher. I spent a year studying Chinese calligraphy with him. When I started, he showed me how to grind the stick of ink with a few drops of water in a blue-grey inkstone to get the proper consistency. Then he showed me how to hold the brush. I told him I was left-handed—memories of first grade. *Never mind,* he said, *It doesn't matter,* and he picked up the brush with his left hand and wrote a line. Since I couldn't do this with either hand yet, I decided to start with my right. Eventually, I learned to write the opening stanzas of the *Tao Te Ching* in Chinese with my right hand.

One day I gave Shirfu a handful of magic mushrooms. He didn't know what they were. I told him they were meditation mushrooms and that they were very strong. A few days later, I was in bed with Toni in Bolinas, and Shirfu was in Berkeley, when I sat up straight and shouted, *Shirfu has eaten the mushrooms!* I rushed to the living room and stood in a meditation posture Shirfu taught us called the Test of Fire. We were supposed to hold this posture for an hour. I was up to twenty minutes to half an hour by then. But that evening, I stood for a full hour—as I started to sweat I stood and mentally talked Shirfu through, letting him know that I was with him, he was not being poisoned, he would not die or become ill, and it would pass.

At our class the next day, for the first time Shirfu wore Buddhist meditation beads wrapped around his wrist. That class was the hardest hour and a half of work I've ever done—not that it was fast or hard in the usual sense. The movements were deep and slow. After only a few minutes, we were in a full sweat. By the end of the class, we had lost gallons of water from moving so slowly and deeply.

Shirfu smiled at us and said, *Now you know the difference between chicken soup and mushroom soup.*

That was all he ever said.

* * *

Toni and I would ride our bikes into town to teach each morning, go for walks along the cliffs, and sometimes hike out to Bass Lake to swim naked in the cold clear water. It was during a bliss-filled afternoon at the lake, after we'd made love on the grass, that I told her she was the clearest manifestation of light I'd ever seen. This is still true today, but at the time, that didn't change my reluctance to commit to a long-term partnership or the future. But I had truly fallen in love—for the first time in my life.

I felt like the walking wounded. I needed deep contact and healing. When Toni once asked how I was doing, I told her I was knocked down, beat up, kicked in, rolled over, slapped silly, and hurt all over.

Toni became my nurse. I would spend days at a time at home, writing my novel, practicing tai chi, and painting Chinese calligraphy, while listening to Music for Zen Meditation and looking out our living room window at Agate beach and the vast ocean beyond.

Sometimes we would lie naked in each other's arms on the deck together and fall asleep to the sound of the waves.

I was now incarnate in the life I desired when I was hitching in Big Sur two years before. How was it possible? After moaning about the dew never coming, suddenly I was living on the coast, in a supportive community, with the love of my life, and writing a novel. Sweetest dream if I ever did see one as I drank in the ocean of dew.

CHAPTER 22

Outlaw Town

Toni was much more than I had bargained for. I thought I was getting into a short-term affair. Despite my attempts to run or blow it up, we continued to fall deeper in love.

She would have left me in the first year. She said I was raw voltage and it was easy to get shocked or sometimes burned. She said I was continually telling her of the other women I'd loved in my life. She thought I was giving her signals to leave. I probably was. She thought I didn't love her. I did, and it scared me. I never had any intention of settling down and living a normal domestic life. Yet here it was looming in front of me.

Toni prayed and contacted what she called my higher self and was reassured that I truly loved her and that this was where she belonged. It also helped that she became best friends with Joan. Joan told her I'd done the same things with her. I'd never seen, or been trained for, the experience of a healthy long-term relationship. I didn't have a clue.

Meanwhile, Toni and I laughed together. From slapstick to mental gymnastics, pantomime, impersonations, skits, skats, and skidoos, we loved each other's sense of humor. Sometimes we laughed so hard that we fell over. And we loved the same books and movies. Not only had Toni read John Barth, she could joke with me based on characters from *Giles Goat Boy*—who could have asked for more? And so much more. To have a best friend and an ally, a true partner in love and life, this was totally new to me. One of "our" songs in that blissful first year was a Waylon Jennings hit, "Ladies Love Outlaws":

Ladies love outlaws

Like babies love stray dogs

Ladies love outlaws

Like a miner loves his gold

And outlaws love ladies

Somewhere deep down in their soul.

After our first year together, I told Toni that she inspired me with aspirations for affluence. I wanted to support her and take care of her in the best possible way. When her husband remarried and moved to Piedmont, we rented his house, and Sarah, nine years old then, stayed in the house and lived with us. I started to make money the only way I knew how: I grew marijuana, but this time, I wasn't planning to give it away. The first crop got a late start, and though it was a small beginning, it was a good one. It supported us and paid for a greenhouse. We accumulated cats, two dogs, chickens, and eventually some Nubian goats to go with Sarah's horses.

Bolinas in the seventies was a mecca for cultural outlaws. Just as Catalonia held out against the fascists of Spain, Bolinas also stood apart. One way the unincorporated town defended itself against the onslaught of development sweeping California was by maintaining control of the Bolinas Water Board, which to this day hasn't issued a new water meter since 1971. Between the town's proximity to San Francisco and the time it took to drive over the mountain to reach it, Bolinas retained both a rural character and the culture that writers, poets, artists, craftsmen, potters, plotters, and everyone else you could imagine brought to it.

Alan Watts, Gary Snyder, Lawrence Ferlinghetti and the Beat poets, and countless others made their home in Bolinas at one time or another. At times though, the town also seemed to be a massive outpatient hospital. The Miwok Indians, who used to live in the area, claimed that living on the Big Mesa of Bolinas long enough would drive one mad. In my experience, most of the people were mad when they arrived. My first day after my first night in town, Toni took me to a pottery show at a private home on the Mesa. Bobby Louise Hawkins, a town poet wearing Navajo turquoise and cowboy boots, and her sidekick Judith "Hawk" Westin, with a joint peeking out from behind her ear, beneath her cowboy hat, looked me over from head to toe when we walked in. One of them said out of the side of her mouth, "Fresh meat in town," and I felt welcomed and at home.

Jerry Brown was governor, and money was easy, before the right wing's Prop 13 bankrupted the state. Bolinas set up a school for adult education, and the state paid people to teach classes as long as the attendance warranted it. Everyone in town took each other's classes. I learned to make raku pottery, went on herb walks with Celana Heron and Denni McCarthy, and took a class on writing a novel from Greg Armstrong, the Harper and Row editor of *Soledad Brother*. As certified teachers for post-secondary education, Toni and I were paid to teach Shirfu's Taoist Yoga every morning at eight. Because Bolinas is on the San Andreas Fault, our school was called Fault Line U. Our school cheer was, *Who's at Fault? Who's at Fault? We are! We are!*

It was in this second year that I told Toni it was time to share the love that we had discovered. I told her it would be selfish to keep it to ourselves. What that really meant was that I wanted to have sex with other women. Toni was devastated.

When a protest was organized against the Diablo Canyon Nuclear Power Plant in San Luis Obispo, Toni and I became trainers in non-violent resistance for the Abalone Alliance. Toni, in part to prove herself to me, joined the Bolinas BAND (Bolinas Against Nuclear Destruction.) Because of my criminal history, I stayed home as a BAND-aide, while Toni went off to war. She was arrested and spent ten days in the county jail—longer stretch then I was ever in for. In the heat of battle, while camping out before the big protest, she and Steve became lovers.

By then I had made love with someone else as well. While it was sweet, erotic, and fun, I wouldn't spend the night because I had to get home to my true love. It was a moment of connection and pleasure but not emotional investment. Toni was different. She was not interested in casual affairs; she didn't see the point. Steve Lerner was a Harvard graduate and the son of a famous political columnist. He was a well-bred, bright, sincere, committed, and good-looking man. Someone I had to approve of, and I did. Toni called this her Camelot affair; Steve was her Lancelot. Hurt and jealousy burned me like a fever, though I tried to deny they were there. As much as I didn't want my pain to show, I still bled all over the place and made a general mess while claiming to be fine and angrily denying my true freelings.

Then Kalu Rinpoche came to town. We saw an announcement in the mimeographed *Hearsay News* that a Lama of the Kagyu lineage of Tibetan Buddhism would be speaking at the community center. This was the lineage of Milarepa, the masters of psychic heat, flying, and disappearing, described by Evans-Wentz. I had read the Evans-Wentz series on Tibetan Buddhism in my cabin in Colorado. Evans-Wentz was an Oxford scholar who published the first translations of the Tibetan canon. When I'd read passages aloud to Toni, I told her I wanted to find these people and learn from them, maybe go to Bhutan to find them. Now these Tibetans were coming to us.

With about fifty other townspeople, we went to our first meeting, where I proceeded to get into an argument with the lama. Flies buzzed around him, but he wouldn't bother them. I asked the lama how he could leave the flies alone yet still eat meat. It seemed like hypocrisy to me. I, on the other hand, was a vegetarian who killed flies. It was a lively debate, but I was not impressed as he seemed rigid in orthodoxy, without a free mind. The lama then announced that a temporary prayer room had been set up in a garage on the edge of the mesa where we were welcome for 5:30 a.m. puja in preparation for Kalu Rinpoche's arrival. Kalu Rinpoche was the meditation master of the Kagyu lineage and would be giving a ceremony for the taking of boddhisatva vows.

I had been to that part of the mesa for my first sweat lodge with Dennis Banks of the American Indian Movement while he was hiding out from the law after the shoot-out on Pine Ridge, so I knew the location. I went to the morning puja and learned to pray in Tibetan. But after that first morning, I was the only one who continued to show up—the so-called puja leader didn't even show. Each morning I walked by flashlight to sit, meditate, and pray. It was such a precious time. Just before daybreak, the birds began to sing, and the air was fresh with the scent of the herbaceous growth on the cliffs overlooking the sea. I didn't know how to do a puja, so I focused on the Rinpoche and prepared myself to make a connection with him.

When Toni and I arrived to meet Kalu Rinpoche and take our vows, we were late. We tried to sneak into the back, but the lama had saved seats for us up front. We took our vows to enlighten all beings, willing to return again and again to the world of suffering until everyone was free. Locks of hair were snipped, red string tied around our necks, and new names were given. Toni was named White Tara, the goddess of compassion, and I became the Lion of Dharma. Then the officers of the new dharma center were announced: the Lion of Dharma was to be president and White

Tara was to be treasurer. The Lama said that because I came to Kalu in a dream I was to run the center.

The dharma center was established in our larger bedroom, while Toni and I moved into the living room. To come to puja, attendees had to walk past our marijuana garden. Every morning at 5:30 we chanted, visualized and did prostrations. The number of people joining us quickly dwindled. Soon there were only three of us. Eventually the pujas stopped.

That was the time Toni and I also decided to get married. We set a date, prepared wedding invitations, and started treating each other like husband and wife. It was unbearable. We canceled the wedding until we could marry without taking each other for granted or resenting each other for feeling trapped. We waited another eleven years.

Our crop that second year of '78 was a big success. We enlarged the greenhouse and had the money for Toni to go to England to study acupuncture. Originally I had thought I might do it because I was already studying to be a Taoist scholar, but Toni was a more serious student, willing to put in the time and pay the dues. When she returned, I continued to cook and clean house while she studied for her boards. I was the househusband who also ran our little farm and tended the marijuana patch.

The crop of '79 was going to be the big one—the one that would lift us out of poverty. When I'd left Oregon, I wanted to have $100,000 in the bank, and now significantly more than that was a real possibility. This crop was grown bio-dynamically. English garden master Alan Jevons wedded the arcane cosmology and gardening potions of Rudolf Steiner with the intense double-digging the French practiced. Jevons set up a display garden in Santa Cruz in the early seventies and trained a cadre of devotees in French Intensive Biodynamic Gardening. From that cadre came my garden guru Larry, a big-mouthed, strong-backed sweetheart from Brooklyn.

For many weeks, the Bolinas biodynamics class practiced transplanting marijuana seedlings from flats to cans to larger cans in my yard. Larry and I double-dug all the beds by hand, which was a massive undertaking. Because of the class's enthusiasm, we had started so many plants that by spring, I had a small nursery selling female plants to the growers in town. I sold over a hundred and kept another hundred. Part of the money from the nursery sales went to set up a community garden in the town, which still exists.

Biodynamic gardening really works. Our plants quickly grew into trees, and it was all we could do to keep them trimmed below the fence line. We raised the fence twice, but that still wasn't enough, as main stalks grew so large you couldn't grasp around one with one hand. Each plant was yielding well over two pounds of dried flowers. It was a perfect growing year. My garden was an open secret. Most of the town knew about it. José, the town fire chief, would alert us, the Bolinas Border Patrol, whenever the radio chatter indicated a sheriff's car was coming to town.

Along with much of the town, our neighbors were also growing. They were wild, alcoholic, gypsy street people who had raucous drunken parties, while we OM'ed and tried to put an invisible shield over our garden. As we feared, the neighbors got busted, and during their bust the deputy looked over the fence from their backyard, our one vulnerable spot. When the deputy came to my door I once again felt that familiar sinking sensation of sickening nausea, the pain and overwhelming sadness flushing my face with the burning humiliation of another failure. Our dream was over.

I'd been working on my next novel when the deputy came in. It was called *Cash Crop: The Biography of an American Guerilla Farmer*, and the front page was open on my desk:

When 28-year old Mike Giacomi, deputy sheriff for West Marin County, walked in past the redwood gate to Levi Jewison and Laura Roberson's seaside home, he saw three things the had never seen before:

First, he had never seen so much marijuana growing in one spot before. As he slowly walked through the yard, examining the 15- to 20-foot tall plants, he made his second unique sighting. In the middle of a particularly lush spot, he saw Levi and Laura both totally naked. Laura was sitting in Levi's lap with her legs wrapped around his back. What made this scene unique for the officer was that Levi and Laura had their eyes closed. They appeared to be so deeply into meditation as to be unaware of his hulking presence.

But the third and certainly the one sight that most impacted this young officer was the town's men and women who'd already assembled there when he turned back to the gate to call for backup. They were armed with everything from pitchforks to shotguns, and they were waiting for him in clear defiance.

As he stared, with his mouth hanging open, trying to digest all of this new input, someone muttered, "Motherfucker. Looks like the grassroots revolution's begun."

So you're a writer? the friendly deputy asked as he searched the house and saw my manuscript on my desk. He asked if I smoked this stuff, and I told him it was a sacred herb. He let me keep the stash he found in my desk drawer. He really was a good man.

The sheriff was called in from over the mountain when this turned out to be more than a garden with a few plants. It was such a major operation that the deputies brought in volunteers to help all of us harvest and load the crop into dump trucks. The harvesting took hours. No one was prepared for what they found. They had to call in more dump trucks.

During the confusion I watched Toni walk over to take back my seed collection from the pile of confiscated plants and dried pot. I never wanted or expected her to do this, but she knew how important my seeds were to me. I had seeds from all over the world as well as strains I'd been developing from the sweetest psychedelic plants, like the Purple Mango from a cross of African and Thai plants. That simple act of courage bonded Toni to my heart for life. After a life of going it alone, I now had a partner who would continue to shine when tested in the fire.

The bust made the front page of the *San Francisco Chronicle*. They called it "the redwoods of marijuana." It set a county record that still stands. Because the sheriff didn't get a warrant, though, I was never arrested, and he lost his job.

This was the time of Ronald Reagan's election and the right-wing counter-revolution. It was clear that our time was over and that the counter-culture revolution was not going to triumph. Acid dreams gone up in smoke and an alternative way of life dealt a mortal blow.

It was time to head over the mountain and re-enter society as what I then called being *a white man*. I was thirty-two years old with no material assets, no career, no business, and no direction. I was wide open for whatever was next, and I knew that whatever might happen, something unknown was present and trustworthy.

CHAPTER 23

Making It in the White World

With a little of the money we made from the crop of '78, I'd bought some tribal rugs for our concrete living room floor. I had no idea what I was doing when I bought the rugs, but now I had to sell them to get some money. To do that, I had to find out more about them.

One was from Turkey, another from Afghanistan, and a third was made by a tribe in Southern Iran, whose name I couldn't remember. Sometimes when I smoked, I would look at these rugs for hours. Observing the artistry became my meditation, as I began to see structure and detail I hadn't seen before. I examined how the knots were tied and started to see the imperfections in a design as well. I'd never noticed that the border was not exactly the same on either side. The closer I looked, the more I saw.

When I sold one of the rugs to an antique shop for more than I'd paid for it, I knew I was on to something and continued to study. I went to every rug shop in the Bay Area and looked at every tribal rug I could find. I knew I was not interested in the city rugs, the Persian rugs most people bought.

The patterns and colors I had first seen in Peru were now calling me into deeper study. One of the many things I loved about my belt from Peru was that the pattern in the six-foot-long strip never repeated itself. It was as if the weaver was speaking a language in code and transmitting a message through time. I started to see this in the tribal rugs as well—for example, how a small camel was woven into a border to replace a geometric pattern. These small changes and imperfections seemed to be consciously woven into the design.

I learned to discern whether the dyes were naturally or chemically based and learned the names of the dyes used. I loved the subtle variations in the shades of indigo or madder or cochineal, a bright purple-red made from an insect. I learned that the Germans introduced aniline dyes in the nineteenth century, and I could see when they began to be used by the different tribal groups, out in the far reaches of beyond.

I read every book I could find and looked at photographs of hundreds of rugs, and soon I could differentiate the tribal patterns and designs and date which quarter of the nineteenth century a rug belonged to. As my eye developed, I could buy a rug from one shop and sell it to another. In the trade, I was now a picker.

In the 1950s and 1960s, the old Armenian and Iranian carpet dealers bundled the outside of their rug shipments with cheap tribal flat-weaves, called kilims. These were throw-away items to them and would lie around the back corners of their shop, while the large Persian rugs and runners were sold. We in the new generation of sellers considered these throwaways tribal collectibles. We loved the saddle-bags, cradles, and small pieces that had been woven on back-strap looms by tribal nomads.

The old dealers labeled a whole class of tribal rugs Bukhara because that was the name of the trading center where the tribes sold their wares. As long as I could find a shop that still had some Bukharas, I would find a treasure. The new dealers like myself could name the different sub-tribes of the Turkomen from Northern Afghanistan and Turkestan. They were no longer simply Bukharas but Tekkes, Yomuds, Ersari, and half a dozen other small nomadic tribes of Central Asia.

I subscribed to all the major rug auction catalogs around the world and had my first rug show in Bolinas at Commonweal less then a year following my crop bust. There was a joke in those days that old drug dealers didn't die—they just dropped the "d" and became rug dealers. Something about marijuana increases our aesthetic sensibility. The Hindus call marijuana the Goddess Saraswati; she bestows culture, poetry, and taste. She certainly bestowed these on me and many of my tribe because suddenly there were hundreds of antique tribal rug dealers sprouting up across the country and the world. Dozens of books were published, as the field had a renaissance.

There was a lot of cash in the counter culture community, and people were looking for a place to put their money. Antique tribal rugs took off as an art form. The rock bands and their roadies, the growers, dealers and smugglers, all had money and were in love with the tribal textiles. Every week a few friends would drive down from the Northern California hills with crops and drive back with rugs.

The following year I was part of a group that put on the first tribal rug exhibit in Marin County and published a book called *Tribal Visions*. The year after that I went to London to the First International Textile Conference and befriended the auctioneer from Christie's. My first textile discovery was also published in *Hali*, the international tribal rug journal. It was of a rare early-nineteenth-century prayer kilim from central Turkey; the only other example of this work was in a museum in Istanbul. I'd bought it for a few hundred dollars and later sold it in Vienna for a few thousand. I could not believe it! I was now an authority on tribal art, which was also the name of my new company. I was making legitimate money. I wasn't yet "a white man," but I was off the reservation.

A few years later when I branched out, it took me around the world and to my next test. I'd found a rare early-nineteenth-century Salor tribal rug in a small rug shop in Sausalito. It had a baseball-sized hole in it, so the shop owner had bought it for a hundred dollars and sold it to me for three hundred and fifty. The Salors were a minor tribe of Turkmen; after military defeats they faded from the scene, leaving only a very few and very old rare pieces behind. This Salor rug was a major score for me. I wholesaled it for three thousand dollars the next day. Short on money, the dealer who bought it traded me two Ming Dynasty Chinese hand-scrolls. Suddenly a new art form opened up to me.

The scrolls were clearly old. Examining them under a magnifying glass, I could see that the paints used were mineral-based lapis lazuli, cinnabar, and gold. I fell in love with what I saw. I took the paintings to the Asian Art Museum, then a part of San Francisco's De Young Museum in Golden Gate Park. I met Steve Little, the curator, who helped me see what I had and became a mentor to me.

I began to study Chinese painting. Once again I bought and read a small library. I went to meet Professor Cahill at UC Berkeley, who had written three of the major books on the subject. I sold one of the scrolls for three thousand dollars and kept the other. My investment of three hundred dollars netted me three thousand dollars and a painting.

I went to my first Asian art auction at Butterfields in San Francisco and found an exquisitely drawn seventeenth-century Tibetan tankha of White Tara, Toni's Tibetan name. It was in a cheap, scratched, and broken frame and was labeled "Glazed Tama" by the auction house, a made-up name, which showed that they didn't know what it was. I sat in the first row, bid seventy-five dollars, and then stood up and glared at everyone behind me, daring them to bid against me. No one did.

I had this painting properly framed, and it is still in our entry hall at home.

At that same auction, I also bought a line drawing of a Buddha on brown paper. I bought it for a hundred and seventy-five dollars.

I thought it was Chinese, but it turned out to be Japanese. It also turned out to be a model that was made from a drawing handed down since the seventh century to teach Buddhist monks how to paint the Buddha. There were notations on the edges of the drawing in different locations that showed where to fill in the color between the lines and which color to use—like my old coloring book from Brooklyn, but with annotations. It was signed by a famous eighteenth-century painter. I didn't know any of this when I bought the drawing; I just saw that it was a great drawing. I later sold it to a museum for five thousand dollars.

I was shocked to discover that Chinese paintings were still quite affordable. At that brief moment in time, there was almost no interest in classical Chinese painting, except for the rare and very best. Most of the Chinese in the world were kept out of the picture because they lived in Maoist China, which kept the market thin and weak.

I flew to my first Asian art auction in New York in 1980. While in New York, I visited the Chinese painting court in the Metropolitan Museum of Art and saw my first Sung Dynasty fan paintings. They made a deep impression on me. At Christie's the next day, I bought two ancient fan paintings in the same Sung Dynasty style. I kept them hanging on our wall for decades, never seeing anything like them for sale again.

I began going to the spring and fall auctions in New York every year. One year I couldn't make it and called Arnold Chang, the Chinese painting auctioneer at Sotheby's. Due to a snowstorm keeping most people at home, he had an unsold handscroll by my favorite painter of the early Ching Dynasty. I bought it for five thousand dollars while on the phone with Arnold. That's the most I had ever spent on anything. The next year, when I sold it for twenty-five thousand dollars at Christie's, I knew I could make my living this way. I couldn't read Chinese, I couldn't even read the artists' signatures or seals—I really knew nothing at all about

Chinese painting—and yet I trusted my eye and my taste and relied on my intuition.

I never spent more than five or six thousand dollars, which was a large sum for me, and I only spent that much three times. This kept me on the margins. The really great ancient masterpieces were going for hundreds of thousands. I learned from examining them closely at each sale. But the market was weak below the first and second tiers, so I hunted for undiscovered bargains.

At one sale in New York, I met the great collector and curator C. C. Wang, not to be confused with C. S. Wang, the Chinese painting specialist and auctioneer at Christie's. C. C., as he was known, was in his eighties then. There is now a wing at the Met displaying his vast collection, spanning several generations of his family collections. A book of his painting collection is still is one of my all-time favorites. C. C. took a fondness to me and pointed out forgeries, which in most cases were going for much more than I could afford, which I would have bought if I could. I didn't really care about the authenticity of the paintings; I was just appreciating what moved me.

I bought a painting attributed to my favorite painter of the Ming Dynasty. Because the attribution was questionable, I was able to get it for six thousand dollars. When the curator at the De Young moved to the Freer Gallery, a part of the Smithsonian in Washington DC, he published a paper on this painter, and a photo of my painting appeared as an example of an important early work. The photo bore the attribution "From the Eli Jaxon-Bear Collection." Too much, right?

The two paintings I bought at my first New York auction for sixteen hundred dollars and twenty-five hundred dollars were cheap enough that I could afford to keep them. They are my favorite paintings for the time period and style they represent. One is on the cover of one of the editions of my book *Sudden Awakening*. When I finally sold these paintings a few years ago, they went for a hundred and twenty-five thousand dollars. A Chinese collector on the phone with Sotheby's bought them. The Chinese are now fully in the market and I am long gone.

CHAPTER 24

Finding a Way to Serve

Toni and I moved out of Bolinas and into Mill Valley during this time. I had given up on finding a teacher who could help me transmit what I had realized. I had to find a way to do it myself.

Toni set up her growing acupuncture practice and was steering us now. She was also doing her best to hew off my rough edges so that I could pass in society. Well, what I call pass is what she called integrate. But in truth, I couldn't fully integrate. It's like learning a language for some people. If you move to a foreign country at a young enough age, you generally pick up the language easily and can often speak it like a native. However, if you go to a new country when you're older, you tend to have an accent and fit in rather than fully assimilating. I was entering a culture I had walked out of decades earlier, when I unplugged the TV in 1968. I left without ever learning to speak the language, much less engage in small talk. I would always only be passing to some small degree.

To address my arrogance and general inability to get along with people, Toni insisted I take the **est** training. I took the training, but I fought the trainers tooth and nail. I agreed not to smoke grass during the week of the training, which was one of the rules, if the trainers would agree not to use caffeine and nicotine during that week. I couldn't see how their drugs of choice were any holier than mine. Three trainers yelling at the top of their lungs in my face meant nothing to me. But I promised Toni, so I obeyed the rules. If nothing else, **est** showed me how to dress like a successful white man. I bought a suit and tie at Wilkes Bashford on Sutter, San Francisco's best-dressed mayor Willie Brown's shop of choice.

In my efforts to blend and fit in I started reading the *San Francisco Chronicle,* which we called the Comical. I always took the sports section first when we shared the paper at breakfast so that Toni could scan the front-page news. I felt talking sports would help me fit in. I started reading about the Warriors basketball team and the 49er football team. I'd never watched a game, let alone considered attending one, and I certainly didn't know all the rules, much less the strategies or plays. I didn't really care. Over the years I would read about players joining the team, having a career, getting traded or hurt or cut, but never actually see them play. Several times I'd come across a photo of a player and be shocked to discover I had their race wrong based on their name. I mean Chuck Jacobs is African American? Who knew?

This sports mind parasite, what Richard Dawkins calls a meme, inhabited a very small part of my mind, but it slowly grew. Thirty years later, in Australia, I found a pirate Internet station broadcasting American sports from Sweden. Stranded in Sydney for a few days I started watching the Warriors' basketball games. Then came the 49ers on the same pirate station. I've been watching ever since. But I can't remember ever having a sports conversation with anyone that I couldn't have gleaned from that day's paper. Years of useless information cataloged, stored, and taking up room in my fading memory banks. I can name all the Warriors point guards starting with Sleepy Floyd. But I have no use at all for such information except as a receptor site for a digital-stimulation fix I am now mildly addicted to.

Well, I have tried to find a use for this information. As I watch my memory deteriorate over the years, I have used lists of words to see if I could recall them. One test required naming the five New York Mafia families, and another required remembering that after Sleepy Floyd came Mookie Blaylock, Muggsy Bogues, and Bimbo Coles, all point guards for the Warriors when having a nickname was a requirement.

Toni next guided me to a Joseph Campbell seminar. She often said that I was the engine and she was the rudder. She steered our life away from the rocky shoals on which I'd become accustomed to crashing. I loved my week with Joseph Campbell. He was a natural renaissance man who transcended culture and loved to tell stories. For a week we learned about the spiritual traditions of the world and their commonalities while we enjoyed slides and skits performed by the group.

At dinner Campbell spoke of his student days in the 1920s and the enormous importance of Spengler's *Decline of the West*. He said that when he was in college, everyone felt that Spengler was right but had no idea how to stop the coming collapse. Campbell was then a Reagan Republican though he was embarrassed to tell us this. He saw Reagan as trying to stem the tide of decline and the hippies as the barbarians at the gates. He was wrong about Reagan but right about us hippies.

On the plane down to see Joseph Campbell, I read a book Toni gave me called *Frogs into Princes*. It was a transcript of a workshop with the founders of Neuro-Linguistic Programming. I have always been embarrassed to be associated with or even to say NLP. When I had to say something, I would say Neurolinguistics and at least drop the "Programming," a word I found offensive to describe working with people. If we had to use the word at all, I would have preferred "Deprogramming"—Neurolinguistic Deprogramming. That's better.

But names aside, NLP covers an incredibly powerful set of insights and strategies for personal change based on the pioneering work of Gregory Bateson. Gregory Bateson, one of the great thinkers of our time, was a polymath. One of his most impactful areas of exploration was the use of language as the interface between internal experience and the external world. He saw that language both shaped experience and was shaped by experience. In his book *The Ecology of Mind*, he says, *The map is not the territory,* and explains how language creates our map of the world and keeps us living in the map and calling it reality.

Bateson was teaching at the Esalen Institute at the time when Richard Bandler was there studying with Fritz Perls. John Grinder, Bateson's neighbor, was a professor of linguistics at UC Santa Cruz. Together they all made startling discoveries about the patterns that underlie conscious interaction. They framed insights into the structure of consciousness into a therapeutic context, based on the standard therapy of the time: Cognitive Behavioral Therapy CBT. They upgraded CBT and made it possible for anyone to produce profound changes in thoughts, feelings and behaviors, the three realms of CBT. I saw this work as a way to communicate the possibility of waking up and in that it could be a vehicle for my service in the world.

NLP was extremely powerful and value free, and apparently the founders were value free as well, so they peddled it to the highest bidder. They bragged about using NLP at a local Mercedes dealership, resulting in a 30 percent rise in sales. They taught Madison Avenue how to sell and the CIA how to enter someone's mind and change it for their own purposes. The worst part showed up years later when Richard Bandler was found in a motel room with a coke dealing biker, a gun and a dead prostitute. He was tried for murder, but lore has it that NLP got him off. It was such an embarrasement to be associated with this, but for me, I saw the enormous potential NLP could have for true service. I went to a three-week training on the campus of UC Santa Cruz to become certified as an NLP practitioner.

For the most part, the establishment psychotherapists criticized NLP for a variety of good reasons, but I believe that it came down to NLP being a threat to their profession. After my three-week training and certification I could have a private practice and help people change their lives in a relatively short amount of time. The speed of both the certification and the cure threatened those who'd spent years becoming certified and then got paid for years to cure their clients.

A month after the training, Toni and I opened a clinic for acupuncture and neurolinguistics on Sacramento Street in San Francisco's Pacific Heights. Soon after opening our clinic I stood up at an **est** seminar and offered a free session to all four hundred people. As my clients flowed into my office, I understood why it was called a private practice: I practiced in private and got paid for it.

One of my first clients was a nurse from a local hospital. She came because she was about to be fired for falling asleep on the job. I noticed that she had a slight speech impediment. It sometimes seemed that a word would get caught somewhere before it came out, and some words came out slurred. At the time I didn't know the word aphasia, which described her condition. She told me that seven years before she was in a serious car wreck and suffered severe brain damage. For a few days she was restrained in a straitjacket. After years of therapy, she was told she had some permanent damage and what she was left with was the best possible result she could hope for. She told me she'd learned to live with the aphasia, but the falling asleep was threatening her job.

I had just read an article on the brain and speech in the popular magazine *Omni*. The article mentioned that the brain was capable of transferring learning and language from a damaged site to its other hemisphere. It also mentioned that speech was encoded in our neurology in a different way than music. So, I guided this woman into a deep trance and had her sing the alphabet as she visualized the letters singing and dancing from one side of her brain to the other. We did four sessions like this. I found that I could regress her to moments before the accident but not into the trauma directly after the wreck. Each time we sang the alphabet together, something stabilized. Within a few weeks, she reported that she was no longer falling asleep on the job. Her aphasia had virtually disappeared as well. She told her friends, and soon I had a full practice.

She sent another nurse to see me. This one told me that her boss was tapping her phone. The first thing I asked her was if she had called me from home. She said she hadn't, so I told her to call me only from a line that could not be tapped. In this way I entered into rapport with her, which is one of the greatest gifts NLP gave to me. In the past, I was always sure that I was right and told whoever I was with what I saw. People would agree or disagree and often pretended they agreed but later disparaged me. It never occurred to me to enter rapport with whatever appeared before me. I was firmly conditioned to break rapport, in shock and confrontation. I found that entering rapport allowed for a deep connection and the possibility for true healing.

To enter rapport, the therapist has to start from a place of not knowing. This was revolutionary to me. I had spent all of my life knowing, categorizing, and presuming. As a wise guy, I had to know everything and have an opinion about everything. If by some remote chance I didn't know something, I either made it up or obfuscated and deflected so that nobody would notice. The challenge of not knowing revealed the possibility of discovering how another individual consciousness could twist itself into a story of suffering.

NLP demonstrates that all experience has a mental, emotional, and physical component. Back in my cabin, Gurdjieff was the first person I'd read who had said that humans are three-brained creatures; a decade later, I was learning how those brains functioned and could be worked with therapeutically. NLP sliced through each of these brains—the physical, emotional, and mental—to uncover the subcomponents that made an experience pleasant or unpleasant, fearful or joyful, for example. By changing just a few of the subcomponents of an experience—perceived temperature, for example, or the route an experience took from the emotional body to the mental body—the experience changed without the circumstances or content of that experience changing. For example, a woman came to me with a phobia of driving over bridges. By having her change the location of the voice in her head that she called thinking, as well as having that thinking appear as singing whenever she approached a bridge, she found that it was actually pleasant to drive over bridges. She managed to plan a route driving over half a dozen bridges on her way to her next appointment with me to give me the good news.

NLP also demonstrated that all language is a trance induction and that everyone is living in a trance of their own creation, a waking dream each of us calls reality.

When applied from an open and expansive perspective in service to the truth, NLP can spell the end of victimhood. Instead, NLP became the motor of the self-help industry spawning inner-child work and then coaching as a career choice. Rather than helping people to wake up from the dream of the egoic self, the self-help industry was selling an "empowered" ego-self imagining it creates prosperity.

After I completed all the levels of training and was certified as a trainer, I went to an evening of fire-walking with John Grinder. It was quite simple. Turn off the internal dialogue and the mental pictures of getting burned. I'd had many experiences of stopping my mind in dangerous situations so this was pretty simple for me. For those who had trouble turning off the internal dialogue John suggested an internal mantra of *cool moss*. Within a few hours everyone in attendance walked across the coals. I assisted at the next fire-walk and learned how to make the fire and spread the coals. This second time around, I experimented with allowing a thought to rise while walking and felt a small burn blister start in that moment. A few months later, I was the leader of my third fire-walk, taking a group across the coals on the coast of Marin.

Although fire-walking proved popular and a money maker, with Tony Robbins, a fellow participant, building an empire of self-help based on fire-walks, it wasn't where I was interested in going. Tony's model was *Passion Pride and Power*, which I saw as the deadly sins. He was more about strengthening the ego, and I was interested in the end of the ego.

I was soon leading NLP trainings at Lone Mountain College, at UC San Francisco, and at Esalen Institute. I used NLP to help people wake up from the trance of personal reality. My program literature opened with a passage from Aldous Huxley's *Doors of Perception*, in which he explains that we are viewing life through dirty windows, seeing only the patterns on the glass. If we we cleanse the filters of perception we would catch a glimpse of the unbelievable totality. Aldous Huxley of course was using magic mushrooms and LSD to clean his windows while NLP was a way to non-psychedically see the patterns and cleanse the filters of conditioned existence.

Toni had a waiting list of patients and worked with two treatment rooms to fit them all in. My NLP practice was thriving as well, and I was selling tribal art and Chinese paintings on the side. Ming Dynasty scrolls depicting ancient processions were mounted along the walls of our offices. It was the yuppie wave, and it was carrying us along. Hippies and Yippies became Yuppies in the blink of an eye.

I met an accountant Ken Casey, someone my age from my old neighborhood in Queens, who went to Archbishop Malloy high school. He became our financial advisor and has steered us financially until today. He got us incorporated and told us that the company could afford a $5,000 car and recommended we buy a $15,000 car because through depreciation and tax write-offs the government would pay the rest. Now Toni and I drove new sports cars and instead of the Bolinas Free Box, I was buying my clothes at Mayor Willie Brown's shop of choice.

The remedy for any lingering belief in free will is to see that you're being carried by a wave that is also carrying a generation. This puts to rest any idea of a "me" charting my destiny. The tide came in and schools of fish were washed along. Toni and I were washed along with everyone else. How could it have been otherwise? We were going with the flow.

In 1983, the owners of the house we were renting needed to sell. They were speculators in a down market. The house was only a one bedroom, but because of its ideal location, on a half acre in the banana belt of Mill Valley, the short easy walk to town, its complete privacy and idyllic green views, it was worth $250,000. With our accountant's help we bought it with $10,000 down. From the farm in Bolinas and getting our clothes from the free box to a two career family in Mill Valley seemed to happen overnight. Within an instant of time we were in new lives along with a house and a mortgage. That is the nature of dreams.

I liked to cook and from the beginning was the cook in our relationship. One evening for dinner I made watercress soup and crepes with a morel mushroom sauce. We had a glass of Chardonnay and with a comfortable fire in the fireplace we put on a video.

The video was a documentary called *Shoah*, which examined the Holocaust from the mundane perspective of the simple logistics involved. Instead of horrific footage of the camps and ovens, Nazi bureaucrats were interviewed about precise train schedules and boxcar loads of human cargo being shuttled to incineration. The details of the carnage were meticulously recorded on carbon copies. While watching this video, I felt a sudden enormous pain in the bone of my left forearm. It felt like my bone had shattered. But there was no apparent cause for the feeling. I kneaded my arm with my right hand, but the pain was deeper. I fell inside, and suddenly I was running through a sewer in the Warsaw ghetto. I had a gun in one hand, and my left forearm was shot through. A woman was running behind me. I turned a corner, and there was a sudden explosion of heat, fire, and white light. It blew me out of that lifetime.

A dream within a dream.

Now I was in the comfort of my home again, in Marin County, at the top of the world. Who could explain any of it? Overwhelming gratitude left me laughing and crying on the living room couch.

*   *   *

A few years later Toni led me to the enneagram. I first encountered this symbol while reading Gurdjieff. Oscar Ochazo, the founder of the Arica Institute, said that he met a Sufi who taught him the enneagram and the spiritual basis of Arica. Oscar taught what he learned to Claudio Naranjo, a Chilean psychotherapist, who then taught it in a Gurdjieff study group in Berkeley. Helen Palmer, Kathleen Speeth, and Hamid Almaas were part of that group. I learned from them, from Kathy Speeth, who grew up with Gurdjieff, Jerry Perkins, one of her students, and from Claudio. Helen was a friend over for dinner, but I never worked with her.

I immediately resonated with the enneagram. It was shockingly familiar. It showed me the difference between ego and true self, and it blew me away. It was being taught as the enneagram of personality, but that seemed self-evidently wrong. People with the same fixation can have very different personalities with obvious examples in each fixation. For example, Bill Clinton and Idi Amin have the same character fixation but very different personalities. The enneagram shows us the deeper structure that personality emerges from. Instead of our true character it shows us the defect of character covered by character fixation.

With the enneagram it was possible to make very clear distinctions of ego on the mental, emotional, and physical levels. It gave me the subtlest map I'd encountered of the arising of fixated mind. The real possibility the enneagram presents is the willingness to stop indulging in egoic identity.

The enneagram gives us a map of who we are not but people were using it to identify who they believed they are. As the enneagram became popular, people were learning and teaching it in order to become a better ego. The enneagram divides the ego into nine different types, and people were making the fixation number part of their personal identity. They went around declaring, *I am a four,* for example, and they would first use that to justify their patterns of egoic living and then work on being a better number, a more positive or more developed or more evolved number.

I saw that the basic triangle of the enneagram—anger, fear and neediness—was an overlay on the true Self. When egoic fixation is overlaid on the true self of Consciousness and Love, ego is born as an angry, fearful, needy somebody.

The Sufi teaching on black holes and essence, which is laid out beautifully in A. H. Almaas's books, can be applied directly to the enneagram as well. Using hypnosis in this context, I could now see how to drop through the fixation and out the black hole, just as I had in my cabin in Colorado.

Hypnosis, NLP, and the enneagram melded into a new whole, bigger than their parts, and my teaching expanded and took off. Dick Price, cofounder of Esalen with Michael Murphy, saw something in me and took me under his wing. He said that Esalen was a place to try new things and gave me the space for my teaching to develop. I loved him dearly for it. My work evolved into what I called Leela Therapy.

Through a Hopi medicine singer I knew, I was introduced to my Uncle Henry, a medicine pipe holder of the Arapaho and head of the Native American Church. We built the first sweat lodge at Esalen, and for the next decade, Uncle would lead sweats at my meetings as we prayed for our oppressed sisters and brothers around the world.

I was making real money for the first time in my life. I had a career that I loved serving others, a life-partner that I loved even more, and the best of the Bay Area. The dream machine was peaking.

CHAPTER 25

Dharma Combat

In April of 1983, I flew to Hong Kong in search of paintings.
Steven Little at the De Young had put me in touch with the
Chinese painting curator at the Chinese art museum in Hong
Kong. He introduced me to several families selling paintings from
their homes in the backstreets of Kowloon. I scoured Hong Kong
and was dismayed to find that not much was available and the
prices comparable to New York. So that the trip wouldn't be a total
loss, I bought a Ming Dynasty fan painting by a second-tier artist.
Rushing to a date with a local Hong Kong girl, I left it behind in a
taxi that sped off into the twilight.

I had planned on staying for a month to search for paintings,
but after a week I was ready to leave. I was in the travel office
making my reservations to return home when I was told that
the Chinese government had just changed the law that allowed
unescorted American tourists to enter the country. I arranged
my visa and a one-way ticket and arrived in Beijing the next
day. I found a *Fodor's Guide* at the airport and picked a hotel near
Tiananmen Square. The taxi dropped me off and drove away, but
the hotel was closed, boarded up for repairs.

I was now in the middle of Beijing and could speak only a half
dozen words of Chinese. Unlike Hong Kong, nothing in Beijing

was written in English, and no one spoke it. There was a strong military presence, and most people were on bicycles. No taxis in sight. I began to walk. And so I found my way around the old city of Beijing and to the Peace Hotel, built by the Russians in 1954, just on the outskirts of the Forbidden City.

Each morning I walked to the moat surrounding the Forbidden City where I practiced tai chi. Men walked their song birds in bamboo cages, opera singers made good use of the palace walls' acoustics, and small groups assembled for tai chi on the grass.

One morning after my workout a man in a jogging suit introduced himself and invited me for breakfast. He said that judging by my stretches I had done hard work and that he'd never seen those stretches before or that form of tai chi. For breakfast he offered me hot buns and butter, although he said many of his Western friends were on a diet and so passed on the butter.

Are you Russian Jewish? he asked. How could he know?

Nissi and I became close friends. He was an English teacher at Beijing Normal University, and his wife taught accounting. He made the room we were having breakfast in himself although he was not a professional carpenter by any stretch. The room was a small part of a communal courtyard in what had once been a private home. Nissi was a second generation Christian, from the landlord class. His parents had converted with the Baptist Inland Mission. Jesus Christ meant compassionate love, a new idea that seemed right for the time. For a persecuted minority Christianity held a meaning closer to its origins with the early martyrs. During the Cultural Revolution Nissi was sent to forced labor. He helped to build the subway in Beijing. An old woman who was a former tutor for the royal family was on his work crew. Nissi would help her with her load, and she would surreptitiously tutor him, helping him memorize the epic poetry of thousands of years of culture.

Nissi had me stay for dinner to meet his family. His mother and father had both been doctors in the old days. During the Cultural

Revolution, his father was sent to the countryside, where he had a stroke. Now he lay paralyzed, slowly dying in the back room. Nissi's mother, a kind and quiet woman, made us a delicious simple dinner of *jao-tzu,* or potstickers. They were shocked that I could use chopsticks, and even more that I use them with my left hand. No one in China uses the left hand for chopsticks. It's the dirty hand. While we were eating a local communist block captain came in unannounced, sat down on a chair, and watched us. We ignored him and carried on our conversation.

After dinner as we sat alone in Nissi's room he told me that he loved the piano and that he loved to play the Western classics. I was traveling with a new Sony Walkman Pro, which had a unique feature of dual headphone jacks. I also had two sets of headphones and my favorite piece of music, Keith Jarrett's *Köln Concert.* I offered Nissi some grass. He had never tried it but was curious. We smoked and then put on the headphones and listened to Keith Jarrett. Nissi was blown away when he realized that the music was improvised.

I felt very much at home in China. Nissi and I rode bicycles around Beijing, and he took me to see an American movie playing at the university. I remember it as an old black-and-white murder mystery with Jimmy Stewart playing a psychiatrist. It had a Freudian theme about the subconscious; Freud was very hip and cutting edge with the university intelligentsia at that time.

I longed to see Hangzhou and to walk around West Lake. I had some ancient romantic attachment to the place although I hardly knew anything about it. Nissi helped me purchase a train ticket, and we parted ways. I spent a week walking in Hangzhou, meeting people and drinking Dragonwell tea, my favorite tea, *picked before the rain* being the early premium harvest, only available on years when the weather cooperated. I'd purchased the tea when I was in Hong Kong and had now brought it back to where it was grown. I drank it out of a glass, proletarian style. I did, however, have a classical old tea pot. It was one of Nissi's father's last possessions. The inside had been cured from a lifetime of use. Nissi gave it to me as a parting gift.

I had been an idealistic supporter of Mao and the Cultural Revolution. Now I had to face the horrors done in the name of revolution. A year later, I helped Nissi and his family recover from the results when I became his sponsor and helped him come to the States. Nissi got a scholarship to Bob Jones University, which allowed him both to leave China and get a U.S. visa. The scholarship required him to work full-time.

When he landed, we took Nissi to Maui. We took him whale watching and then scuba diving. While he was putting on his tank, it suddenly occurred to me that maybe he'd never been in the ocean before. *Oh well, Eli,* he said, *I was once in a pool in China.* With his scuba tanks already on we discovered that Nissi could not swim but was willing to go along with whatever I proposed. We took him down and held his hands as we guided him through the ocean. His first time in the ocean and he was scuba diving. We woke up early one morning on Maui to the sound of a car crash. He had never been in a car before Maui and Nissi was teaching himself to drive with our rental car.

After a short while at Bob Jones, Nissi wrote to us saying that the place was worse than communist China. The next year he attended Harvard on a scholarship. Within a few years, he had his master's degree and was working on a second. When we visited him in Boston, he had two cars and a trick of switching license plates to avoid tickets.

I sponsored Nissi's wife as well, and she earned her master's in accounting at Harvard as well. Because her English wasn't good, Nissi took the same courses with his wife, in addition to the classes in his master's program. He and his wife had the two highest grades in accounting.

Nissi also had to work full-time while he was in school. He worked as a waiter in a Chinese restaurant, and one evening he met Jimmy Carter and enjoyed a conversation with him. Several years later he owned two apartment buildings in Boston, got a job with a high tech company in Silicon Valley, and went back to China as a U.S. citizen. He now has a house in Beijing and another in Boston.

*   *   *

After Hangzhou, I went to Shanghai before returning home. I couldn't get a connecting flight to Hong Kong, but there was a flight leaving in two days for Osaka, Japan. I took it. I thought I would visit my old friend Rycho, who was now the head of a Zen Temple.

Choshoji Zen Temple is over six hundred years old. Built on the site of a sacred Shinto rock, it is in the heart of the hot springs area of the southern island of Kyushu. A short cobblestone street leads to the temple gate. Though the ancient gate is closed to traffic with bamboo poles, it has pedestrian openings on either side. Once in the gate there is a Koi pond to the right with a tea house overlooking it. Across the lawn ancient flat stones make a path to the front entrance.

Leaving my shoes in a rack, I stepped onto the polished ancient wood floors. Their dark luster spoke of silent centuries. The large zendo off the main entrance had a tatami mat floor and sliding wooden walls that were open to the spring breeze. A twenty-foot tall statue of Quan Yin, the goddess of mercy and compassion, was visible behind the zendo.

I was escorted to meet the oldest living Zen master. I imagined he might not be too thrilled to see me. While his eldest son, Rycho, lived with us in Berkeley, he renounced his position and family obligation, declining to take over his father's temple. His brother took his place for four years, but then he was killed in a motorcycle crash. That's when Rycho returned to Japan to take on his responsibility. He arrived in Japan with shoulder-length hair, sparkling Day-Glo purple shoes, and John Lennon glasses.

Knowing I would meet Rycho's father, I bought a present for him while I was in Shanghai. I chose the finest calligraphy brush I could find. Now sitting at the table with him I discovered that the oldest living Zen master was blind. I was giving a paintbrush to a blind man.

He held the brocaded box containing the brush and felt the silk and the small ivory-like clasps. Like a small boy filled with wonder, he made it clear that the box alone would have been enough. He opened the box with a laugh that was loud and sharp, like two Zen blocks clapping. He told me that the only love left for him to enjoy was calligraphy. He said that his old brush was too worn, and he showed it to me. It was true. It was the same size and weight as the one I brought, but the new brush had better quality bristles made of wolf's hair. He held the new brush in both hands and said I must be a messenger of Avalokiteshvara, the deity of compassionate aid. He spent the next several days painting calligraphy for me to take home. (When I returned two years later, leading a group of Americans in a workshop we called *The Buddha, the Goddess, and NLP*, he painted calligraphy for everyone in the group with this brush). I called him *Ojiisan*, grandfather.

I was given a small monk's room, behind the sitting hall. The view from my window, framed by bamboo, was the Goddess of Mercy, Quan Yin. I was in bliss. Sitting zazen, exploring the local hot springs, shopping by bicycle in the mornings for fresh fish at the market, I was immersed in timeless beauty.

During our first meeting, I told Ojiisan that I'd come looking for antique paintings. After several days, he told me it was time to go to Kyoto on a buying trip and then to quickly return. Rycho drove me and another monk, who was flying to Tokyo with a sitar for a concert, to the airport. We entered the airport together: me in jeans carrying my attaché case, Rycho dressed in sky-blue Esalen sweats, and the monk, who was a very large martial arts master with a shaved head, carrying his sitar wrapped in towels, which made it look like a machine gun. Airport security immediately followed us. We separated at the gate, since I was going to Kyoto and the monk to Tokyo.

After I went through the metal detector and my attaché case was x-rayed, two officers in white gloves stopped me. They asked permission to search me. I agreed and became silent inside. They did an extremely thorough body search, and then they opened my briefcase. I found out later that the Yakuza, the Japanese mob, had just murdered someone using an imported white mobster as the killer. All airports and train stations on the southern island were on high alert. When security saw our trio enter the airport we set off all the alarms.

While the two police who searched me stood by my side flanking me, a third officer started at one end of my briefcase. He picked up my pen, opened it, took it apart, and examined it inside and out. He put it back together and went to the next item. He picked up my camera, took it out of its case, took off the lens, and proceeded to minutely examine the lens and body. Next, he picked up my calendar, flipped through it page by page, and then held it upside down to see what might fall out. My notebook was examined in the same way. I stood and watched, empty and still. I dared not give rise to a thought.

He picked up my cardboard box of Dr. Chang's Licorice Tea, which contained a large baggy filled with California sinsemilla. I watched in silence. He looked under the box and put it back into the briefcase without opening it. The two officers next to me then snapped to attention, saluted me, bowed, and wished me a safe trip. I thanked them and headed to the runway.

In Kyoto I went to Shinmonzen Street, as Ojiisan had instructed me to do. It is the only street in the city with a block of antique painting shops. I was shocked to see two six hundred year old thangkas in the shop windows. For shockingly little money, I quickly bought four paintings. Two ancient world-class Thangkas, worthy of any museum, a black ink scroll of bamboo and song birds by a famous 16th Century Zen painter, and for a few hundred dollars a Chinese album leaf from the 17th century in the style that I love from the southern Sung.

Over the next four years, I returned to Shinmonzen many times but never again found anything remotely interesting. This window of opportunity opened for a moment and then it was closed and gone.

Seven years later I loaned three of the paintings to the Honolulu Academy of Arts. If life isn't a dream, how is it possible that the curator who was there then was my old acquaintance Steve Little from the De Young Museum? I hadn't heard from him since he published my handscroll while at the Freer on the East Coast. If this were a movie, such coincidence would seem contrived. With Steve's guidance, the Honolulu Academy bought my paintings for $50,000 and featured them in a book produced for a special show called *Visions of the Dharma*. The rare fourteenth- and fifteenth-century tankhas I'd found were the stars of the show and attributed to the Eli Jaxon-Bear Collection but really a gift from Ojiisan.

Paintings in hand I quickly returned to ChoShoJi. Midori was waiting for me. Before I'd left I had watched her silently folding kimonos on the tatami mat of the temple. Her long black hair had fallen in front of her face, as a sunbeam created a glowing halo of light. She didn't see me watching her while she folded the indigo cloth in a ballet of silent timeless movement. I watched her in bliss.

Now, on my return, I was being showered with gifts, and I was overflowing with gratitude. Midori had spent her junior year in the United States so she could speak English. We smoked together, sat zazen, and then made love in my room, with Keith Jarrett playing on my Walkman.

Was it a lifetime we spent like this? The sweet simplicity of timeless routine with no calendar or clocks. Zazen was imbued in the atmosphere, radiating from the tatami and the soji. And the almost invisible presence of Ojiisan, the blind Zen master, was a fragrance of the subtlest sort permeating the silence.

One day a phone call shattered this blissful dream. Rycho had given LSD to one of his students, who had a bad trip and called Tanaka-san in the middle of the night. Tanaka-san was the head of Saikoji Monastery and had been given responsibility for Midori by her parents. Since she was not ordained, she could not stay at his monastery. He learned that Rycho's temple was open to lay people so he sent her there. The phone call alerted him that the temple where he'd sent his charge was a drug den. He immediately called Midori. Ever honest, she told him that we were sleeping together and that I had given her marijuana. He ordered her immediate return. I chose to go with her.

Before we left Choshoji, Ojiisan called me in for a private meeting in which Midori served as translator. He presented me with a Zen teaching fan. Passing on the fan is something given to a dharma heir and traditionally would go to his son. I was shocked, and Midori was astonished.

But Master, she said, *you don't even know him.*

Without my eyes, I see with my heart, he said.

I was now the dharma heir of Ojiisan of the Soto Zen lineage of ChoShoJi Zen Temple on the island of Kyshu.

On the train Midori shocked me yet again. *I remember you as a Mongol,* she said. I'd been feeling that lifetime so strongly in those days. I tried writing about it when I first moved to Bolinas, about riding into a village, pillaging and then falling in love. Just a few weeks before leaving for China, I wrote a poem called "A Mongol Horseman's Lament."

I loved Chinese culture, but I had to face the horror and shame of once riding in and helping to destroy it. My past life as a killer and destroyer of culture helped me to understand and forgive the Nazis.

I remember you riding into my village and taking me as a third wife, Midori said, with her head on my shoulder, as we held hands on the bullet train to Kyoto. The gentle rocking of the train created a hypnotic soothing background as Midori softly spoke. *I have often been your second or third wife. But we have such beautiful babies. I don't really mind.*

How could she know the perfect thing to say?

When I left the States I told Toni I would bring back a wife for us. She laughed. We often joked that we both needed a wife now that we were working so much. Midori was clearly part of the divine plan.

When I first met Tanaka-san, the head of Saikoji Monastery, in the mountains south of Kyoto, Midori and I ritually prostrated ourselves at his feet in the customary fashion. He sent us off in different directions to make our living space.

At afternoon tea, everyone in the monastery sat around a long table in the small dining room, sipping tea and watching expectantly. Rather then sit cross-legged, because of my training with Shirfu I was able to be in a more formal posture upright and sitting on my knees with my butt resting on my heels.

So, you were born in the year of the Wild Boar, Tanaka-san said after looking up my birth year in his book. It was our first meeting, and he probed to see what he could find. *Our Prime Minister, Nakasone, is also a wild boar and a good friend of Reagan. You must be a big businessman.* He showed no visible disappointment except for the slightest hesitation, when I told him I was neither a businessman nor a fan of Reagan or Nakasone.

Originally, I was to go to the United States with Suzuki Roshi, he said. *But at the last minute I was needed here, and Rycho was sent in my place. So you are the one that Rycho met in Berkeley.*

I winced internally. I had corrupted his charge Midori with sex and drugs, and now he knew that I was the one responsible for Rycho returning as a psychedelic Zen priest. Rycho stole Tanaka's chance for a trip to the States and I was the one who corrupted Rycho with his first acid.

This man had reasons to hate me. Being hated was nothing new to me. I've often been deeply hated in this lifetime. But here with Tanaka-san I understood why I was hated. I didn't need to defend against it or feel wounded by it. I didn't need to assert my innocence, withdraw, or project negativity back at Tanaka-san. My past strategies weren't operative. This was simply the context for our meeting. For three days, we met each afternoon for tea and dharma combat.

After the first meeting Tanaka-san tried to push me on Vietnam. He learned though that we were not only on the same side but that I had given up the university and my career to fight against the war, which impressed the young monks. He persisted with me, but nothing he tried was working.

So maybe I should leave this monastery, take LSD, and follow you, Tanaka-san said through clenched teeth. He was large for a Japanese man, more of a samurai than a monk. His broad face and shaved head were flushed with anger, though he smiled politely.

Then I would have to come here and do your job, I replied. *Any path can lead home. It is the heart of the seeker not the path that is important. As you know, there is no problem with the appearance of multiplicity if you know it is empty.*

How do you know it is empty? he could barely contain himself.

LSD showed me, I said.

So, you think you can just take a pill? You think that you don't need practice? His contempt and outrage were boiling just below the surface.

I quoted to him from my favorite Zen story of Hui Neng, an uneducated woodcutter who one day delivered a load of wood and overheard the *Diamond Sutra* being recited and instantly woke up. Hui Neng went to the reigning Zen patriarch, whose monks had been reciting the sutra on their rounds of collecting alms. He was seen as an illiterate peasant and sent to work in the kitchen. For sixteen years, he worked in the kitchen. When the master was ready to pass on his robe and begging bowl to an heir, he asked that sutras expressing the depth of realization be submitted to claim the seat as the next master. The winning sutra was selected and posted on the wall:

> The body is the bodhi tree.
> The mind a mirror bright.
> We must work hard and polish it,
> night and day,
> so that no dust can alight.

Hui Neng came out of the kitchen, and because he was illiterate, he asked to have the winning sutra read to him. When he heard it, he asked to have someone write his reply:

> The body is no bodhi tree.
> The mind no mirror bright.
> Since at the root nothing exists,
> where can dust alight?

I wasn't so presumptuous as to recite the whole story, but presumptuous enough to recite Hui Neng's reply.

This was just too much for Tanaka-san. All of Soto Zen, in every monastery and temple, chanted the *Diamond Sutra* at five in the morning. Soto Zen is the lineage that descended from the Sudden School of Hui Neng. So I was reciting the founder's sutra to one of its lineage holders, Tanaka-san. If smoke could have come out of his ears it would have. As he stared at me I could see his thoughts that I was a miserable miscreant, misusing the sacred Zen canon and spouting it back at him of all people!

You compare your emptiness with Hui Neng! he sucked air through his clenched teeth, in disgust and dismay.

Emptiness is emptiness, I said quietly, and through some grace, my mind dropped into silence. The room dropped into deep silence as well, and it was over.

The next morning our routine started out the same. Getting up for 4:30 zazen, chanting the Diamond Sutra, and then cleaning up for breakfast. Breakfast proceeded in the same way. We each had a neatly wrapped bundle, to be precisely opened, with each hand gripping a corner of the cloth, and in one fluid motion revealing three bowls, one inside the other. We removed each bowl with practiced hand movements and placed each one just so. We ate with our chopsticks as if at West Point, each movement forming a straight line from the bowl up and then a horizontal line to the mouth. Such precision kept every movement conscious. When we finished, we always left a little soup and a yellow pickle after we'd put the last of our food on a plate for an offering. We used our chopsticks to hold the pickle and slosh the soup to clean each bowl, moving from the larger to the smaller. Then we ate the pickle, drank the soup, restacked the bowls, and retied the bundle, with the chopsticks pointing out in one move, just so.

After breakfast Tanaka-san invited me for a walk. We walked up behind the monastery into the mountains, for maybe an hour, until we reached a ridge and looked down onto a pristine lake. As we looked out at the view Tanaka-san asked if I'd brought any LSD to these holy premises. I lied and assured him that I hadn't. I detected a touch of disappointment. It was the wrong answer.

We took a path down to the lakeshore, where Tanaka-san picked up a small stone. *You can tell the depth of silence by listening to the splash,* he said, as he tossed the stone into the lake. The kerplush was deeper and longer than I'd ever heard before. Much deeper than the splash on the bridge with my grandma. The silence in this small valley was vast and deep.

Tanaka stood on a small outcropping over the lake and suddenly started chanting in a beautifully deep and resonant voice that exploded into white light.

Time stopped. The universe disappeared.

When the world reappeared, I was in full prostration at his feet, laughing and crying. Our eyes met in deep recognition, and love exploded between us.

At that instant, just yards away, a large wild boar walked out of the woods to graze by the shore of the lake. We looked at each other in silent wonder.

That night we had a party. Tanaka-san announced Eli-san's spontaneous realization of Zen. He broke out the sake and the beer and we sang songs until midnight. After I sang the songs from my civil rights repertoire and Bob Dylan, the group wanted me to teach them a song, so I sang them a song by Joe Hill, an old Wobbly song *Solidarity Forever.* Perhaps they are still singing it in a little monastery in the foothills.

*   *   *

My wife, in her irrefutable wisdom, would not allow a second wife, even one who was willing to be the second wife. After promising Midori that Toni would love her as I did and that all of us together wouldn't be a problem, I had to tell Midori she couldn't come back to the U.S. with me.

Now that the Zen monastery was no longer an option for hiding from her destiny, Midori's family arranged for her marriage to a truck driver in Kobe. She has two children and stays in contact. I just saw her daughter's wedding pictures. I still feel the pain of the emotional damage that was done.

I had a vision of all of us living happily ever after. I wanted to take care of Midori and was lost in the hedonistic bliss that rides alongside true love and calls itself love. I painted myself as a romantic, believing it was possible for us to love each other equally, and I believed my own propaganda.

Toni saw the practicalities, the inevitable jealousies and estrangements, and through her clarity, I was able to see that my vision was biased by my desire. I saw how my sexual acting out caused suffering, even when done openly in the name of love. This was a lesson I needed to learn again and again.

CHAPTER 26

The Anvil

An old Hebrew teaching story:

God said to Adam: I have good news and bad news, Adam. The good news is that I have enough parts left to give you both a brain and a penis. The bad news is that you only have enough blood to use one at a time.

In 1984 I led a group called The Journey Home at Esalen, and while I was there, I was introduced to Wolf Büntig. He was running Zist, a center in Germany and invited me to teach there.

Invited to teach in Germany. Germany! And not just Germany, but Bavaria. Not just Bavaria, but the Black Forest! For me, the Black Forest was a terrifying Hansel and Gretel nightmare, with evil lurking about in its shadows like a Mississippi swamp.

In Germany I found human beings just like myself. Some were open, some closed, but with no essential difference. German society in the 1980s was very different from the U.S. and the way it is now, thirty years later. In the early eighties, Germany was still under a dark cloud. The atmosphere was heavy, and people in general were uptight and guarded. But in my groups, the culture was the same as with the people at home, except that the Germans were more serious.

I found that the wounding of the German psyche by their Nazi past made these people more serious and more ready for something deeper. I liked my time there and started going regularly. I continue to have meetings in Germany today. I deeply love the people in our sangha. How ironic that I love Germany and deplore the Zionist state of Israel.

My first enneagram book was published in German, and then in Hungarian.

By this time, I'd become an examiner on the board of the American Council of Hypnotist Examiners and started holding month-long trainings for certification in clinical hypnosis at Esalen. Invitations to hold month-long retreats at an institute in Vienna followed. Soon I was holding month-long retreats at Esalen in spring and fall and in Vienna in the summer. I also held advanced retreats on Maui, Formentera, and Sardinia.

In the blink of an eye the world changed, and Toni and I went from dressing out of the free box in Bolinas to teaching around the world, with a clinic in San Francisco and a home in Mill Valley. We continued to love each other's company. We had similar tastes in music, art, literature, and movies. We never watched television. In 1968, when Jean was watching the Democratic Convention and I was out on the street, I realized I would rather be living life than watching it. Toni and I were on the same wavelength.

We loved each other, and our lives were blessed, except for one thing—sex. It was the only fault-line that ran through our relationship and threatened to destroy it. When we started seeing each other I made it very clear I was not monogamous. I cited scientific evidence proving that monogamy is genetically inherited and not everyone has the gene. I for sure did not. And even when the gene was present there is clear evidence that monogamous birds, paired for life, will cheat if given a chance.

When we bonded, we had a year of monogamy, but I broke it soon afterward. It was our war. I blamed her jealousy and need to control for the lack of harmony, and she told me I was not facing the suffering I was creating. I wasn't monogamous, I would tell her, but I was loyal. I would never leave her for anyone else. I wasn't searching for anyone to take her place. She did fulfill me. But . . . I just wasn't wired that way.

We tried different strategies over the years to manage this. At a time when we were monogamous, Toni's ex-lover was coming to town. He was an artist, a painter, and her first real lover after her divorce. She still had strong feelings for him. We made a new exception to the rule so that it was allowed once, if an old lover should come by.

I continued to feel that if you couldn't be with the one you love, love the one you're with—as long as I was upfront and clear that I was in a committed relationship and that the affair was just for the moment. I justified my sexual desire in every way possible. Eventually, I couldn't help but see that she was right. I could hear what Toni said was true in the moment, but it didn't stick.

I saw her pain and didn't want to cause that pain. But I kept returning to my reasoning, telling her to trust that I was hers and would never leave her. *If you give up your jealousy, everything would be fine. The pain will be gone.*

What I had not yet realized was the intimate bonding that occurs in the limbic brain and how we carry each other's emotional taste and essence with us. I had to realize that in the moment I am with my lover, I am excluding my partner, if only on a subtle emotional psychic level. Since we are all psychic, when a limbic cord is wounded by exclusion, it creates pain.

After our advanced training on Maui in April of 1988, a woman who was working with me on my new German book stayed after the group was over to finish up our work together. When we finished, I took her to dinner, before the airport. We ate grilled mahi-mahi with a Macadamia nut sauce and wasabi butter, sitting oceanfront at Mama's. The warm tropical air was filled with the scent of Plumeria blossoms, and the full moon danced in liquid silver on the gentle waves lapping the shore. We drank a '78 Chalone from my collection. Its rich buttery roundness filled the scene with a golden light. By the time we hugged and kissed goodbye, we were drunk and stoned.

Toni saw us from her car. That night, at 2:30 in the morning, furious, she woke me up. *We have to talk,* she said.

Later. In the morning.

No. Now.

But I'm drunk and stoned. In the morning. I didn't understand why she should be jealous or hurt by this innocent dinner.

No! Now!

By then, Toni had become my teacher. It happened one year before when she came home early and walked in on me with an old lover. Even though this was part of our old-lover-comes-to-town-once arrangement, she was enraged, hurt, and jealous. Sitting in her bed crying, Toni came to realize that a part of her was getting off on the suffering, and then something shifted. She told the truth to herself, in the middle of her emotional nightmare. She was actually getting a kind of pleasure from her pain. Her commitment to the truth paid off. She took responsibility when she saw this about herself, and she stopped. In that moment, she woke up. She was no longer a victim. She was suddenly clear and present. From that moment on, she became my teacher.

From then on, it was not my lust versus her jealousy. I could always sort of win those battles. But now it was my lust versus her clarity. She said we were on a mission together, and she was not interested in wasting her precious time processing our emotions. She was right. I got it in that moment, and I felt clear about the future. But there was no place for that insight to stick. I did get it in that moment, but in a future moment, the insight disappeared. Then I acted like a bimbo, just a girl who couldn't say *no.* I didn't hunt, but I was fair game if I was lured and caught.

Toni once said that she became my teacher because she really listened to what I taught. She said I needed to take one of my own workshops. What was clear was that once she was not willing to indulge her ego fixation, mine became apparent to both of us, and I had to drop it. The roles were switched, and she was calling me out on my stuff. It was hard to take. I often fought and resisted, but the deeper truth was that I was thrilled to meet my match, a teacher who could go one better. I surrendered.

So in the middle of that night on Maui, I woke from my sleep, and in my willingness to sit up and face it all, I was suddenly sober and present and clear. I saw how my drunk and stoned mind made excuses, and I saw that I had to break through this pattern.

At first, I denied there was anything going on with this woman. I could feel what Toni was talking about but kept it out of sight. But Toni stayed with me long enough that I told the truth to her, and to myself. My lies were not conscious lies, but subconscious. Not telling the truth to myself, I could defend the lie as if it were true. When I saw the sexual dance I was doing with the other woman, I really saw it, and I thanked Toni. This ability to work so deeply together opened up amazing levels of intimacy.

The next day at the beach, we continued to work it out. Toni's crystal clarity showed me that I needed to commit myself to monogamy. I saw that when I had sex with someone other then my wife, somebody always suffered. I could see this only because Toni was able to stare me down and hold her own, without getting back into her ego. That day on the beach she was brilliant. I surrendered to her. I fell at her feet and kissed them.

This is the energy of the satguru, I said.

What's a satguru? she asked. This rarest of the rare, the satguru, who transmits the truth on all levels, as an emanation of divine being, was her destiny.

I proposed to Toni there on the beach. We would be married one year later, in a cave in Haleakala Crater, in the heart of Maui.

CHAPTER 27

Initiation

In the year between my proposal and our marriage, Toni and I landed in Casablanca on an October evening. Soldiers sauntering around with AK47s slung over their shoulders set the mood at the airport. We took a taxi out to the kasbah, exhilarated by the ocean breeze as our car hugged the coast on an unlit and bumpy desert road.

We entered the kasbah through an eight-foot thick wall, built to repel desert marauders. We passed camels spending the night in stalls located in the middle of the wall. Once past the inner courtyard and a stable of horses, we found our way to the front desk. We'd been invited here for a Sufi conference on trance and healing.

For the past several years, I had continued leading hypnosis certification trainings in Austria. The month-long trainings now took place in a twelfth-century castle in the Austrian countryside. Several of the students at these trainings were also students of a Moroccan Sufi teacher, Jabrane, who'd heard of us through his students. He invited us to Morocco.

After checking into our rooms, we followed the music out to the beach, where a large tent holding a few hundred people was filled with French and Germans—and a Gnauer Sufi clan. Open on one side to let in the cool ocean breeze, it felt like we'd walked into an Arabian Nights tale. The tent was made of large arabesques of red felt and velvet, which caught the candlelight and gave off a rosy glow. Because we just finished teaching in Munich, we arrived on the evening of the second day of this event. We missed the introductions, the program overview, and the structure of what was to come. We found out that the conference was in Arabic and French, with translation into German, so we wouldn't have understood anything that we missed any way. We joined the group after the ceremony had been going on for some time. We were drawn into the hypnotic music as we watched people trance dance in the middle of the floor.

We later discovered that the Gnauer Sufis were once palace slaves from the Dogon Tribe on the west coast of Africa. The "Dog People" claim they were dropped on Earth from Sirius, the Dog Star. For them, music is a literal phoning home. When the Dogon were captured and sold in the slave markets of North Africa, some were made servants in the palaces in Morocco. Here they met Islam and the Sufis.

Sufis are the ecstatic mystics of Islam. Throughout the Islamic world the Sufis are often a brotherhood of enlightened tolerance in search of a direct mystical experience of God. There are many different Sufi schools and practices for attaining oneness. Some Sufis twirl and are known as whirling dervishes originating in Konya, in the central mountains of Turkey. Some are beggars, while others have trades, like Kabir, who wove carpets in Varanasi, in India. The music we heard is the most hypnotic I've ever experienced, a blend of the Gnauer tribal rhythms and the subtle harmonics of the Sufi stringed instruments and vocals. A different order from the new age music we use in the West to help induce trance or any of the other trance styles of music. There is a high-pitched drone that seems to circulate and spin as it moves from ear to ear, riding above the drums and through the harmony of the voices.

La Yeshay a sixty-year-old Black man with greying nap and beard was the leader of this clan. He circled the perimeter of the circle as the musicians played. When La Yeshay saw that someone had gone into trance he brought them into the middle of the circle to dance. This is how the Gnauer heal psychological disorders and transcend to altered states for spiritual purposes.

That first night we sat in the back and watched. Many people were up dancing, but the evening was dominated by a six-foot-two German woman with long black hair and dressed all in black. She was screaming and beating her head.

Ya! she slapped her head with one hand.

Nein! and she slapped her head with the other.

Yah! Nein! Yah! Nein! Yah! Nein! Yah! Nein!

She did this for the last two hours of the ceremony but didn't seem to find relief or resolution. She looked like a possessed black witch. No one interacted with her. Her energy destroyed the mood. It was impossible to hear anything but her screams. This was not a good start.

The next night the ceremony started at midnight. As soon as the music began I felt it moving me to another plane. I'd been to Grateful Dead concerts and had seen the Rolling Stones on acid but I'd never had music transport me in this way. I closed my eyes and fell inside, into a vast dark silence where there was a spinning like wind in a funnel. The wind whirled around the silent emptiness at my center. An image rose up from the depth of the emptiness. It was a Buddha. I merged with the image and the thought arose, *I am Buddha*. The image of Christ appeared. I merged with it, and the thought arose, *I am Christ*. I was startled to see an image of Moses, and the merging continued, *I am Moses*. Next was an image of Mohammed: *I am Mohammed*.

These four images rotated around me on the wind, like petals. I was the silent hub. The images rotated faster and faster, and out of the center, I arose, along with the thought, *I am Sufi*. I experienced myself blossoming from the lotus petals of Buddha, Jesus, Moses, and Mohammed. When I later reported this experience to Jabrane, the conference organizer, he told me this experience was a traditional Sufi initiation, often written about, but he'd never witnessed it.

I opened my eyes and La Yeshay took my hand and led me into the circle. The music was in control of my body, which moved in fluid and unknown ways. I saw the German woman from the night before dancing near me. I saw that she was creating psychic sex slaves with her movements, attracting two weak-minded women who danced in her orbit. They were being drained on some level that I could see but not describe. I danced around her, and through the dance, I broke first one link and then the other to the two women. The freed women were dazed, like chickens in shock, and wobbled to the circle's edge with no understanding of what had just happened.

After the second woman was psychically cut free, the black witch went into a rage and attacked me. We danced. Our dancing was her thrusting and my deflecting. At one point, my right index finger came up into the air signifying One; my whole body felt like the embodiment of One. The German woman reacted strongly to this. At first, she tried to attack, but some force came over her as she stared at my uplifted finger. She was mesmerized, and something inside her began to surrender. Then a deeper level of attack surged up. Unable to hurt me she began to hit her own head.

She was shouting *Nein!* as she raised her two fists to hit herself. I grabbed her wrists. She was bigger than I am. I looked up into her eyes. She struggled violently, but I couldn't let her hurt herself. Somehow I was able to hold on to her wrists. She was unable to scream. From some deep vastness, words come out of my mouth. I sounded like I was speaking to a three year old: *It's all right. Just a bad dream. You are here now. It's over.* The woman collapsed to the floor and sat quietly for the rest of the night.

My dancing over, I left the circle with Toni. I couldn't believe what had just happened and wanted to hear Toni's view. We sat behind a large boulder on the beach and smoked Moroccan hash. Toni told me about her initial concern that I was acting inappropriately. Then she told me about her surprise when she saw the results and understood that something else was going on. I felt the hash coming on and started to slightly shake and tremble as my body unwound.

Suddenly, I heard a commotion from the tent. I was no longer in an altered state from the music. I was stoned and decompressing. I felt helpless, defenseless, and uncertain of what to do. The familiar dread in my belly warned me of impending danger. There was shouting and the threat of violence coming from the tent. I walked over to the tent and saw three local Moroccans, who were not part of our group, standing over a Moroccan in the tent who was seated as part of the circle. One of the three locals was shouting at the seated man, while his two friends stood by to back him up.

La Yeshay and his crew were in a dangerous position. Blacks were still second-class citizens in Morocco. Still worse, these Blacks were from Marrakesh, in the mountains; this was not their territory. They were strangers invited by the conference organizer. They looked very worried.

I looked for Jabrane, but his seat at the power spot guarding the circle was empty. He slipped off hours ago with a new girlfriend. I had no idea what the shouting was about. Perhaps the local man sitting in the tent was a thief hiding in the circle. I couldn't be sure whether he was part of the group. Perhaps these were shopkeepers and they'd caught him. These men could have been in the right. Still, something needed to be done.

I stepped between the seated man and his accuser. The accuser started to shout at me, explaining everything in French. I stood empty and open. I listened for several minutes as he shouted in my face. When he stopped for breath, I said, *Je ne comprende pas Français.*

The man was taken aback. *Rien?* he shouted. Nothing?

I shrugged and smiled and gently said, *Rien,* and the trance was broken.

Maybe it was that I was told this fellow in French that I couldn't speak French that made two hundred people laugh. Whatever it was, the three men left, and La Yeshay hugged me and brought me to him. He sat down on a chair and I sat on the floor next to him. I rested my head on his knee and he stroked my hair.

La Yeshay invited Toni and me to be his guests at a special dinner. At the dinner we were seated on either side of him. We ate only with our right hand from a communal tajine, and while we ate, we learned that tripe had been prepared as a special treat in our honor. This was a new one for both of us. Toni tried not to eat, but La Yeshay insisted and fed her. All the while he told her in French to pay attention and not let this man get away. He said she must eat a lot to get very big so she could have my babies.

He has very strong bakara, healing power, La Yeshay told her. *He needs several babies at least.* Toni and I caught each other's eye and silently laughed at our private joke.

La Yeshay wanted us to come to Marrakesh where he would marry us. Though Toni and I had been living together for eleven years and I had already proposed and been accepted, we weren't prepared for a ceremony here. I finally promised to return alone the next week when the group reconvened for the full moon in Marrakesh.

While the group continued its tour of Morocco, Toni and I flew to Vienna to teach a workshop on the enneagram. The workshop ran through Sunday, but I had promised to return to La Yeshay and getting a flight out of Vienna to Morocco was not easy, so I flew out Sunday and left Toni to finish the workshop.

I flew from Vienna to Paris, connecting from Paris to the last seat available to Marrakesh. I bought the last seat on a one-class plane. My seat turned out to be a front-row aisle seat, and unbeknownst to me, my seatmate at the window turned out to be a famous movie actress expecting an empty seat next to her. When the plane landed I was the first one off, while the actress walked back to be with her entourage. I was the only one off the plane and walked onto a red carpet on the tarmac. As I walked toward the terminal, a band started playing, women trilled in that Berber way, and belly dancers started dancing and I was showered with rose petals. I was surprised and started laughing at the cosmic jokester. At that point, none of us—the band, the dancers, nor I—realized that the show was for the actress still on the plane.

When I arrived in Marrakesh I found that inside the ancient walled city is the inner walled compound of the royal palace and inside the east gate of this inner wall are former slave quarters. This is where La Yeshay and his clan lived, in small huts built into the surrounding walls, around a courtyard with an ancient tree and a water spigot.

The German woman's dark spell had not returned. She was friendly and happy to see me. She thanked me and gave me a gift, a small stone bear. We had a banquet of mutton, and as the honored guest I was given the sheep's eye to eat. The music and dancing went on from midnight to the dawn as I was brought into this Sufi clan as a son.

If ever I need a refuge I have a home in the old slave quarters of Marrakesh.

PART VI

FREEDOM

Another strung-out soul

Is beaded on Buddha's necklace . . .

CHAPTER 28

Leaving the Kingdom

Freedom's just another word

for nothing left to lose.

—Janis Joplin

By 1989, a decade after we'd left the farm in Bolinas, we were established in a good life doing good work in the world, and we were happy. We had made it. Then we felt a call. We didn't know what it was, but we both felt it. I told Toni it felt like a spiritual promotion. Something big was in the air.

I was attached to our house in Mill Valley, which we had bought for $10,000 down and would soon be worth $2 million, but we had to let it go. We had to give up our security and position and comfortable life and start again. We closed our clinic, sold the house, and moved to Maui.

On Maui we began to plan our wedding and to look for our new center. We came across a real estate ad for a 22-acre protea farm, with a five bedroom main house, a guest house, a workers' house, a heated pool, tennis courts, a protea flower crop, and landscaped gardens. It was going for $1.2 million. Compared to anything in Marin County this was incredibly cheap. We had to check it out.

At the end of a pristine country lane we came to two square stone pillars and a gatekeeper's cottage. The drive to the main house was lined with horses grazing in a pasture behind a white split-rail fence. We pulled into a parking area for a dozen cars. The property was impressive. The kitchen in the main house was set up for commercial use with two of everything: two Wolf ranges, two Sub-Zero refrigerators, commercial-size stainless sinks, and a manager's office behind the walk-in pantry. The property was completely private and had a view of Maui's mountains to the west and of the beaches on both the north and south shores. A producing protea farm could bring in income and agricultural tax write-offs.

From the sale of our house we had enough for a down payment. I offered to buy the place for the asking price. We envisioned a center, the Pacific Center for Sacred Studies, which would bring all the enlightened traditions together in a new synthesis. Applegate commune 2.0.

But that was the year the Japanese real estate bubble was peaking, when the Japanese bought a Hollywood film empire, the Empire State Building, and Hawaii, among other trophies. A Japanese businessman offered an extra $200,000 for the farm, all cash, and we lost the dream.

Joan and her kids were all living on Maui by then, and she found a farm for us to rent, which was an almost impossible task. To find a completely private farm that was very affordable was a pipe dream All the private farms had been snatched up and subdivided decades ago and were now occupied by the owners. But Joan did it. An old and rundown Japanese family farm, it was one gulch over from the one we tried to buy, completely private and affordable but higher up. It was so high on the mountain that the pipes once froze in the winter. The local couple that owned it was building a new home farther down the mountain where it was warmer. Joan was giving their daughter piano lessons, so for $800 a month, we rented a nine-acre farm complete with a farmhouse and dozens of avocado, cherimoya, loquat, persimmon, and plum trees. This farm wasn't for sale but would be our base while we found our ideal center.

A student from Esalen who had experienced the power of our work had just sold his business and retired. After selling the business, he had an extra $3 million that he hadn't planned on and wanted to give a million to us! That sent us off to explore all the islands. We found the treasure we were looking for back on Maui: forty acres of the old Thompson Ranch was for sale in Keokea, serene undeveloped backcountry of rolling hills overlooking the south shore.

We explored the land and found under the thigh-high grass that it was the site of an old Hawaiian village. We brought a local Hawaiian friend with an ancient healing lineage to the site, and he identified two Hawaiian heiau temple sites. He also found a rare vine that the Hawaiians used for healing broken bones. This land had been a healing place. The land was very hilly, so that a dozen small houses could be in close proximity to one another and still be completely out of view. Each would have views of the ocean and sunset. It was the perfect idyllic Polynesian scene.

We put a down payment on the land and went into escrow, while setting up our nonprofit. Everything seemed to be falling into place. We also found the perfect place to hold our wedding party, one of the original Baldwin mansions. The Baldwins came as missionaries and ended up owning much of Maui. The mansion for our party was then owned by a wealthy televangelist, who rented it out by application to worthy Christians. We wrote a letter and he deemed us worthy. The next year the house was bought by Reagan's Treasury Secretary and no longer available to people like us.

We had our wedding in a cave in Haleakala. When we assembled at the top for the two-hour hike into the crater it was storming. A cold, driving rain made visibility almost zero, which matched people's desire to get out of their cars. Most didn't. We had no rain gear and had just driven up from the warm sunny beach. As we stood on the rim, wavering, Toni announced that she was going in if she had to marry herself! I fell in next to her. A few of us cut holes in plastic garbage bags and put them over our heads. Five others followed us in the blinding storm. We couldn't see or hear each other for the rain and roar of the wind as we walked silently down the trail.

We got to the cabin we'd reserved below and lit a fire to dry off. We took off our clothes to dry by the fire in the stove. Standing in our underwear, we looked out the window and couldn't believe our eyes. Out of the sheets of rain a rider appeared in a great coat and leather hat. He looked like an apparition from the Civil War as he rode his mule to our cabin. He made his way in and stomped his feet to shed water. German John was a mountain man who stood six foot two with a great bushy beard. When he spoke he shouted with the throatiness of a biker in a bar.

How the hell are ya? I'm German John! I heard some damn fools were having a wedding here today, and I figured if you made it, I would too.

We looked at him in amazement. He seemed to have stepped out of another world, another era. He reached into his great coat and pulled out a bottle of rare old Armagnac.

I've been saving this bottle for a dozen years, and I never knew why. You people must have some power to bring me and this bottle to you today.

He passed the bottle and it warmed us. Wolf, who first brought me to Germany, and his partner, were two of the people who walked in with us, and they recognized German John! There had been a special about him on German TV. He was a seaman who jumped ship on Maui and became a cabinetmaker. John told us he'd been trained by a Hawaiian kahuna. We hadn't planned on a priest for the occasion, but here he was.

And then the shocker: *The kahuna who trained me was from the old Thompson Ranch.*

We told John we were in escrow to buy the South 40 of the Thompson Ranch, and he told us the ranch's story. A German seaman jumped ship in the 1850s and changed his name to hide from the law. He married a Hawaiian girl of some nobility and the king gave them a pie slice of land they called the Thompson Ranch.

The rain stopped, and we proceeded up a hill to a small cave. John had us join hands, as he said, *I don't know if you people know anything about energy or believe in it, but the energy is very, very strong here right now.* I glanced at Toni and we smiled. We all closed our eyes, as John chanted in Hawaiian and led us in a short ceremony. Then Toni and I exchanged our vows. They came out spontaneously in the moment. We both said the same essential thing: that we are dedicated to each other's freedom and enlightenment, that we dedicate our marriage to this, and that if our marriage ever becomes an obstacle to that, the marriage must go. When we hiked out of the crater it was a perfect sunny day.

The next day we had our party. People had flown in from all over the world. The party started with a female vocalist accompanying herself on a harp, moved on to a Hawaiian music duet, and ended in the evening with a blues band. We served cases of a delicious 1979 French champagne I bought five years before, after tasting it at a dinner at Chez Panisse.

Toni and I realized half way through the wedding reception that the man with the money for our center hadn't come, although he was on the island and expected. We had to go through the last half of the party acting as though nothing was wrong, while the collapse of knowing he had backed out of the land deal sank in. Shades of my mother putting on a happy front at my bar mitzvah. Now I knew what it was like to be my mother that day. Our dream was so close yet so far away. Years later Oprah ended up buying the whole Thompson Ranch, not just our forty acres, as well as everything else as far as the eye could see.

We had no idea what good luck this would turn out to be.

While I was on Maui nine months later, Toni met Andrew Cohen, a spiritual teacher who was then in Larkspur, California. She went to him with her problem: *My husband says that my jealousy around his sexual promiscuity is just my superego. Is this true?* He sneered at her for bringing this kind of question to his holy meeting. Andrew had a confidence, though, that drew Toni toward him. She asked me if I would be interested in meeting this teacher when I returned. To her surprise I was very enthusiastic. I had been going to see whatever spiritual teacher happened by, checking them out and challenging them without ever finding one that could give me what I was still searching for.

When I opened my eyes from the sitting meditation at Andrew's gathering, he had already walked in. He was sitting in a large armchair in front of the room. His shakti was very strong. It was the first time I'd felt shakti like that since Muktananda. Muktananda's shakti was perfumed with incense and wrapped in dancing girls in saris. Andrew's shakti was crystal clear and penetrating. Sometimes he was sarcastic and arrogant, but beneath that was a stunning clarity of presence. It stopped me in my tracks.

I then read Andrew's book describing his meeting with his master. Andrew had come in an ordinary vipassana student and left a satguru in a matter of weeks. His letters to his teacher in his book displayed a very deep realization and profound understanding. I may have met my teacher. I had to deeply examine my situation.

Andrew was a snotty Jewish kid from the Upper West Side. He was at least ten years my junior. His rudeness and arrogance were a problem for me, as well as his age and inexperience. That I would have to take this young arrogant Upper-West-Side Jew as my master was a huge challenge. On the other hand, I thought Muktananda was a CIA tool at first, and he had profoundly affected my life. I saw that my objections to Andrew were my ego's objections and what a powerful antidote to spiritual pride it was to accept this kid as my teacher. So be it. I was grateful for whatever form the teacher might take.

I met some of Andrew's students. One was a very pretty female therapist from Boston with a shaved head. She said she was told to shave her head to help fight her vanity and attachment to looks. I saw several other members with shaved heads. One student told me that Andrew had him take his new car to a wrecking yard and watch it be crushed. I didn't have a problem with this. Whatever it took, I was willing.

I had examined myself for much of the night and now I was ready. As we sat in meditation before he arrived I fell deeply inside. Suddenly an image of a teacher's head, someone I didn't know, appeared directly in front of me. We looked into each other's eyes, and the head floated forward and turned to fit over mine. As our heads aligned, there was an explosion of light, and everything disappeared. I opened my eyes and had the unusual experience of sitting as formless consciousness. I was ecstatic. I couldn't find my body or any boundary. I was in deep bliss.

When Andrew asked for questions, I reported my current state and the events that led to my sitting in front of him with no body. He wasn't impressed. He asked me if this was some Tibetan technique. I wondered what he saw that I didn't. I was open and eager. Years later I realized that he saw me through the filter of "the cheating husband."

After the meeting I followed him outside. I threw myself at his feet and told him, *I am ready now. Whatever it takes. I am ready.*

He looked at me and smirked. *Slow down,* he said, *not so fast.*

The next day Toni and I left for Esalen to lead the month-long. I opened by letting the group know that I had met someone more awake than I was. I told them I couldn't really sit there as their teacher and invited everyone to drive up to Marin for Andrew's next meeting. About a dozen people drove up with us. It was a four-hour drive, a one-hour wait, a two-hour meeting, and a four-hour drive back. Toni and I were happy to do it.

Andrew then announced that he was leaving for India to visit his guru. I asked if I could go as well. He told me that it was private. No one else was invited. I asked for his guru's address so that I might go at another time. He wouldn't give it to me—that was private as well. I thought to myself that if Andrew had found a true guru, there must be others. I wanted to find someone now and told Toni I had to go to find a teacher. I told her I would go to the frontiers of Pakistan in search of enlightened Sufis and to Sikkim in search of enlightened Tibetans.

Meanwhile, each day at Esalen I led a morning zazen sitting meditation. Usually, when I led the meditation, I counted my breath and emptied the mind. During the meditation this time, however, I examined what I was willing and not willing to give up in my quest for a true teacher.

Money. I had gone from pauper to prince. It wouldn't be pleasant to give up the comforts I now enjoyed, but ultimately this was not a problem. My personal survival was not a problem. Mother Earth had always taken care of me, and I trusted this implicitly, even if she put me back in the dumpsters. Besides, I was past my expiration date of thirty, so every day was a bonus.

Sex. I saw the suffering I had caused. I didn't want to create suffering from my pleasure. If I have to cut my balls off, so be it. I would not cause harm again. If this meant a lifetime of celibacy, I was willing. This wasn't my preference, but I was willing.

Marijuana. This was a holy sacrament. When I smoked, I invoked Shiva and gave thanks in deep gratitude. Grass opened my mind and helped me see whatever I was avoiding. It was a kind of truth serum. It was my first teacher and my ally. The goddess of marijuana had taught me so much from gardening, to cooking, to music and art. I enjoyed how she felt inside me. But I was ready to give her up if that was what was required. Whatever it would take.

Toni. I broke into sobs, and snot ran down my face as I sat in zazen. I didn't move to wipe my face. I sat motionless and held the huge scream and painful cry that were bursting in my chest. I ran out of the room as soon as the meditation was over. Sobbing, I walked across the campus back to where Toni was waiting in our bedroom. I couldn't give up my love for Toni. I wouldn't give her up for my enlightenment. If this was what it took, I was not willing. I was only willing to give her up for *her* enlightenment, if that was what was needed.

Toni thought I was mad. She said that the teacher, Andrew, was right here, and I was running away. Joan, who had come to sit with Toni, agreed that I was running away from the truth. Her solution was for the three of us to sleep together. Both Joan and Toni said I was having a midlife crisis. Nobody thought it was a good idea for me to go off with no idea where I was heading.

But I did have criteria: I wanted to wake up in the nondual reality I had experienced with Andrew. I was searching for someone more awake than I was. If I couldn't find that, then at least I wanted to find Sufis who could transmit deeper insight into the enneagram.

My training at Esalen was over in mid-November, and I was ready to go. To finance my trip, I sold my wine collection. Starting in the early eighties, when wine was still cheap, great bargains could be had. I had amassed a fifty-case collection, from bottles of 1945 Lafitte to the great vintages of Napa and Bourdeau of the late seventies and early eighties. I'd bought wine futures and paid two hundred dollars for a case of 1982 Latour, now considered one of the best wines of the century. I sold the case for $1,600. Today that is the price for one bottle, if you can find it.

By the end of December, I had my visa and my plane tickets for India.

CHAPTER 29

The Call of Freedom

I landed in Delhi on New Year's Day, 1990. My plan was to make Delhi my base and from there get a visa for Pakistan and Sikkim. I found a small local hotel, away from the downtown of Connaught Place, in the relatively quiet residential neighborhood of Sunder Nagar. The Kailash Inn was once a private home that had been converted into a small hotel. It had nine rooms. Mine was upstairs in the back, over what used to be a garage.

A father and his sons ran the inn. One of the sons, Ahmet, befriended me and asked what I was doing in India. I told him I was looking for Sufis, and he told me that I was just a short drive away from a Sufi village, named after the sixteenth-century Sufi saint Nizamuddin.

I took a taxi there. In fifteen minutes, I was back in time on the dusty streets of Nizamuddin. This village had not changed much in the past several hundred years. The winding tiny dirt lanes, sometimes only wide enough for one person to walk along, were surrounded by mud walls that hid homes and inner courtyards. I looked into an open courtyard door and saw a water buffalo, a naked baby on a bed made of strings across a wooden frame, piles of manure stacked into flat cakes for fuel, and dust everywhere.

Except for the dust, it was hard to believe this place was a short drive from downtown Delhi.

I found the shrine of Nizamuddin in the center of the town. It is a beautiful marble edifice, with cool marble floors for the barefooted pilgrims. The mausoleum in the center of the courtyard is also made of marble, a soft rosy white marble. The walls are carved into screens of prayer-arched filigrees. The local Muslims in charge asked me to sign the guest book and make a donation. I signed as Ali, instead of Eli, to make it easier for everyone. I am Ali, a brother, a seeker of God—in Urdu, I am a *paisab*.

I first sat in the courtyard and watched the pilgrims from different parts of the Muslim world come through with their various headdresses and garb. I then made my way into the cool darkness, to sit beside the raised marble coffin. It was strewn with fragrant rose petals, and beams of sunshine played through the filigree, lighting the darkness. I dropped into deep silence and prayed. I called for help to find a true teacher.

After I prayed, I went to eat at Karim's, a nearby local restaurant. I took a table in the corner and waited to be served. A well-dressed man in a Western suit and tie came in a few minutes after me and sat at a table to my left, with his back to me. The waiter went to his table to take his order first, and I fumed in my New York fashion. *Hey! I was here first!* was the energy I was emitting. The well-dressed man sensed my annoyance, and while turning toward me, said to the waiter, *I will pay for whatever this gentleman wants.* Then he asked if he could join me. I encouraged him, and he sat with me at my table, helping me with suggestions of the house specialties.

I learned that he was a government minister in the Ministry of Textiles and was in town just for the day on business. When I told him my mission, he told me that his sister wrote books on the Sufis and that he knew all the real ones. As we talked I couldn't quite believe this was really happening. It was right out of an Idries Shah book. I was a reader of his Sufi tales and had written to

Idries Shah at his publishing house in London before I set out on my journey announcing my mission and asking for his help.

It was my first day in India and help arrived. The minister drove me back to my hotel in his chauffeured government Ambassador, a local car that looked like it came out of a sweet 1930s cartoon, with its little state flags on the hood above the headlights. Off the top of his head, he wrote down a list of half a dozen names of Sufis and said that he would give me more upon his return home. He would be flying to Bombay in the morning but would return to his home in Lucknow in two weeks.

Using the ministers list, I spent the next two weeks meeting Sufis. First I met a Sufi in Nizamuddin. I entered his courtyard and was invited to sit while a small meeting was going on. I introduced myself as Ali and was introduced to the other men. One of the men was a member of Congress who was about to recite his latest poem. He was introduced as the world's foremost poet of Urdu. It was an urbane, intelligent and warm meeting of men gathered in a rose garden hidden behind ancient white walls. I enjoyed it very much, but it was not what I was looking for.

I went to old Delhi next, behind the souk under the shadow of the Red Fort. I wound my way through the ancient lanes and found the home of one of the most revered Naqshbandi Sufi saints. I brought tea biscuits as an offering, and we enjoyed a pleasant afternoon. He was a kind man, open-hearted and interested, but this was not the connection I was looking for.

I went to the mosque in Nizamuddin when a Chishti Sufi saint arrived. I sat through my first Muslim service and was befriended by two young Pakistani businessmen, who lived in London. They translated for me. I learned that if I wanted to put my name on a list of about two hundred people, the saint would pray over the list. I passed and snuck out before the prayers over the list began.

Using the list of names and hamlets provided by the minister, I continued my search. I hired Ahmet, the innkeeper's son, to be my driver. We went to tiny villages in the Gangetic Plain, the vast floodplain of the holy River Ganga. At one place, the Sufi had gone on *haj,* a pilgrimage to Mecca, and I spent the day with his students. Wherever I went, I didn't find what I was searching for.

When I returned to Delhi, my visas had come through for Pakistan and Sikkim. I made a reservation on Pakistan Airlines to fly into Lahore. Since I could not make the reservations until I had my visa, my flight was booked for a full two weeks ahead. So I had two weeks to kill and decided to go to Lucknow to get the rest of the Sufi names from the government minister.

Once in Lucknow I made an appointment to take the minister to lunch. I stayed at the Carleton Hotel, which used to be the palace of a minor nabob of the old Mughal sultanate. It was once an elegant place but was now filthy and rundown. I would walk up to the roof along a spiraling staircase that was inside an unused crenellated tower decorating a corner of the hotel. The steps and niches were littered with empty bottles, some broken, all dusty and covered with webs. At the top of the stairs was an ancient door that opened to the roof. I could sit unobserved up there and look out over the neighborhood.

I remembered reading in Andrew's book that his teacher lived in Lucknow. Lucknow, the capital of Uttar Pradesh, is a city of several million people. How to find him? When Andrew said I was not allowed to visit his private teacher, I went off to find another teacher and never thought to take the name of Andrew's teacher along with me. I phoned Toni in the States and she could only tell me that his name was Poonja.

On the roof I smoked my holy herb and called for help. Off in the near distance I saw something unusual. It looked like a scrap of black paper that had caught a draft of warm air, perhaps something that escaped from the piles of burning garbage on the street. It was floating up into the air. But I'd never seen a piece of garbage float that high before. Suddenly it seemed to jerk. Did it really move? Was I hallucinating? It went back to drifting on the air currents, and for another moment I wasn't sure. As it drifted back down toward the earth, it suddenly made a volitional move again. I was not hallucinating. Then a red square appeared and they danced together. I knew that this was my sign. Like signal flags they were showing me where this Poonja lived.

Later when I told Poonjaji this story, he showed me the kites of the boys up on the roof across the street from his house. I had never before seen kites that were small, square, and without tails. They had served their purpose well.

I rushed down from the roof after seeing the dancing squares and asked for a phone book. The P's were torn out. I went off in search of another phone book with P's. I found a Poonja listed. When I asked where 422 Narhi was, I was told that it was in the Narhi Market, right where I saw the black and red squares. It was only a short walk from my hotel.

CHAPTER 30

Home

I walked through the old Narhi Market, its small lanes lined with fruit sellers, yogurt makers, and other food stands. I asked directions and was pointed to a small street that ended by a tree. The tree, painted in colors and festooned with ribbons had a small shrine set up in the hallow of its trunk. Dried patties of water buffalo manure were neatly stacked, and fresh patties were drying on the wall. I turned the corner and went up the lane.

The day was January 19, 1990, my 43rd birthday.

I knocked on the door. A friendly man answered and said, *Come in. He is waiting for you. Please go upstairs.*

My breath stopped and perhaps my heart as well. He is waiting for me? He. was. waiting. for. me?

I walked through a small open courtyard. It had a sink with a spigot on the wall to the left, a squat-style latrine off to the other side, and a kitchen with a table across the back. I walked up the unrailed white stucco stairs and on to a small balcony that ran around the second floor. I stuck my head in the first open doorway and heard a voice say, *Come in, come in.*

He was sitting on his bed, in a tiny room. The room was large enough for a single bed and a chair. He was my build, maybe two-hundred pounds, six-feet tall, and his head was shaved. He sat at the head of his bed with his legs crossed and his eyes burning bright.

He had two items on his wall. One was a large poster of his guru, Ramana Maharshi, which he later gave to me and is now in my bedroom. The other was a Sri Yantra, the sacred symbol for the sound of Om. I had fallen in love with the Sri Yantra years ago and commissioned a traditional Tibetan yantra painter to paint a Sri Yantra for our organization. It hung on my office wall and was on our letterhead. It had been our logo for the past ten years. When Toni and I first taught in Budapest, while Hungary was still behind the iron curtain, we entered the organizers' apartment and saw a huge Sri Yantra painted on their living room wall. We knew we were home then, even in a communist country.

As I did with every teacher I visited, I brought an offering. This simple act of respect I learned from Swami Muktananda. This time I brought a special Indian sweet, made of finely ground cashews, cooked down with sweetened milk to form a thin and chewy fudge. The top of it was covered with silver paper.

He put the sweets aside and asked me to sit on the bed with him. Then he asked me what I wanted.

I am ready to wake up! I said as I fell into his eyes.

He laughed a laugh of joy and looked deeply into my eyes. In that moment, there was no doubt. My journey was over. The journey that started in Brooklyn, that started when I was born, forty-three years ago to the day, the journey that had taken me all over the world had come to an end.

I absolutely knew that I was looking at my own Self. My search was really and finally over. All the experiences, from fighting in the streets, to jail, acid trips, Peru, Japan, Morocco, and all the other places and events, had brought me here, to the end of seeking. I had found what I was searching for. Eighteen years to the day since the night in my cabin in Colorado.

In my therapy work, I would sometimes have a person under hypnosis visualize their older, wiser self from the future visiting in the present or their past. This moment was nothing like that at all. What I had walked into was a different order of reality. Hyper reality. Here, in the flesh, was my very own Self. No other. In the flesh. Of this there was no doubt. My own Self looking back at me and loving me.

In all of my spiritual searching, starting with my reading in my cabin and with everything that followed, I never knew for certain if I was deluding myself. I never knew if there was a space brotherhood or a Shangri-La Valley or lamas who could fly. Maybe, as I secretly suspected, even in the moment, it was all delusional mind projection.

This was not that. This was absolutely true. This moment was certain, beyond mind, beyond doubt. This meeting was out of time and space, yet manifesting consciously in the appearance of form.

I understood in that moment Swami Muktananda's direction to worship him as the God that was in me. Here was the God that was in me, in a human form, looking back at me. I did not have to be told to worship. I fell in love. My devotion was pure.

In my mind, his body even looked like mine, down to the bumps on our noses. There was absolutely no doubt in me, no hesitation. Nothing didn't fit. This was not squinting to make it *seem like*. My mind stopped, and I fell into bliss.

He began to speak.

A boy came here recently to see me, he said. *It was so urgent he flew here with only the clothes on his back. I had to lend him a warm sweater because the weather has been quite cold. He didn't mind. He had only one question that he had to have answered, and when this question was answered, he would fly back to his duties. His question was, 'Is it my will that creates the universe?'*

He stopped and looked deeply at me.

He stopped me in my tracks. This was what I was searching for. I didn't know the answer to that question. I knew the answer theoretically, but I had not realized it. At last. Someone who could take me beyond. I sat unable to answer.

He looked at me for a few moments and smiled, then slightly nodded his head toward me waiting for an answer. I couldn't say anything. He then reached over, picked up a small booklet, and read to me from the *Hsin Hsin Ming*, by the Third Zen Patriarch— Hui Neng's spiritual great grandfather! I could not believe it. The living embodiment of all that I'd been searching for not only spoke perfect English, he was reading Zen sutras to me. And not just any Zen master, but the one who was the root of my lineage.

A living Buddha! A Zen master sitting on his bed, alone with me and loving me. It was simply too much. I broke out into sobs, uncontrolled tears of laughter and bliss. He laughed too and playfully slapped me.

That timeless moment I had experienced as a child in Brooklyn was now here as the permanent reality. I had found what I'd been searching for my whole life. Those moments when time stopped and the world froze into stillness were so precious, but were too soon lost again to the next moment's crashing appearance.

Those timeless moments appeared and disappeared without my being able to control or change anything. But now those moments, which seemed to appear and disappear, were revealed to be the ground of being, of life. Silent emptiness was not a state but the living truth of existence. My search for those moments had led me to the final still point that is unmoving and unchanging and prior to all states. The timeless, spaceless reality I had experienced on LSD was now realized to be my unchanging self.

*   *   *

I gave him my money and my passport and told him I no longer had a desire to wake up. I simply wanted to sleep outside his bedroom door and serve him. He laughed and playfully slapped me, and we laughed together. He didn't keep my money or my passport. The only thing he ever requested of me was to send him a tape of my laughter.

He said that souls hitchhike from womb to womb for millions of years before they ever hear of the possibility of freedom from the cycle of incarnation. I told him that I had taken Bodhisattva vows and had promised to come back.

My God! I'm glad I found you! he declared in mock horror. *You would have brought me back too!* We laughed until I rolled on the floor.

He then said something that sank in very deeply. *To light candles is one thing. But to light a candle that lights other candles. This is something else.* I sensed that this was his desire, and all I wanted to do was fulfill his desires. So I desired to be the candle that he lit, that would light other candles.

That night I sat on the roof and examined my renunciation. What was it that I was required to renounce? My life? I knew my life was a dream. I would gladly give this life in service to Papaji. I could gladly give the life of this body; if it meant I die now of a stroke, so be it. In fact, I gladly give the life-force of this body so that he may live longer and spread the message. I visualized pouring the life force from my body into his.

I could give up the world. I could give up my pleasures. And then I saw that I was still identified as a soul. That too! Not just the solar system, but the whole universe! Soul, God, world, everything! The enormity of it hit me. I knew that I was immortal consciousness, though it was still confined within a very subtle boundary, like stars floating in the sky. Now, all the knowing, all the boundaries, everything had to go! The entire universe had to go. All universes gone!

Now, I was ready. Now, I could honestly say, *I renounce everything.*

The next morning, I told Papaji what I had realized, that it was so much bigger that really everything had to be renounced.

He smiled at me with love and said, *It never existed. If you see anything at all, you are dreaming.*

CHAPTER 31

Apotheosis

I finally received a letter from Toni. I had written to her about what was happening with me and around me and told her I was being prepared for a seat in this lineage. I told her that Papaji said he had plans for me beyond my wildest imagination. In her letter, Toni said that she could feel Papaji's transmission through my letters. She said they filled her with bliss, that she recognized my awakening and bowed in service to that. She told me she prayed for her own awakening as well.

Toni's letter showed me her complete willingness and her lack of arrogance. I saw her purity shining so brightly. I saw that she is a perfect teacher. Without her, I would not be here now.

I saw that awakening expresses itself in all manner of being. Some who awaken become hermits, sometimes never speaking again. Others, like Nityananda, who was Muktananda's guru, are known for sitting naked in trees and throwing rocks at anyone who would come near. And then there is Ramana Maharshi, who woke up as a sixteen-year-old boy and lived the life of a saint and a renunciate.

I saw that I am more likely to sit naked in a tree and throw rocks. My personality is not a satvic one. I don't easily get along with people. Toni, on the other hand, is the honey queen, in the best sense. Her purity far surpasses that of anyone I know. Her ability to stay true while getting along with people is remarkable. It was clear that it was Toni's destiny to be a true world teacher.

After a few weeks, Papaji called me into his room to say that he had been testing me and that I was ready. I could feel the first movement of pride arising inside me. Before he could finish his next sentence, I said, *Papaji, my wife is the satguru.* With that statement I abandoned the role he had so graciously prepared me for and offered to me.

This is apotheosis, I now realize as I write this!

I realize now what I did not get in reading *The Hero's Journey* on my return from Peru, or finally even in writing this memoir. The previous chapter was called "Apotheosis," the merging with totality, leaving nothing behind—but here it is, a chapter late, so I will have to change the chapter headings.

I had gladly left the kingdom behind when I went to find my teacher. And I renounced even my soul in my surrender to him. But now, this was renouncing the kingdom to come. I am nobody, I am nothing, I am complete, and I am fulfilled. And the pattern is complete as well! The world disappears in bliss!

I am only now getting the enormous cosmic joke of my own life.

*   *   *

I promised I would return with my wife in one month's time, but as she is a goddess, not a yogi, I wanted to find suitable accommodations for her. Papaji, Surendra, and three of us from satsang then took a second-class sleeper to Haridwar, a holy city on the banks of the Ganga to find a place for my wife. We had a feast on the train, prepared by Papaji's granddaughters, who came to the station to see us off.

CHAPTER 32

Finale

Here comes the sun . . .

—The Beatles

Toni met Papaji at the banks of the Ganga in April of 1990.
She fell into his eyes and never looked back.

*You know how I love my beloved Ganga. Your wife, Mrs. Toni, has
somehow mysteriously entered my heart, I have to give her a very special
name. Now, whenever I think of my beloved Ganga, I will think of her.
She is a satguru. She has the purity, nobility, and satvic nature to take
this transmission to the West. Her name is Ma Gangaji, and people will
come from all over the world just to sit in her presence.*

I became Gangaji's first devotee, the first to call her Gangaji.
Over the years as people elbowed past me to see her, I became
Mrs. Gangaji, which made us laugh into the night.

And it came to pass that Gangaji carried the transmission
of a silent mind and liberation to the West. From that night in
my cabin in 1972 to this moment, my life-time search is over.
Freedom is being passed on to countless others and a new
generation of truth seekers is waking up. I am fulfilled. My
mission is accomplished.

FULFILLMENT

On September 6, 1997 I was abruptly awakened from deep sleep in the middle of the night. I sat up in bed, laughing and sobbing and crying at once. I knew in that moment that Papaji had died. I remembered his teasing us with a refrain:

When I was born everyone was laughing
and I was crying.
Now that I am dying everyone is crying
and I am laughing.

His body is gone, but his transmission of freedom lives on in countless hearts around the world. He brought satsang to the world, and the world is waking up.

About the Leela Foundation

Eli founded and teaches through The Leela Foundation, a non-profit organization supporting world peace and freedom through universal Self-realization.

For more information about the Leela Foundation please visit www.leela.org. On Facebook visit both: Leela Community and The Leela School of Awakening.

Eli Jaxon-Bear is the author of *Wake Up and Roar; Sudden Awakening* and *From Fixation to Freedom*. He has worked as a mailboy, dishwasher, steel-worker, teacher and organic farmer. He was a community organizer with VISTA in Chicago and Detroit and was in a doctoral program at the Graduate School of International Studies in Denver, Colorado. He has been living with his partner and wife since 1976. They currently reside in Ashland, Oregon.

Eli meets people and teaches through the Leela Foundation. www.leela.org.

Also by Eli Jaxon-Bear

Wake Up and Roar (1992, 2016)

Sudden Awakening (2012)

From Fixation to Freedom: The Enneagram of Liberation (2000)

Lied der Freiheit (1998)

Cosmic Jokes and Teaching Stories (1990)

*Healing the Heart of Suffering: Using the Enneagram
for Spiritual Growth* (1989)

For color photos, video clips and more, go to:
outlawmakesithome.org